Diana

By the same author

Cesare Borgia
Disraeli
Princess Grace
George VI
Sacheverell Sitwell
Elizabeth: A Biography of Her Majesty The Queen
America's Queen: The Life of Jacqueline Kennedy Onassis
Lucrezia Borgia

Diana

SARAH BRADFORD

VIKING
an imprint of
PENGUIN BOOKS

VIKING

Published by the Penguin Group

Penguin Books Ltd, 80 Strand, London WC2R ORL, England

Penguin Group (USA) Inc., 375 Hudson Street, New York, New York 10014, USA

Penguin Group (Canada), 90 Eglinton Avenue East, Suite 700, Toronto, Ontario, Canada M4P 2Y3
(a division of Pearson Penguin Canada Inc.)

Penguin Ireland, 25 St Stephen's Green, Dublin 2, Ireland (a division of Penguin Books Ltd)

Penguin Group (Australia), 250 Camberwell Road,
Camberwell, Victoria 3124, Australia (a division of Pearson Australia Group Pty Ltd)

Penguin Books India Pvt Ltd, 11 Community Centre,
Panchsheel Park, New Delhi – 110 017, India

Penguin Group (NZ), cnr Airborne and Rosedale Roads, Albany,
Auckland 1310, New Zealand (a division of Pearson New Zealand Ltd)

Penguin Books (South Africa) (Pty) Ltd, 24 Sturdee Avenue,
Rosebank, Johannesburg 2196, South Africa

Penguin Books Ltd, Registered Offices: 80 Strand, London WC2R ORL, England

www.penguin.com

First published 2006

1

Copyright © Sarah Bradford, 2006

The moral right of the author has been asserted

The permissions on pages 415–16 constitute an extension of this copyright page

Set in 12/14.75pt Monotype Bembo
Typeset by Rowland Phototypesetting Ltd, Bury St Edmunds, Suffolk
Printed in Great Britain by Clays Ltd, St Ives plc

A CIP catalogue record for this book is available from the British Library

ISBN-13: 978–0–670–88166–6
ISBN-10: 0–670–88166–x

For William

Contents

List of Illustrations

Picture Credits

Alpha Photo Press: 54, 57, 58, 65.

From the Collection at Althorp: 3.

Camera Press: 1, 8; SPEN/AL: 6, 7; Diana Memorial Fund: 17, 24; Ian Burns: 34.

Daily Mail/Associated Press: 16.

Colin Davey: 52.

Empics: 12, 13, 25, 36.

Getty Images: Central Press/Hulton: 2, Fox/Hulton: 22; Keystone/ Hulton: 5; Ian Tyas/Hulton: 10; Tim Graham Photo Library: 9, 11, 18, 21, 23, 26, 28, 30, 31, 43, 45, 46, 47, 51, 59, 62, 63, 64, 66.

Liverpool Post & Echo/Stephen Shakeshaft: 19.

Mike Lawn: 37.

Mirrorpix/Mike Malonay: 15: Gavin Kent: 38.

National Portrait Gallery, London: 4.

Rex Features: 14, 20, 27, 29, 32, 33, 35, 39, 40, 41, 42, 44, 48, 49, 50, 55, 56, 60, 61, 67, 68, 69, 70.

Photograph by Leona Shanks: 53.

Prologue

How was it that for just over sixteen years, between her glittering marriage to the heir to the British throne and her violent death in a Paris underpass, a young, unsophisticated girl shook the British monarchy to its foundations and became a worldwide celebrity? Diana Spencer was just twenty when she married, not yet twenty-one when she became the mother of the future King, and an international celebrity at just thirty-six when she was sensationally killed in a car crash. In 1981, when Diana Spencer married the Prince of Wales watched by a worldwide TV audience of millions, she was just another teenage English rose, a typical 'Sloane Ranger'. By the time of her death in August 1997, she was an icon and a royal rebel, a glamorous figure both worshipped and reviled, 'the most hunted woman in the world', as her brother put it at her funeral service. In the days after her death the British Royal Family – even the popular and respected Queen herself – became the target of a tidal wave of criticism. No one who was in London during that time, or who watched the run-up to the funeral on television, will ever forget the experience or the irrational, danger-ous emotions which the death of Diana had stirred in the British people. For the Royal Family its recent history could be seen as pre-Diana and post-Diana, such was the impact this young woman had upon the ancient institution and people's attitudes towards it.

Diana's luminous presence and undoubted gifts of empathy with the suffering held up a mirror to the monarchy which appeared stuffy, remote and out of touch. She groomed her sons to be in touch with the age: she had a clear view of how William should set about his royal task when the time came. Her own approach to what she saw as her job was utterly professional and could not have been carried out by a woman suffering the psychological problems attributed to her.

At the same time, it would be wrong to ignore the fact that the pressures of her life, her rejection by her husband and the public demands made upon her did indeed bring out some of the worst aspects of her character – deviousness, manipulativeness and a deep-rooted suspicion which led her to drop friends and servants in the most brutal manner.

The emphasis on her image, her beauty and her photogenic qualities turned Diana from an ordinary British teenager and elevated her to the level of Jackie Kennedy and Marilyn Monroe, with whom she empathized. She had an instinctive understanding of celebrity in the modern world with all that such status involved. In the end her celebrity killed her: it could be said that she connived in her own death, deliberately inviting the attentions of the paparazzi in the last days of her life.

1. The Country Girl

'In the Spencer family the gender issue is a big one . . . Women are very much second-class citizens' (a Spencer cousin)

Diana Spencer was born to the sound of applause. Her birth took place at 7.45 p.m. on a warm summer evening, 1 July 1961, in the bow-fronted bedroom where her mother had been born before her, overlooking the lawn where the annual cricket match organized by her father was nearing its end. Yet far from being a cause for applause, Diana's birth was regarded as a disappointment. As a girl she could not be the heir to the Spencer name that her parents so desperately wanted. Moreover, she was the third girl born to her parents, Frances and Johnnie Althorp, heir to the Spencer earldom, and had confidently been expected to be a boy, so much so that at the time of her birth the local newspaper reported her father as saying 'they had not yet decided on a name'. Since all Spencer male heirs were traditionally christened John or Charles this was understandable in the circumstances. The new girl's Spencer namesake, Diana (1735–43), was the short-lived sister of the 1st Earl Spencer.

Diana's father's family, the Spencers, was one of the most aristocratic in England; her extraordinary bloodline included the children of two Kings, a Duke, and a saint. A web of titled ancestors made her an eleventh cousin to the heir to the British throne, Charles, Prince of Wales; she was even distantly connected to the first President of the United States, George Washington. (Through her grandfather's marriage to American heiress Frances Work she was a seventh cousin to both Humphrey Bogart and Rudolph Valentino.)

Diana's family connections and the location of her birthplace could be said to have determined her royal future. Park House, where she was born, was the property of the Queen, and had been leased to Diana's maternal grandfather, Maurice Fermoy, in 1931 by King George V. It stood on the Sandringham estate in Norfolk about half a mile from the main house where the Royal Family frequently spent their holidays and the church where they worshipped. Diana had connections on both sides with the Royal Family: Lord Fermoy had been friend and shooting companion to Kings George V and VI, her father had been equerry (a privileged position as royal dogsbody reserved for members of the armed forces) to the Queen, Elizabeth II, and was a frequent guest at Balmoral shooting parties. Both her paternal grandmother, Cynthia Spencer (born Lady Cynthia Hamilton), and her great-aunt, Lady Delia Peel, were close friends and ladies-in-waiting to Queen Elizabeth, the Queen Mother, as was her maternal grandmother, Ruth, Lady Fermoy. Another Spencer great-aunt, Lady Lavinia White, who died in 1955, had been a close childhood friend of Queen Elizabeth. Park House could even be seen from the top windows of the Big House at Sandringham. She was, in a very real sense, 'the Girl Next Door'.

The Spencer family estate was Althorp in Northamptonshire but Diana rarely went there as a child; her fierce grandfather, Jack Spencer, the 7th Earl, and his heir, Diana's father Johnnie (Viscount Althorp at the time of Diana's birth), did not get on. She grew up with her roots in north Norfolk, a remote corner of one of the most isolated and rural parts of England, a county of gently rolling countryside under a vast sky. The Sandringham estate surrounding her birthplace is, in contrast, a sandy heath dotted with towering pine trees. The cold grey North Sea with its sand dunes and reeded marshes lies a short distance from Park House. North Norfolk is the territory of large estates and ancient families living the sporting and social life of a closed circle, largely barred to outsiders. Diana's parents, Frances and Johnnie Althorp, fitted perfectly into this background.

On Diana's mother's side the family were Anglo-Irish from County Cork: their name was Roche and their title Baron Fermoy.

Diana's great-great-grandfather, Edmund Burke Roche, was elected to Parliament and made a baron in the mid-nineteenth century; his second son, James Boothby Burke Roche, 3rd Baron Fermoy, married, in 1880, an American 'Dollar Princess', Frances 'Fanny' Work, daughter of a successful Wall Street broker. It was the usual alliance of American money in exchange for European title which became current practice in the nineteenth century and, as so many of such marriages were, it was unhappy and ended in divorce in 1891. Fanny's father, Frank Work, had little use for Europeans and after the divorce he told his daughter that her children would only inherit his fortune if they became Americans. Fanny's twin elder sons, Maurice and Francis, were sent to the cream of American schools and colleges, St Paul's School, Concord, New Hampshire, and Harvard, but despite this they refused to become Americans on their grandfather's death in 1911 and successfully challenged the conditions of his will. With $2.9 million (roughly £28–30 million today) apiece they turned their back on America and in 1921 left for England where Diana's grandfather, Maurice, now 4th Baron Fermoy, settled in Norfolk, becoming Member of Parliament for King's Lynn; a position he held from 1924 to 1935 and later from 1943 to 1945. On a trip to Paris, he met the beautiful, talented and ambitious Ruth Gill, a paint manufacturer's daughter from Aberdeenshire. Ruth was studying to be a concert pianist at the Paris Conservatoire but without much hesitation she gave up her career to marry Maurice, who was attractive to women, extremely wealthy and had a title to boot. They married in 1931, when she was twenty-six and he forty-six, and had three children: Mary, born in 1934, Frances, Diana's mother, born in 1936, and Edmund, born in 1939.

Maurice and Ruth Fermoy settled at Park House, a convenient base for Maurice because of its proximity to his constituency. He was outgoing, jovial and much liked by his constituents, a notable communicator, willing to burst into a speech at any time; on visits to local hospitals he would sit on the side of patients' beds and chat happily away with them. Ruth, backed by the Fermoy money, was a generous and skilful hostess. 'They had wonderful tennis parties and things like that which nobody else had in those days,' a Spencer relation recalled. 'Because of the American money they lived in a style that nobody else seemed to then.' There were rumours that some of the Norfolk grandees sneered at the couple, at Maurice for his 'American trade' connections and at Ruth for her modest background. 'The sort of Norfolk hierarchy – dubbed "county-bound" by a Spencer contemporary [Lady Margaret Douglas-Home] – wouldn't have anything to do with them, and rather rejected them,' said an aristocratic contemporary of Ruth's. 'And because they lived at Park House [so close to Sandringham] the King and Queen took them up. Queen Elizabeth never liked that sort of ostracism and snobbery.'[1] Diana's mother, Frances, was born on 20 January 1936, the day of King George V's death at Sandringham; even at that stressful time, his widow, Queen Mary, noted 'the birth of Lady Fermoy's baby' and sent Ruth a congratulatory note.

Diana never knew her grandfather, who died in 1955, but her grandmother, Ruth Fermoy, was to play an important part in her life, not least for her close royal connections based on her valued friendship with the Queen Mother whose woman of the bed-chamber she became. Like her friend the Queen Mother, Ruth had a Scottish steel about her. 'She was a very, very mysterious woman,' the Spencer relation said, 'always very elegant and gentle and quiet but there was another side to her – less gentle.' Ruth Fermoy was socially ambitious, adopting the attitudes of the aristo-cratic circles she had joined on her marriage. She was delighted when her daughter Mary married Anthony Berry, the son of Viscount Kemsley, ecstatic when Frances became engaged to Johnnie, Viscount Althorp, only son and heir to the 7th Earl Spencer, with vast acres of Northamptonshire, and an historic stately home, Althorp. Now titled herself, very rich and outstandingly beautiful, she turned her back on her middle-class Aberdeenshire background to cultivate her royal and aristocratic connections. Her rigid adher-ence to the conventions of her adopted class and of the courtier circle was to have dramatic repercussions on Diana's early life.

Frances Burke Roche, whom Diana was to resemble both in

looks and character, was a beauty with fine features, luminous blue eyes, long, slim legs and blonde hair. She was also as strong and independent minded as her mother, Ruth, if not quite as tough. Frances herself said of Ruth, 'I don't think I've ever known anyone with as much confidence. She made up her mind and went for it. She didn't waver over anything.' The same words were echoed of Frances by her friends. 'Frances was the strongest character of anyone I've ever known,' said one. 'She was forcible, dynamic, energetic and very intelligent – had she had a better education she would have been a very contributive person – she had leadership qualities. She had terrific power over men – she was funny but one of the most dominating female characters I've ever known and she was like that at seventeen.' And at seventeen, what Frances wanted was Johnnie Althorp as he then was; she had first seen him when he visited her school, Downham, when she was just fourteen. At seventeen and just after leaving school, her parents launched her on the marriage market for upper-class girls known as the London Season, a daily round of balls, cocktail parties, house parties at weekends and certain sporting events such as the unmissable Royal Ascot. During that Season, Frances met Johnnie again, they fell in love and became engaged, despite the fact that Johnnie had been expected to marry the beautiful and charming Lady Anne Coke, daughter of the Earl of Leicester, owner of a great estate, Holkham, in Norfolk. As head of the great Norfolk family, neighbours of the Royal Family at Sandringham and close friends of the late King and of Queen Elizabeth, the Leicesters were leading lights in the hermetic world of north Norfolk royal and aristocratic society. Lady Anne confessed that she 'adored' Johnnie, though many of her friends did not, finding him 'unkind'. Still less did they like Frances who ruthlessly cut Anne out and took her man.

Johnnie Althorp liked dominant women. Tall, handsome in a bucolic way, charming and impeccably bred, he was a catch in social terms despite the tight financial lead on which his father, the 7th Earl, kept him. Any available money – and there was not a great deal – was devoted to the maintenance and restoration of Althorp. (The exception was the sale of one of the jewels of the

Spencer collection, a magnificent Holbein portrait of Henry VIII, which paid for Johnnie's Eton education, and is now in the Thyssen collection in Madrid.) As was the case in many aristocratic families (and indeed, historically, the British Royal Family) the heir and his father did not get on. Jack Spencer was irascible, difficult and eccentric: his nickname in society was the ironic 'Jolly Jack'. His passion for the family house, Althorp, seemed to have left him little room for other affections and the thought of passing on his treasure to his son was painful in the extreme. Althorp was his temple, and as its custodian he regarded himself as the temple priest, spending hours polishing the silver in the butler's pantry although he had a butler to do it for him. Unlike his son, he disliked human contact, particularly with those he regarded as 'the lower orders'. Among the numerous bees in his bonnet was an aversion to his driver looking round when he got into the car, the signal for departure being the sound of his door slamming shut. As Lord Lieutenant of Northamptonshire he used an old Rolls-Royce with chauffeur; on one occasion after an official dinner, Spencer got out to relieve himself, the wind slammed the door before he could get back in and the driver, knowing perfectly well what had happened, gleefully drove off leaving him in open country in the dark. He was a crashing snob with a dread of anything middle class. Once, lunching at Clarence House, he told Queen Elizabeth that he would never go into a house where people ate fish with fish knives because it was so middle class. 'Whenever he came to lunch after that,' said one of Queen Elizabeth's circle, 'we always had fish with fish knives.' 'He induced respect in many, and fear in almost all,' his grandson Charles Spencer wrote.[2] Unsurprisingly, Johnnie's childhood memories were not happy ones. He used to dread the train journey home and would hide in the shadow of the carriage, hoping his father had forgotten to collect him. At Althorp, when he felt the atmosphere thickening, he would climb into the false ceiling of a bathroom and hide there with his terriers as companions. 'I fear these solitary moments were relatively frequent,' his son wrote.[3]

Jolly Jack's wife, Cynthia, daughter of the Duke of Abercorn, was his complete opposite, beautiful, sensitive, charitable and greatly loved. 'I have never heard anyone say a word against her memory,' her grandson wrote, 'and she is still very much alive as a paragon of sweet nobility ... The word most often used to describe her is "saintly".'[4] She had served the Queen Mother as lady of the bedchamber but even more the local people for whom she had done an enormous amount of voluntary work. When she died in 1972 of a brain tumour, the county's hospice was named after her. Johnnie, who had loved her deeply and seen her too little because of his difficult relationship with his father, was devastated. Some of Diana's gentleness and empathy with the sick and suffering came from Lady Cynthia, whom she resembled in looks. Diana, aged eleven, came to believe that her grandmother Cynthia watched out for her as her guardian angel.

Diana's father was a typical product of his age and class. He was educated at Eton, served as an officer in the Royal Scots Greys and, on the strength of his family connections, had acted as equerry to both King George VI and Queen Elizabeth II and accompanied the Queen on her post-Coronation Commonwealth tour in 1953. By then he was engaged to Frances; they married on 1 June 1954 in a grand society wedding at St Margaret's, Westminster, attended by one thousand guests including the Queen, the Duke of Edinburgh, the Queen Mother and Princess Margaret. The young couple were very much in love but their circumstances were unequal from the start. Frances would have to finance the marriage. Johnnie, once described by his commanding officer in the Royal Scots Greys as 'very nice but very stupid', tried to find a job as a banker but was turned down by his old friend and partner in Hoare's on the grounds that 'mathematics was never his strong suit'. He then enrolled as a student at the Royal Agricultural College at Cirencester, the traditional option for the landed gentry and aristocracy (unkindly dubbed 'clotted cream': rich and thick). They lived first at Rodmarton, Gloucestershire, in a rented cottage and then at Orchard Cottage on the Althorp estate in uncomfortable proximity to Jolly Jack.

Happily for them, after the death of Frances's father, Maurice

Fermoy, in 1955, his widow Ruth had offered to let them take over the lease of Park House. At the same time Frances, having inherited her share of her father's fortune, generously bought Johnnie a 600-acre farm at nearby Snettisham for £30,000. While Johnnie farmed at Snettisham and the family land at North Creake and looked after his charities, particularly the National Association of Boys' Clubs, Frances set about the business of producing babies. The pressure was on her to bear the male heir but her first two children were girls: Sarah, born in March 1955 nine months after the wedding, and Jane born in February 1957. She had a miscarriage but when finally a son was born, on 1 January 1960, it was not a triumph but a tragedy. John Spencer was born malformed: he died ten hours later, unable to breathe, having been taken away from Frances before she could hold him. It was a pain she never forgot.

Something in the relationship fractured after John's death. Johnnie Spencer insisted that Frances was responsible for her continuing failure to bear a healthy boy and she was sent to a Harley Street gynaecologist for humiliating tests and treatment. 'It was a dreadful time for my parents,' Charles Spencer said, 'and probably the root of their divorce because I don't think they ever got over it.' A Spencer cousin and a friend of Frances, said: 'The death of John was a deep tragedy in their lives. Afterwards there was a sadness in both of them which had not been there before.'

Diana was intended to be the replacement child, the longed-for heir. By the time she was born, her parents' marriage was in trouble, which the arrival of yet another girl did nothing to improve. The Norfolk married life which may have suited Frances as a young bride became confining for a woman with wider horizons. Her dashing husband had become considerably less dashing as time went by, settling all too comfortably into his country squire surroundings. 'Johnnie was the best company when he was a young man,' his former fiancée Lady Anne Coke said, 'but then he just became boring, wrapped up in his children and his country life.'

Diana convinced herself that she should have been a boy and

that, being a girl, she was a disappointment and regarded as a lesser being. 'I do know that in the Spencer family the gender issue is a big one and even when there was a son and no pressure to produce an heir, the female children are of less account than the male. Women are very much second-class citizens in the Spencer family,' a Spencer relation said. By the time the longed-for heir, Charles Spencer, was born in May 1964, the marriage was beyond repair. Johnnie, as long as his irascible, eccentric father lived, had virtually no role to play beyond gentlemanly farming, cricket and shooting. Essentially a weak man, he resented the intellectual and financial dominance of Frances. There were rows, sometimes, it is said, descending into violence. Frances was bored with her husband and her life in staid, enclosed, predictable Norfolk society. She was only twenty-eight and wanted to spread her wings.

The inevitable happened: she fell in love with another man, Peter Shand Kydd, whom she had met at a London dinner party in 1966. They met again on a joint skiing holiday with their respective spouses early in 1967. This time interest turned into powerful attraction and they began a secret affair. In the summer of 1967 Frances and Johnnie agreed on a trial separation: with the two older girls now at school, Frances would take Diana, aged six, and Charles, aged four, to London for the weekdays. Both were enrolled in London schools and returned to Park House and their father for weekends. The family were reunited at half-term in October and again for Christmas. By then the thought of continuing with life at Park House had become intolerable to Frances. She was headstrong, a character trait that Diana would inherit, and at Christmas 1967 she confronted Johnnie with a request for a divorce. An affair, however, was one thing, divorce quite another. It was a tradition in English upper-class families at the time that everything should be done to keep the family together and to avoid the scandal and humiliation which the request for a divorce by the wife would involve. Johnnie was not merely hurt but bitterly angry, determined that Frances should be punished and seen to be so. She would not be allowed to profit from her crime by keeping the children. She could leave, but as an outcast. He declared that the children would be sent to school in King's Lynn, that they would stay with him and not return to London.

In the subsequent custody case, Ruth Fermoy took her son-in-law's side and gave evidence against her own daughter. The deep-seated reason for this apparently cruel action seems to have been a combination of shock at her daughter's behaviour and extreme snobbishness, manifested in her determination to take the Spencer side: 'It was the name and the shame,' a Spencer relation who knew Ruth well said.[5] 'When I asked her why she did that,' a friend said, 'she said it was because Charles must be brought up at Althorp . . .' 'She had a very ruthless streak. It was the most extraordinary thing to do. It split her family. Ruth's funeral was one of the saddest and creepiest I have ever been to. We sat on one side of the church with Charles and Diana – who had separated, I think, but came together for the day – and on the other side of the aisle was the Fermoy family, and there was Frances, and they didn't talk to each other, husbands and cousins who were all not talking to her. It was the most terrible thing.'[6] Ruth, she said, in a phrase which was to become a litany in court circles later on, blamed the 'bad Fermoy blood' for Frances's behaviour. 'I remember Ruth saying that the trouble was her husband's family. They are what you call "bolters". They were all American bolters. A very unfortunate gene.'[7]

Diana, six at this time, was old enough to sense the strained atmosphere and, as she later recalled, to overhear the bitter rows. Opinions are divided as to whether an overwrought Johnnie actually hit his wife or not. Both are now dead so the truth cannot be known; the rumour that he did may have arisen because Frances later based her grounds for divorce on a plea of cruelty. Frances had come back for Christmas with the intention of having the children with her in London but, when she left this time, she left for good. Years later Diana, pouring out her heart on tapes for Andrew Morton's explosive book, *Diana: Her True Story*, remembered as a defining moment the crunch of tyres on the gravel as her mother drove off. 'I'll be back,' Frances told her, but she never did return to Park House.

The happy, undemanding childhood life at Park House fell apart. Diana saw her father unhappy and withdrawn, couldn't understand why her mother was no longer there, heard her little brother Charles sobbing for his mother in the night. Her longing for love and her fear of abandonment, her horror and fear of divorce and determination that it should not happen to her and to her children was born at that moment. Torn between love for her devastated father and her absent mother, Diana suffered what was to turn out to be a deep and psychologically crippling wound.

2. A Norfolk Childhood

'She has been accused of making too much of losing her mother through divorce in the late 1960s, but in truth the loss ran deep within her' (William Deedes[1])

Diana's despair at the departure of her mother would be at the root of her later view of herself as a 'victim', something to which she returned over and over again, particularly when faced with a television camera or a tape recorder. She had a strong streak of fantasy and self-dramatization in her make-up, and as a child had a reputation for lying: one day on the school run, a local vicar's wife told her: 'Diana Spencer, if you tell one more lie, I'll put you out of the car.' Even her brother Charles Spencer later agreed that as a child she had a tendency to lie. Some people, including the Spencer family, tended to dismiss Diana's claims of unhappiness. 'I think in her perception it seemed like that but it wasn't the reality. It was much happier than she felt it was in retrospect,' a cousin said. Yet a man who was close to her before she began her relationship with Prince Charles was convinced that the departure of her mother 'had a very severe, dramatic effect on her'.[2]

People who witnessed the early days after Frances's departure tend to bear out Diana's view. A cook, engaged by Lady Fermoy, who arrived shortly after Frances left when Diana was six, had a very different impression of life at Park House at the time. 'It was not in my recollection a happy household. Lord Althorp was absent a lot of the time and not cheerful . . . Diana was very quiet, kept herself to herself. The children never cried [during the day] but did sob at night when they had gone to bed.' A Norfolk neighbour remembers giving a birthday party for one of her sons at the time: 'It was July and all the children were enjoying themselves in the garden except for poor Diana – she refused to join in and I said to the young nanny who was with her, "What can we do to encourage her to join the other children?" Her answer was: "Nothing, she is a very sad little girl." This was just after her mother had bolted.'[3]

Years later, in 1992, Diana would claim in tapes recorded by Peter Settelen, 'My father told me about five years ago that he would find me on the doorstep: "You didn't speak. You just sat there. You just, you know, you just never spoke."' Diana, at six, was just the age when her mother's unexplained disappearance hit hard: her sisters, aged ten and thirteen, were better equipped to cope; Charles, at only three, cried for his mother at night but was unable to understand or rationalize her departure from his life as Diana did.

But if Diana was shocked and confused by her mother's unexplained disappearance from her life, her father was equally so. When he was at home he shut himself away: 'He was really miserable after the divorce, basically shell-shocked,' Charles Spencer said. 'He used to sit in the study the whole time.' Frances's name was never mentioned. Emotions were raw on both sides: 'Frances went through agonies when she lost her children,' a contemporary recalled.[4]

Luckily for Diana, she was initially unaware of the bitter behind-the-scenes battles between Frances and Johnnie both over the terms of the divorce and the custody of the children. Frances lost all the way down the line: in two custody cases when Ruth Fermoy sided with Johnnie against her and in the divorce case in which her cause was not helped by Mrs Shand Kydd, whose own divorce petition cited Frances as the co-respondent. When Frances petitioned on the grounds of cruelty, Johnnie countersued by reason of her adultery. Frances lost and costs were awarded against her. She was publicly branded an unfit mother, a 'bolter' (after a character in Nancy Mitford's *The Pursuit of Love*, 1945) and an adulteress. The Althorp divorce caused an upheaval in Norfolk society where Frances was widely condemned for what was seen as her desertion of her children.

Diana was not, however, too young to be sensitive to people's curious stares when they attended church at Sandringham or were taken by Ruth Fermoy to Ladyman's tea rooms in King's Lynn. Although there was nothing beyond bald announcements in the London newspapers about the proceedings, all north Norfolk from top to bottom of the social scale knew about it and most of them sympathized with the deserted father and his children.

A Norfolk neighbour left a widower with a number of children around the time of the Althorp divorce used to employ house-keeper/nannies who had previously been at Park House. 'They had usually left Johnnie Althorp and were full of stories about the awful [atmosphere] . . . how Frances would ring the children up every night just as they went to bed, and always upset them. It was a very unhappy set-up.'[5]

Whatever Diana's recollections of her sadness in the first year after her mother left, as time went on that view became a distortion of the truth. Mary Clarke, whom Diana's father engaged to look after the two younger children in February 1971, remembered: 'When I look back to life at Park House, I do think to myself what a wonderful free and easy life we had. Always I remember just laughter and jokes. Diana was a real tease.'[6] Diana spent the first fourteen years of her life at Park House, a solid Victorian mansion built of the rust-coloured local carrstone with large bow win-dows, a servants' wing and stabling. It was no architectural gem, but the Spencer children remembered it as 'lovely'. The house was large and roomy with open fires in every main room including the nursery, while background heating was provided by huge Edwardian radiators. The entrance led into a flagged hall with huge stone slabs, from which a stone staircase with wrought-iron balustrade led to the upper floor. Off the hall there were big, light rooms with marble fireplaces, bow windows and cornices with tongue and egg moulding. A large cedar tree, planted at the time the house was built, still stands on the lawn in front of the house, cattle graze in the fields beyond and surrounding trees provide shelter from the icy winds blowing in from the Wash to the north and the North Sea to the east. The windows look out beyond the lawn to green fields and to the south over Sandringham Park.

Mary Clarke's memory of life at Park House was very different from the unhappy household of a previous employee's recollection. 'I was impressed from the start by how happy and self-contained the children were,' she wrote, 'and how they always found so much to do to amuse themselves.'⁷ A cousin remembers Park House as 'a great family house, everything was family about it, nothing daunting. You felt it was well used and enjoyed but predictable. Not opulent, nothing of that kind, just cosy and predictable.' Diana kept a huge collection of stuffed furry animals in her bedroom; poignantly, she referred to them as 'my family'. There were lots of live animals: Johnnie's black Labrador gun dog, Jill the springer spaniel, Diana's bad-tempered cat Marmalade, and her collection of hamsters, rabbits and guinea pigs. 'She loved animals when she was a child,' her mother said. 'I think you want something to love, and she loved everything that was small and furry or had feathers. She had rabbits, guinea pigs, hamsters; a long succession of animals to care for. She outgrew it and took on people . . . But the animals were super-comfortable and rather well catered for – well looked after, well cleaned out. She had a great consciousness they were dependent on her. She did the dirty work.' There were ponies in the fields and stables, Diana could ride by the time she was three, although after an accident in which she broke her arm her enthusiasm for horses disappeared. There were swimming and tennis parties with the children of the local gentry when Diana liked to show off her diving skills. The family owned a beach hut at Brancaster where they picnicked, and also played and paddled on the huge beach at Holkham.

Diana became used to playing to the camera at an early age. Her father was a passionate photographer, snapping away on every occasion to fill the albums which he dedicated to each of his children. His early pictures registered Diana's shy habit of looking upwards from under her fringe, a habit which never left her. But, like all stars, she never took a bad picture: the camera loved her and she instinctively responded to the lens levelled at her. She had the capacity to pose but yet make the pose look natural, a lifelong characteristic. Wherever she was, she communicated with the camera.

The Spencer children were, with the exception of Diana, all bright academically. Her failure to keep up with her siblings in this area gave Diana a secret inferiority complex which she balanced by her belief in her own instinct. 'Diana was not stupid,' a cousin said of her. 'She was intelligent with this very, very quick wit.' Sarah, six years older than she was, the elder sister whom she hero-worshipped, was named after the Spencers' formidable ancestor, Sarah Jennings, Duchess of Marlborough, and had many of her namesake's qualities. 'She is a most interesting character,' a cousin said of her. 'The most complex of them all I would have said. Very strong, very alive and alert, intelligent. Not terribly nice. An interesting woman but tough, without Diana's gentle side. She knows what she wants.' Sarah had that foxy look inherited from the red-haired Spencers and the overwhelming confidence of her mother. Jane, the least assertive of the four, managed to spend more time with her mother and Diana did not become close to her until later. Charles, another red-headed Spencer and academically the brightest, was an equally strong character but wary, controlling and complex in his relationships. When he grew up, a relation was to say that he was a control freak and that they all, even his mother, were 'terrified of him'. But during their childhood Diana mothered him and the two were very close. 'I've always seen him as the brains in the family,' Diana told Morton in 1991. 'I still see that. He's got S levels and things like that. I think that my brother being the youngest and the only boy was quite precious [to the family as the heir to Althorp] . . . I was the girl who was supposed to be a boy. Being third in line was a very good position to be in − I got away with murder. I was my father's favourite, no doubt about that.

'I longed to be as good as Charles in the schoolroom. I was never jealous of him. I so understand him. He's very like me as opposed to my two sisters. Like me he will always suffer. There's something in us that attracts that department . . .'[8]

In the absence of their parents, the children congregated in the big kitchen begging for treats from the cook. It was a pattern in Diana's behaviour: even when she grew up and married she preferred the company of her staff to that of the 'grown-ups'. The kitchen or the butler's pantry was where she felt at home. The children had a nanny who was so young and inexperienced that she was more of a childminder than a nanny; they ignored her for the company of the cook. Ruth Fermoy, living four miles away at nearby Hillington, was the distant power in the household, hiring the staff and supporting Johnnie. The staff was headed by a couple, Johnnie's former army batman, Mr Smith, and his wife, who lived over the stables and ran the house, doing most of the work, including the shopping, except the nannying and the cooking. They were devoted to Johnnie and aloof with the other staff, the nanny and the cook, whom they treated as outsiders. They all lived off the estate so venison and pheasant featured largely on the menu. 'Bought food', food from the regular shops, was rarely allowed. Vegetables came straight from the garden. The children complained – 'Can't we have lamb chops' – but to no avail.

The children reacted differently to their situation: although Sarah and Jane, being older and at boarding school when the separation happened, were less affected, Sarah at least reacted by being naughty, as indeed to some extent they all did. Sarah was the worst behaved, 'a horror' an employee recalled: she would bring her pony into the kitchen and ride it round the table despite the cook's protests. Diana remembered being extremely badly behaved towards the young and inexperienced 'nannies' who were imposed on them, sticking pins into their seat cushions and throwing their clothes out of the window. Both parents were so traumatized by feelings of guilt (on Frances's side), humiliation and despair (on Johnnie's), that they spoiled the children and exercised little parental control. Like many children of divorce, the Spencers manipulated their parents to get what they wanted. Diana became extremely adept at pushing and cajoling for what she wanted in the certainty that no one would say no to her Machiavellian behaviour, which she would indulge in with devastating effect years later.

Ostracized as a bolter, Frances never came back to Norfolk. Park House, for all its amenities, conspicuously lacked a maternal figure. Ruth Fermoy and Cynthia Spencer did their best to cheer the children, teaching them bridge and card games. Lady Margaret Douglas-Home, Jolly Jack's sister, was a stimulating presence in the children's life; known as 'Aunt Margaret', she was in fact their great-aunt. As Charles remembered, 'Aunt Margaret was a life-enhancing force, her deep and generous laugh always at the ready, a passion for gossip evidence of an enquiring, rather than a malicious mind. To visit her in her small cottage in Burnham Market . . . was to experience humour of the greatest breadth, and intelligence of a rare intensity . . . Few were not bewitched by her mischievous chuckle.'[9]

After her divorce was made final in April 1969, with Johnnie granted a divorce on the grounds of her adultery and given custody of the children, Frances had married Peter Shand Kydd in May 1969. Before that there had been agonizing weekend visits by the two younger children to their mother in London: 'I remember Mummy crying an awful lot and every Saturday when we went up for weekends, every Saturday night, standard procedure, she would start crying. On Saturday we would both see her crying. "What's the matter, Mummy?" "Oh, I don't want you to leave tomorrow . . ."' It was, as Diana said, 'devastating' for a nine-year-old. 'Holidays were always very grim because we had a four-week holiday. Two weeks Mummy and two weeks Daddy and the trauma of going from one house to another and each individual parent trying to make it up in their area with material things rather than the actual tactile stuff, which is what we both craved for but neither of us ever got. When I say neither of us my other two sisters were busy at prep school and were sort of out of the house whereas my brother and I were very much stuck together.'[10] A year before she died, Ruth Fermoy, looking back, told a cousin, 'I feel those two younger ones have been very, very damaged by the separation, divorce, which the older two hadn't.' Years later Diana told one of her mother figures how difficult it had been for her because 'her mother would buy her a dress [then] her father would buy her another one. And there were always these disputes. And for holidays, for ever. Torn between the two . . . she loved her father but I don't think she really loved her mother, she felt sorry for her mother sometimes . . . but she didn't trust her . . .'[11] The children, according to people who knew them, had an 'awful upbringing' with no rules beyond eating everything on their plates and writing thank-you letters.

Again Diana was exaggerating: the sadness of the early years after the divorce blotted out the happy times of her Norfolk childhood. As Mary Clarke wrote: 'A child who was truly, deeply traumatized, would not be able to maintain the contentment Diana continually displayed, apart from those occasional hiccups, throughout the time I knew her.' These 'hiccups' were prompted by the children's returning from their time with their mother: Charles took the situation quite naturally but Diana behaved strangely, the result perhaps of her mother's emotive farewell: 'Don't worry, you'll be all right, you'll settle, don't forget what I said, please ring me.' When Mary Clarke told them how happy their father would be to see them, Diana glanced sideways at her and said how sad her mother would be to be all on her own. Charles, used to his sister's dramatizations, said sharply, 'You know Mummy is not on her own, Diana, and you always say that about Daddy too.' When they reached Park House, Diana's bubbly self was replaced by a shy, deliberately withdrawn, little girl. She thought that if she appeared too excited to see him he might think that she was happier with him than with her mother. When Johnnie held out the prospect of a tea party at Sandringham with Princes Andrew and Edward, Diana said she didn't want to go, pleading a headache; showing a strength of will characteristic of her, she resisted all her father's attempts to persuade her.[12] Whether this was a misguided attempt to show loyalty to her mother by punishing her father, or whether she felt that the distress caused her by their split deserved to be demonstrated, is impossible to tell. Similar incidents were to occur later in life when she behaved in the same way to her husband.

According to Mary Clarke such royal invitations were rare; the two families did not often socialize. The Spencer children took their royal neighbours for granted and were not in awe of them. Among the few occasions when they did see the Royal Family was Sunday church which they attended only when the Queen was in residence; Johnnie thought that the Queen would notice their absence and think it odd. 'We were all shunted over to Sandringham for [sic] holidays. Used to go and see *Chitty Chitty Bang Bang*, the film. We hated it so much. We hated going over there. The atmosphere was always very strange when we went there and I used to kick and fight anyone who tried to make us go over there and Daddy was most insistent because it was rude,' Diana recalled.[13]

The Reverend Reginald Sweet, Latin teacher and chaplain at her second school, however, had a different story to tell: 'Diana was very keen on Prince Andrew,' he recalled. 'He was her great holiday friend. She had all these photographs on her desk and . . . she said, "Mr Sweet, when I grow up I'm going to marry Prince Andrew." I said, "Really, Diana?" "Yes, I'm going to marry him and he's my friend." The impression I got is that they knew each other very well and used to spend time together during the holidays.'[14] Diana's nanny, Janet Thompson, remembered walking into the drawing room at Sandringham to find the Queen playing hide and seek with the six-year-old Andrew and five-year-old Diana. At tea, Charles walked in, very much the elder brother. 'Everything all right? Looks like a good party to me.'[15]

In reality Diana knew that both her parents loved her and that she was her father's favourite. When the children got to know Peter Shand Kydd they liked him very much. 'Peter was humorous, generous, spontaneous and exciting,' Charles recorded. Diana and Charles's first meeting with him was in 1969 at Liverpool Street Station when they arrived off the train from Norwich. Diana remembered saying to Frances, 'Where's your new husband? "He's at the ticket barrier." And there was this very good-looking, handsome man and we were longing to love him and we accepted him and he was great to us and spoilt us rotten.'[16] It was Peter Shand Kydd who first christened Diana 'Duch', short for 'Duchess'.

The name, prompted by Diana's at times haughty behaviour, stuck: not only her family but all her Sloaney friends used it. When Peter and Frances moved to Itchenor in West Sussex, the children spent happy holidays there sailing with him and his three children. His presence made their time with their mother more relaxing and normal. When, after the second custody case, it was agreed that Johnnie and Frances should share the children's time together, Frances and Peter started looking for a proper home with plenty of space. They found an eighteenth-century farmhouse, Ardencaple, on the Isle of Seil off the west coast of Scotland, with 1000 acres of wild farmland and spectacular views. Diana and Charles loved their visits, the freedom, the beauty and the wild landscape – sailing, fishing, lobster-potting. Diana kept a Shetland pony called Soufflé there. At her boarding school, West Heath, she pinned a poster of the island above her bed. Charles Spencer recalled Ardencaple as 'a magical place which Diana and I adored'. Later the Shand Kydds bought a 2000-acre ranch at Yass in New South Wales where they spent six weeks each summer, and the children joined them there.

Diana's education was of the undemanding nature which in those days applied to girls of her age and class. She was first taught by her mother's governess, Gertrude Allen, known as 'Ally', who lived in the nearby village of Dersingham. Ally would collect Diana from Park House and take her to a neighbour's house for morning lessons with the children of the local gentry; while the children ate their packed lunches in the nursery with the owner and the children's nanny, Ally ate hers in isolated splendour in the dining room, her lunch specially prepared by the resident cook. Afterwards she would take the children for a walk accompanied by her ferocious dog.

In January 1968 Diana was enrolled at Silfield private school, a day school for girls and boys in Gayton, on the outskirts of King's Lynn. The school, housed in a large early twentieth-century suburban family house in a variety of architectural styles, was, as a notice board still proclaims, 'founded in 1955 for 5–11-year-olds'. There was a good-sized garden dominated by a large monkey puzzle tree contemporary with the house, and rambling wooden outbuildings including a 30-foot room with wooden panelling and false timbering and a fireplace which served as an assembly and games room. A small school with forty pupils, attended by the children of local farmers and gentry (including Diana's best friend, Alexandra Loyd, daughter of the Queen's estate agent at Sandringham), it was a cosy place with a family atmosphere. Diana was remembered by the headmistress, Jean Lowe, for her kindness to younger children, her love of animals and 'general helpfulness' but not for her academic potential. Later, she was shown up by her younger brother, Charles, who revenged himself for her superior strength and height in their sibling fights by calling her 'Brian' after the slow-witted snail in the children's programme *The Magic Roundabout*. It was here too, the first closed organization outside her home of which she had experience, that she found she was the only child of divorced parents. Sadly, she used to dedicate her work in art class 'To Mummy and Daddy'.

When she was nine Diana went to board at Riddlesworth Hall, some one and a half hours' drive from Sandringham. At first she had resented being made to leave her father, towards whom she had become very protective since the divorce but, despite her complaints – 'if you love me you won't leave me here' – she confessed that she 'loved being at school'. She boasted about being naughty and wanting to laugh and muck about, of taking a dare and escaping from her dormitory to run down the drive in the dark. Riddlesworth was a rectangular classical-style house, standing high with many windows and views over the surrounding gardens and fields. It had the feel of a lived-in house; elaborate light fittings, glass cases of stuffed birds and rather gloomy trophies of large animals were traces of the previous occupants. There were plaster and gilt ceilings in the larger rooms which were light and well proportioned; the general atmosphere was cheerful and friendly. Diana was not among strangers; several of the girls she knew from the surrounding families were there with her: Alexandra Loyd, her cousin Diana Wake-Walker, and Claire Pratt, daughter of her godmother, Sarah Pratt. Pupils were encouraged to bring pets, which were housed in 'Pets' Corner' in the garden within sight of the house. Diana became head of Pets' Corner and brought her treasured guinea pig Peanuts with her. She never carried off any academic prizes but she did win a prize with Peanuts for 'Best Kept Guinea Pig' and the Leggatt Cup 'for helpfulness'. She won prizes for swimming and diving: 'But in the academic department, you might as well forget about that!' she laughed. 'I ate and ate. It was always a great joke – let's get Diana to eat three kippers and six pieces of bread. I did all that,' the future bulimic said proudly. What with the pets and the Norfolk friends, school was merely an extension of her normal life and simple, restricted horizon.

Johnnie Althorp always drove Diana back to Riddlesworth, much as he had joined in the school run to Silfield, and where he was remembered for his easy manner and interest in people. At Riddlesworth, the headmistress, Patricia Wood, said that all the kitchen staff and grounds people particularly remembered him. 'When you talked to the kitchen ladies they couldn't remember much about Diana because she was just one of the little girls, but they could all remember her father. He was a very conspicuous gentleman . . . very tall and noticeable and almost the first thing he did when he brought her to the school after the holidays was to go down in the kitchens and talk to them.'[17] Johnnie was interested in everybody he met, regardless of background, a quality Diana inherited from him. 'My father,' Sarah told an interviewer, 'had an instinctive way with people . . . People would talk to him and he was gripped . . . He loved people. And Diana did too. I don't think that quality has got anything to do with upbringing. I think you've either got it or you haven't . . . it's either in you when you're born, or it's not.'[18]

Aged twelve, in September 1973, after three years at Riddlesworth, Diana followed Sarah and Jane to a new school, West Heath, near Sevenoaks in Kent. Located in another splendid country house, West Heath was the natural progression from Riddlesworth: small – there were only 120 girls – friendly, with the emphasis on happiness and good behaviour rather than academic achievement. In many ways such schools were throwbacks to the fifties, when girls of good family were not expected to do much more than prepare themselves for marriage. 'Hamsters and knitting were what they were about,' a contemporary remembered. 'Everyone came out confident and happy,' a schoolmate recorded, 'and there was very little angst . . . It was a relaxed place.' When Diana arrived, Jane, 'the good Spencer' then aged sixteen, was a prefect with an excellent academic record. Sarah was no longer there, having been expelled for drunkenness two years earlier. She had been a success both academically and in sport, winning prizes and appearing in the school plays. But, brilliant, forceful and wilful, she was bored at West Heath. Somehow, according to her own admission, she laid hands on an astonishing variety of drink. 'I used to drink because I was bored,' she said. 'I would drink anything: whisky, Cointreau, gin, sherry or, most often, vodka because the staff couldn't smell that.'[19] But one day in 1971 the staff did notice: she was drunk and instantly expelled. A few years later there were to be further signs of trouble when she was affected by serious eating disorders.

In her own way Diana was a success at West Heath, although she liked later on to emphasize her image as a rebel. The head-mistress, Ruth Rudge, a keen observer, recorded that when Diana first arrived she was 'wary of adults, often prickly with her peers . . . but was lucky enough to find herself in a group of lively, talented, caring individuals, some of whom she already knew, and soon gained confidence in her new surroundings and found her niche socially'.[20] The friends she made at West Heath, notably Carolyn Pride and Laura Greig, were to become part of her loyal inner circle, supporting her through thick and thin, through the depths of despair and beyond. The trauma of her parents' divorce never quite left her: '. . . she came and talked to me quite a lot,' the matron, Violet Allen, said. 'Of course she missed her mother and father. The other [girls] who had divorces felt the same way. Some accepted it and some had more difficulty with it. No doubt about it, Diana found it difficult to accept. She was vulnerable in some things. I can't put a finger on it, but it probably all had to do with the insecurity and break-up of [her parents'] marriage.'[21]

She learned to play the piano, took lessons in ballet, tap and ballroom dance – her greatest relaxation. She won the school dancing competition one year and cups in swimming and diving every year. She developed her strong sense of sympathy for the suffering and the needy when she visited the mentally handicapped in the local hospital: when there were dances she would manoeuvre the wheelchairs from the front, facing the patients as if she were dancing with them, instead of, as was more usual, pushing from behind. In her day-to-day life Diana was at times fierce in her emotional responses, unforgiving to people who had offended her. 'She had a very strong character,' her headmistress said. 'She went about getting what she wanted . . .' In her last year Diana was named a prefect, and carried out her role so successfully that she was awarded a special prize for service – 'for anyone who has done things that otherwise might have gone unsung,' Ruth Rudge said. 'She was dependable in her own doings, reliable, and went out of her way to help people. She was generous with her time.'[22] When she was not being dutiful and dependable, Diana immersed herself in the romantic world of Barbara Cartland's novels in which strong men wooed virgin brides and love triumphed over all. It was perhaps the worst preparation for life in general and her own life in particular that she could have had.

Just as Diana was creating her own stable world on her own terms at West Heath, life at Park House and her relationship with her father there, the hitherto immutable centre for her since childhood, was about to change forever. The one thing the children had always dreaded happened. A new, powerful woman came into their father's life – Raine Legge, then Countess of Dartmouth. The first inkling they had of Raine's existence had come in the summer of 1972 when Johnnie invited Raine to lunch at Park House. Raine Dartmouth, or Legge as she was always then known, was a formidable woman, a beauty, immaculately dressed, made-up and coiffed, with a sharp intelligence and a will as determined as any of the Spencer children. She and Johnnie had met and fallen in love although Raine was still married to her first husband and was the mother of four children. She was also the daughter of another formidable character, the immensely successful Barbara Cartland, Diana's favourite novelist.

Sarah, it seems, who now had a London life, had heard gossip about her father's friendship with Lady Dartmouth which she had passed on to Diana and her siblings. The children were determined that no one should come between them and their beloved father whom they regarded as their property. When Johnnie told them he had invited Lady Dartmouth to lunch, the children's hackles were immediately raised. Diana's reaction to this immaculate vision, so far removed from the county ladies of their experience, was suppressed giggles. Raine was charming and gracious but oblivious to the children's covert hostility or, if she was not, determined not to let it bother her. In the end Sarah, with no other outlet for her enmity, burped loudly and deliberately. Johnnie said 'Sarah!' to which she cheekily replied that in Arab countries a burp was recognized as a sign of appreciation. Her father was so appalled that he told her to leave the table, which she did. Diana attempted to defend her, only to be told, 'That's enough, Diana.' Loyally, Diana riposted that she did not feel well and asked permission to leave, a request which her father readily granted. It had not been a good beginning.

The children's antennae were quivering at the prospect of this new woman in their father's life. 'We didn't like her one bit,' Charles said. 'As a child you instinctively feel things and with her I very much instinctively felt things.' The next encounter was to be at Sarah's coming-out party for her eighteenth birthday the following year, a fabulous occasion arranged by Johnnie at Castle Rising, a Norman ruin in Norfolk. Raine was among the four hundred guests and had taken a hand in its organization, finding a costume for Johnnie as Henry VIII and for Sarah a dress worn by Geneviève Bujold as Anne Boleyn in the 1969 film *Anne of the Thousand Days*. Sarah was in her element dancing with her boy-friend, Gerald Grosvenor, heir to the Duke of Westminster, and driving off in her father's birthday present to her, a green MGB GT sports car.

Sarah may have been too happy to notice the growing relation-

ship between her father and the Countess of Dartmouth. Raine
was determined to land Johnnie as her second husband. Her first,
Gerald Legge, was already on his way out as far as she was concerned: she frequently gave dinner parties without him. Raine was
dogged, ambitious and devastatingly efficient: by the time she and
Johnnie met again for the first time since his marriage, she had
already led a successful and high-profile public life as a councillor
for Westminster for eleven years, for eight as the LCC member
for Lewisham West, then as a member of the newly formed Greater
London Council, when she had made her name opposing the
licensing of the film of James Joyce's *Ulysses*, which she described
as 'disgusting and degrading'. 'I like things that present life and sex
in a glamorous way,'[23] she declared, true to the theme of her
mother's novels. She had been a great success as chairman of the
Historic Buildings Board; in 1971 she became a member of the
English Tourist Board and headed an advisory committee to
the government on the environment. When she resigned from the
committee in protest at the Covent Garden development scheme,
she became a national figure and a surprising heroine to the liberal
left. 'It is all too easy to dismiss this particular woman . . . as
a good-looking, immaculately dressed, effusive member of the
aristocracy who somehow gets offered positions of power', the
Guardian wrote, '[but] behind the saccharine image there stands an
extremely able politician, a feminine but tough bargainer . . .' In
1972 she was asked to become Chairman of the United Kingdom
Executive Committee for European Architectural Heritage Year
1975. Her mission was to preserve historic towns and buildings;
she wrote a book, *What Is Our Heritage?*, and co-opted Johnnie
Spencer to the Youth Panel to promote the cause in his capacity
as chairman of the National Association of Boys' Clubs. She also
asked him to help with photographs for her book: it was obvious
to colleagues that the couple were in love.

Johnnie was attracted to strong women and, if anything, Raine
was even more forceful and dynamic than Frances. He had been
lonely ever since Frances left: Raine's looks, wit and physical
attraction bowled him over. Being rather slow and diffident he left

her to make all the running. Raine was much brighter than Johnnie but found a vulnerability in him that appealed to her. She mothered and organized him. There was also a strong physical attraction between them (*Private Eye* later reported that en route from London to Northamptonshire they had stopped off at a motel for a few hours). Diana, who had mothered her father as much as she did her younger brother, had always thought of herself as first in his affections. But Raine could give him everything he got from Diana and more. Diana was about to receive a double shock.

3. 'I'm Lady Diana'

'I remember being a fat, podgy, no make-up, unsmart lady but I made a lot of noise and he [Prince Charles] liked that' (Diana to Andrew Morton)[1]

On 9 June 1975, Jack, 7th Earl Spencer, died and Diana's cosy family life at Park House came to an end. At first she was excited by her new title, Lady Diana, so much grander than the former Hon[ourable], and ran round West Heath shouting, 'I'm Lady Diana . . .' It was when she got home for the holidays that the real impact of the change in the family's circumstances hit her. Park House was being packed up in preparation for the move to the Spencer family home, Althorp. Her father was no longer Viscount Althorp but the 8th Earl Spencer. Diana's reaction to all this was to binge on peaches with her friend Alex Loyd at the beach hut at Brancaster.

Diana recalled: 'When I was 13 [actually fourteen; Diana was born 1 July 1961] we moved to Althorp in Northampton and that was a terrible wrench, leaving Norfolk, because that's where everybody who I'd grown up with lived. We had to move because grandfather died and life took a very big turn because my step-mother, Raine, appeared on the scene, supposedly incognito. She used to sort of join us, accidentally find us in places and come and sit down and pour [sic] us with presents and we all hated her so much because we thought she was going to take Daddy away from us . . .'[2] Leaving the house in which she had been born and spent all the years of her life so far was like another abandonment, another stage in her life like the departure of her mother. They had rarely visited Althorp and their feared grandfather and they had not liked it. Charles described it as 'a difficult phase in all our lives: uprooted from our childhood haunts and friends, and marooned in a park the size of Monaco', while the 121-room house seemed to them 'such an old man's house, reflecting my grandfather's Edwardian tastes, in a chilling time warp complete with the permeating smell of Trumper's hair oil and the ubiquitous tocking of grandfather clocks – their ticking always seemed too subtle a sound, getting absorbed in the oak of the floorboards and the fabric of the tapestries'.[3]

While Althorp was never to be 'home' to Diana as Park House had been, it reconnected her to her ancestors in a way which was to make her able to stand up to and even look down on the Royal Family. Even to someone as uninterested in history as Diana, the grandeur of Althorp, and the serried ranks of five centuries of distinguished forebears looking down on her from its walls, could not fail to impart a sense of the historic importance of her bloodlines. A historian friend of Diana's put it this way: 'Diana had sort of vaguely grasped, although being historically ignorant had not completely grasped, that those old Whig families like the Cavendishes and the Russells and her lot and one or two others, they in a way felt they were older and grander than the royal house, that they had put the House of Hanover on the throne when they were just German princelings, absolutely nothing, come from nowhere, couldn't speak a word of English . . . Parliament made George I monarch under the direction of the Whig oligarchy of which her family was a very important constituent founding member. So that in some way she had not married above her by marrying Prince Charles, if anything she'd married beneath her. Now I'm not sure that she ever formulated this view precisely in her mind, but it was sort of there I felt. "Who is he [Prince Charles] to look down on me and to say 'They're praising you because you're married to me, not because they like you'. 'You know, "Who is he to say this?"'[4] Traditionally, the Spencers and their aristocratic connections like the Cavendishes (Dukes of Devonshire) were Whigs who upheld the rights of the people against the overweening power of the monarch, as opposed to the Tory tradition of loyalty to the throne. 'The Tory tradition in the aristocracy,' said the historian Ben Pimlott, 'was deeply loyal to the monarchy; the Whig tradition was basically rather contemptuous. This difference can be exaggerated but there's a grain of truth, not necessarily in their traditions but in their style, and how they related to those traditions. The Whigs were individualists.'[5]

Althorp is not a beautiful house – the warm brick of the original Tudor great mansion was covered over in the late eighteenth century with silvery white tiles which give it a cold appearance – but it is surrounded by idyllic English countryside, the rolling acres of grassland which nurtured the sheep whose wool was the source of the original Spencer fortune. Spencers had occupied Althorp for nearly five centuries since the original John Spencer, known as 'the Founder', had acquired the land in 1507 and begun to build his mansion, acquiring more land, planting trees and creating the surrounding park. The family also owned the magnificent eighteenth-century Spencer House in London overlooking Green Park, but this was rented out in Diana's day. Spencer wealth and possessions had increased over the centuries, some of the more splendid through the first Diana Spencer, daughter of Lady Anne Churchill, whose parents were John Churchill, 1st Duke of Marlborough and his wife, Sarah Jennings, one of the most remarkable and difficult women of her day. The Spencer tendency for falling out with members of the family – it is said Sarah changed her will fifty times – may well have been passed down from her. The Churchill connection was much cherished by the family who were extremely proud of being related to the 1st Duke of Marlborough, whose great victories over the French in the first decade of the eighteenth century had brought him fame and riches and the great palace of Blenheim, named after his most celebrated victory and built for him by a grateful nation. Winston Churchill was born Winston Spencer Churchill: one day Diana's grandfather, Jack Spencer, found Winston Churchill in his cherished Muniment Room, smoking a cigar while researching the life of their mutual ancestor, the 1st Duke of Marlborough. Peremptorily he ordered Churchill to douse his cigar in a glass of water. Sarah, the 1st Duchess, had left her Spencer heirs her great collections of paintings and jewellery and the Marlborough Silver, the reward for the 1st Duke's campaigns, including the lavish gold and silver pieces bestowed on him by Queen Anne after Blenheim.

Diana's ancestors included not only Sarah Jennings, whose pride led her to snub even her sovereign and former friend, Queen Anne, but also another outstanding woman, Georgiana, Duchess of Devonshire, the headstrong beauty whose reckless exploits in Whig politics and at the gaming tables made her the most famous woman of her day. The blood of these distant ancestors meant that Diana was never going to be the mousy little girl some people thought – or perhaps hoped – that she would be. 'Spencers are very difficult and complicated people,' a Spencer relation said. 'The Queen Mother once said to me, "You know the Spencer women are extremely unusual and difficult!" and that's how they are. They also have an unforgiving side to them which seems to run through the family a bit. And I think that that way she had with the inability to sustain friendships and relationships seems to be one of the characteristics of them.' She said of her own Spencer mother: 'She was incredibly like Diana. In the same things. The sort of manipulation of reality, as I call it, and the conflict and then reunion and so on.'[6]

At first life at Althorp when Diana and Charles moved there seemed like a continuation of their childhood, although on a grand scale. Although latterly there had been a butler named Betts at Park House, his services had been abruptly dispensed with when the house was closed. At Althorp, however, there was not only a butler, Ainsley Pendrey, who had served the previous Earl, but a footman as well and seven other indoor servants. 'The early days were very happy ones and jolly good fun, with no bowing and scraping,' Betty Andrews, who started work at Althorp in 1975, told Angela Levin, author of a joint biography of Johnnie and Raine. The children would rush into the kitchen to find something to eat. 'Diana even used to cook for the staff. She loved to make bread and butter pudding for us and rice or milk pudding for herself,' Betty Andrews recalled.[7] Diana, always so domesticated, did her own washing and ironing and often Charles's too. This nurturing, almost domestic slave, side of Diana repeated itself in later life: she would do all the household chores for her sister Sarah, iron shirts for her platonic boyfriends before her marriage and, in the year of her death, do the ironing for Annabel Goldsmith and Jemima Khan on their trip to Pakistan. It was never a Marie Antoinette act, rather a response to a need in herself, to be useful, to show her skills, and to be 'tidy', another of her favourite words. At school people noticed her obsessive tidiness. She even used the word 'tidy' about keeping her virginity for the right man. The atmosphere at Althorp, according to Andrews, was 'happy-go-lucky – all three sisters got on well together'. Diana would toboggan down the grand front staircase on a tea tray, and dance by herself in the great Wootton Hall, designed as the entrance to the house in the early eighteenth century, with pictures and plasterwork reflecting the family passion for hunting.

Raine's presence radically changed the atmosphere. She had always wanted a grand country house, which Gerald Dartmouth had not possessed. Although not yet married to Johnnie, she was ever-present, staying in the India Silk Bedroom across the corridor from Johnnie's room. She began to redecorate the house, paying the cost herself. Johnnie was cash poor, as always, and now faced with a £2 million bill for death duties. She was desperate to marry Johnnie and began to fear that his hostile children would eventually frustrate her. None of them, and Sarah in particular, made any secret of their dislike. Sarah, never averse to talking to reporters, used their inquisitive telephone calls to drop acid into the newspapers about Raine. To one inquiry about Lord Spencer's relationship with Lady Dartmouth, she replied that her father was in bed with Lady Dartmouth and she wasn't going to disturb them. She told another: 'Since my grandfather died last June and we moved from Sandringham to Althorp, Lady Dartmouth has been an all too frequent visitor . . .'[8] When asked why Lady Dartmouth was spending so much time at Althorp, she replied, 'She is helping my father to open the house on a commercial basis. In my grandfather's time he did not care for the idea of the public walking around his house. Lady Dartmouth is writing a guide for it with my father.' Diana's protest was characteristic: a member of the paying public remembered seeing her 'acting the part of Cinderella' sitting beside the fire as the public walked past. The children used to chant 'Raine, Raine, go away' intending that she should hear them.

But Raine did not go away. In May 1976 Gerald Dartmouth obtained a divorce on the grounds of her adultery; two months later, on 14 July 1976, Johnnie and Raine married at Caxton Hall register office in London. He did not tell his children beforehand what he was going to do. Their fury knew no bounds, as he had anticipated. In 1992 Diana told Peter Settelen: 'Sarah rang me up, she said, "Have you seen the newspapers?" So I said, "What?" "Daddy's married Raine." I said, "My God, how do you know that?" "It's in the *Express*." We were so angry, but Sarah said, "Right, Duch" – my nickname was Duch – "you go in and sort him out."

'He said, "I want to explain to you why, um, I've got married to Raine." And I said, "Well, we don't like her." And he said, "I know that, but you'll grow to love her, as I have." And I said, "Well, we won't." I kept on saying we not I . . . I was the little crusader here . . . and I got really angry and I, if I remember rightly, I slapped him across the face, and I said, "That's from all of us, for hurting us", and walked out of the room and slammed the door. He followed me and he got me by the wrist and turned me round and said, "Don't you ever talk to me like that again." And I said, "Well, don't you ever do that to us again", and walked off.'[9]

The four Spencer children had always stood together, meta-phorically and physically. 'They were always very close as young people. Always did everything together, on any family occasion they were always in a group together, quite daunting for other people – it seemed like they were protecting each other . . .' a Spencer relation said. For anyone less concentrated on her goal than Raine Dartmouth, the hostile Spencer children gathered like a praetorian guard round their father would have been deeply intimidating. There had even been moments when she feared Johnnie's devotion to his children would prevent him from marrying her. After the wedding, when Raine became undisputed mistress of Althorp, things became even worse. The children's proprietorial attitude towards their father had not changed, and now they felt excluded. They remained impervious to Raine's charms. When friends were invited to stay at Althorp by Johnnie and Raine, they noticed 'a terrible air of strain between all three girls' which was 'very, very awkward' and that the sisters avoided saying a word to Raine if they could. On one social weekend in Derbyshire where there was a ball for the young at Haddon Hall, a friend of Johnnie's and Raine's sat next to Diana at lunch. 'Suddenly her eyes glinted, and she said, "You're a friend of my stepmother's, aren't you?" He replied, "I hope I'm a friend of your father's too."' – 'It was very unpleasant,' he commented. Sarah, who was in touch with the media, was more active in her enmity – leaking disagreeable stories about Raine to a tabloid reporter.[10] Even Jane, the quietest and least unstable of the Spencer quartet, 'the best of the lot' in a family friend's opinion, could not entirely restrain her hostility. On being asked at a dinner how often she went to Althorp, she replied loudly in Raine's hearing – 'When I'm asked.'

So Diana, like the others, felt a kind of estrangement from her father. She loved him but she saw less of him. He remained a loving father but in her view he belonged to Raine and not to her. It did not help the following year when she took her O levels. She took them twice and failed them twice and as a result had to leave West Heath at the age of sixteen. Diana said, 'At the age of fourteen I just remember thinking that I wasn't very good at anything, that I was hopeless. My brother was always the one who was getting exams at school and I was the dropout . . .'[11] 'I was always told by my family that I was the thick one and that my brother was the clever one and I was always so conscious of that.' 'I used to go to the headmistress,' she added, 'crying, saying, I wish I wasn't so stupid,' she said later.[12] Ruth Rudge denies her ever having done this: 'I never remember walking around with her and feeding her aspirins the night before, which I have done a number of times with other girls, [but] I didn't see any signs of panic when she took exams.'[13] Friends of Diana's have attributed it to 'sheer laziness and the fact that she was never pushed'. She excelled in

the things she liked doing but, when it came to academic work,
she simply gave up even before she started. A relative explained
it: 'I think she was not stupid, she was intelligent and she had this
very, very quick wit, but I think it reflected on her lack of confidence, her inability to achieve at school and sometimes if you're
emotionally damaged in some way you can't sustain concentration
or learning, and I think a certain part of you cuts out the ability to
absorb and process and construct, and I think that's what happened
to her. She certainly wasn't stupid.' The same relation attributed
Diana's backwardness in formal education to her status as a 'replacement baby', the girl born after the death of John: 'I have
noticed in other families where there has been what's called a
replacement baby, that the baby that's been born after a death has
certain things imposed on it which are not really relevant and they
seem to feel things which have perhaps been in other people's
minds . . .' In compensation, Diana developed an almost mystical
belief in the power and rightness of her own instinct which was
to guide her, for better or for worse, through her entire life. She
had, or so she later claimed, a sense of her own destiny, that she
was apart from the rest, designed for higher things. If so, who
needs exams?

Things were changing in all their lives: Raine was extremely
social. There were constant house parties, balls, shooting parties:
the children were banished to the nursery floor to leave room for
the guests. Entertaining became more formal, and under Raine,
demanding and a perfectionist, staff turnover was high. A senior
employee told Angela Levin of the children's reaction to their
stepmother: 'With the exception of Jane, who wasn't too bad, the
children could not have been more difficult and cold to Raine.
There was open hostility, not just to her as a person. They also
disliked the way she dominated and became so possessive of their
father which made them feel they had to compete with her for his
attention.'[14] Rupert Hambro recalled his impression: 'It was as if
she had put an iron fence around him. She also had a way of
making people who played a part in his life before she arrived feel
small. She was totally insensitive to Johnnie's family, his life and

his interests. When you did see him she was his mouthpiece and if you asked him anything, she would answer. A lot of people are incredibly happy in an environment that takes any pressure away from them. I would describe Lord Spencer as being pretty close to that . . .'[15] Johnnie Spencer's aunt, Lady Margaret Douglas-Home, who knew the children well, saw to the heart of the problem: 'I don't think Raine went about it the right way,' she said. 'I don't think she is made to be a stepmother. She must be the only pebble on the beach and wasn't willing to take second place to Johnnie's children. She used to claim all of him the whole time and didn't like them interfering in her life with Johnnie. The children never liked it and they were old enough to know. I was very sorry for them. They looked miserable.'[16]

According to a friend of Raine's the great strength in the Althorp household during this time of strain was Pendrey the butler whom he described as 'droll and amusing and a great pillar'. He and his wife Maudie, the housekeeper, a Norfolk farmer's daughter, were a refuge for Diana, as Mrs Pendrey recalled:

When she came to live at Althorp, she was always shy. She used to blush ever so easily too, used to go scarlet. My husband adored Diana, we all did. She would come and see her father about every six or seven weeks. When we knew Diana was coming for the weekend my husband would get all her favourite food in and make sure she had everything up in her bedroom. She used to sleep in the nursery, in a little black iron bed . . . When she came to Althorp the first thing she did was come and find my husband, because she was a very lovely, very polite little girl – always called him Mr. Pendrey – . . . of course he used to spoil her.

After her father remarried, she used to come and talk to us quite a lot. She sometimes used to come and have lunch with us. She never had airs and graces. Diana was just an ordinary lovely girl. She was very sweet and all the staff loved her. They used to put flowers in her bedroom when she used to come to Althorp. We used to make a fuss of her and make sure she was someone important. My husband said to me, when he saw her start growing up . . . 'You wait. She's going to be someone very special'.[17]

Staying with friends in Norfolk one September weekend Diana had a premonition about her father. By her own account she told her friends that she felt her father was going to 'drop down' and that 'if he dies, he'll die immediately, otherwise he'll survive'. Next day, 19 September 1978, Johnnie collapsed as he was crossing the courtyard at Althorp: he had suffered a massive cerebral haemorrhage. He was taken unconscious to Northampton General Hospital where he developed pneumonia. Raine, despite the danger, insisted that he be transferred to the National Hospital for Nervous Diseases in Queen Square, London, where the facilities would be better. In a deep coma he was put on a life-support machine, and subsequently underwent a four-hour brain operation. Raine was heroic: sitting beside his bed as he lay unconscious, willing him to live. He appeared to recover, then four weeks after the operation he contracted pseudomonas, a rare virulent bacterium unresponsive to normal antibiotics, and was transferred to the Brompton Hospital. There he remained on the critical list and almost died eight times. Raine saved his life. Desperate, she asked her friend Bill Cavendish-Bentinck, later Duke of Portland and a director of the German pharmaceutical company Bayer, whether the company had any drug under testing that might help his condition. Cavendish-Bentinck told her that there was indeed one, Azlocillin, but that it was not yet on the market and that she needed the approval of Johnnie's doctors before it was tried out on him. She bullied them into agreement: 'I'd rather he died my way, doing something, than your way, doing nothing.' Samples were flown from Germany and given to Johnnie. Almost miraculously he recovered. Later he gave Raine a magnificent parure of rubies from Van Cleef & Arpels for saving his life.

Gratitude does not seem to have been among the feelings Raine's devotion to Johnnie provoked in his children. At one point Raine instructed nurses at Queen Square to prevent the children from disturbing their seriously ill father while she was with him. They waited for her to leave before sneaking in. A nurse remembered that they would have Sarah going up in the lift as

Raine was coming down. Unsurprisingly, they were rude to her, Jane being the only one to say hello. Diana, devastated, was in tears, although by her own account she was 'frightfully calm'. 'We saw another side of Raine which we hadn't anticipated,' she recalled, 'as she basically blocked us out of the hospital, she wouldn't let us see Daddy . . . Anyway he got better and he basically changed character. He was one person before and another person after. He's remained estranged but adoring since.'[18]

Meanwhile, Diana's destiny had been taking her away from school and childhood towards a new and unexpected life. Since the previous summer Prince Charles had become involved with her sister Sarah. The two had met when Sarah, as an eligible twenty-two-year-old, was invited to join the house party at Windsor Castle for the racing week at Royal Ascot, at the instigation of Henriette Abel Smith, her godmother and one of the Queen's ladies-in-waiting. Prince Andrew, whom she had known as a child, introduced her to Prince Charles. Despite asking her tactlessly, 'Do you have anorexia?' – she was obviously very thin but denied the illness – the two got on. Sarah Spencer was recovering from a traumatic two years, suffering from the eating disorders anorexia nervosa and bulimia, setting a pattern for Diana's own reaction to stress. Years later Diana told patients at the Priory, a private clinic treating addictions on the outskirts of London, that she had first had symptoms of bulimia in the mid-seventies, attributing it to Sarah's experience: 'It started because Sarah was anorexic and I idolized her so much that I wanted to be like her.' If this is so – and Diana's statements are not always the truth of a situation, but sometimes her rereading of it from a distance in time – it certainly did not affect her seriously. While Sarah, who was 5 foot 7 inches tall, went down to 5 stone 10 pounds, photographs of Diana at the time show no signs whatever of serious slimming. Sarah suffered for two years: it was so severe at first that Frances had her taken to hospital. Frances attributed the illness to Sarah's break-up with Gerald Grosvenor after returning from a three-month stay with the Shand Kydds in Australia. This may be so but

Sarah had already shown signs of addiction problems when she drank to alleviate her boredom at school: the split with Grosvenor may well, however, have precipitated it.

Prince Charles enjoyed Sarah's sparkiness and irreverent wit and they made each other laugh. By mid-July the press were following their relationship: Sarah was seen with the Prince at polo and – always a test of the seriousness of one of Prince Charles's relationships – invited by the Queen to Balmoral. Sarah was extremely attractive, vital and witty: Prince Charles was amused by her but not, it seems, physically attracted. Diana later asserted that Sarah had been surprised that he had never tried to go to bed with her. Sarah invited Charles to a shoot at Althorp in November 1977. Diana was given the weekend off from West Heath to attend, meeting the Prince for the first time in a ploughed field near Nobottle Wood when Charles, according to his official biographer, found her 'jolly' and 'bouncy', a pretty, unaffected teenager. Diana herself recorded, perhaps with the benefit of hindsight, that her first impression was 'God, what a sad man'. Sarah, she said cattily in one of her favourite phrases, was 'all over him like a bad rash'.

At the dance that night at Althorp, Charles showed that he was attracted by the sixteen-year-old's high spirits. Diana said, 'I remember being a fat, podgy, no make-up, unsmart lady but I made a lot of noise and he liked that and he came up to me after dinner and we had a big dance and he said: "Will you show me the gallery [the Picture Gallery, a notable feature of Althorp] and I was just about to show him the gallery and my sister Sarah comes up and tells me to push off and I said, "At least let me tell you where the switches are because you won't know where they are", and I disappeared. And he was charm itself and when I stood next to him next day [out shooting], a 16-year-old for someone like that to show you any attention – I was just so sort of amazed. "Why would anyone like him be interested in me?" And it *was* interest.'[19]

Even her siblings began to notice that Diana had changed. 'She suddenly became sort of magnetic and people were interested in her as a character when she hit about 16,' her brother Charles, between her and Charles but she had realized that she had not had a single weekend away with Charles unless they were at Bolehyde Manor or Camilla was otherwise present. While Charles was away in Australia, she had gone to her father in tears, confessing her doubts about the marriage.[44] At the wedding rehearsal in St Paul's forty-eight hours before the ceremony, Diana said, she broke down, sobbing: 'Absolutely collapsed . . . because of all sorts of things. The Camilla thing rearing its head the whole way through our engagement and I was desperately trying to be mature about the situation but I didn't have the foundations to do it and I couldn't talk to anyone about it.'[45] If she did truly collapse, she did it in private. Eleven-year-old Sarah Jane Gaselee, one of her bridesmaids who was there, recalled: 'I don't think she was stressed by it or anything; it didn't appear that way. What I do remember is that she and Charles were really in love as far as I could see, at that age. I saw them cuddling on the sofa and during the rehearsals they had their arms linked and were skipping down the aisles. It was all really happy, or so I thought.'[46]

But that night, at the Queen's ball at Buckingham Palace, two guests found Diana in tears: Charles had danced only once with her and the remainder of the evening with Camilla, and gone off with her.[47] The story that Charles spent the night with Camilla at Buckingham Palace after the ball as Diana slept in Clarence House is, however, untrue. Diana was not at Clarence House on the night of the ball, but in her apartment in Buckingham Palace, and she and Charles left the ball at the same time. Camilla was at the ball with her husband and in any case it is highly unlikely that the Prince would have taken such a risk at that juncture. The two of them may have spent some time alone together earlier in the evening but the 'spending the night' story, told to James Whitaker, allegedly by Barry (who, however, denied it in his own book), was also categorically denied by Michael Colborne: 'It didn't happen, that's for certain. It couldn't have happened without a lot of people knowing . . .' Later, Andrew Parker Bowles told Nigel Dempster the story was absolutely untrue. Nor was Charles with Camilla on the eve of the wedding: with Diana he hosted a party at Mark's Club in Mayfair for his own staff who had not been invited to the wedding ball.★ Afterwards Diana went back to Clarence House to sleep, while Charles returned to Buckingham Palace, where, after the fireworks in Hyde Park, he spent some time at a window watching the crowds in the Mall and chatting to Lady Susan Hussey.

At Clarence House with her sister Jane on the eve of the wedding, Diana had a fit of pre-wedding nerves and was violently sick. But that night Charles sent her a signet ring bearing the Prince of Wales feathers and a loving note which said: 'I'm so proud of you and when you come up I'll be there at the altar for you tomorrow. Just look 'em in the eye and knock them dead.' From her room at Clarence House Diana could hear the explosions of the magnificent fireworks display in Hyde Park celebrating her wedding eve. It was certainly too late to chicken out now.

★ The party was organized by Michael Colborne and paid for by Ronnie Driver, father of the actress Minnie Driver, who invited some of his showbusiness friends, including Michael Caine.

6. The Beginning of the 'Fairy Tale'

'The essential basis of that tragedy was that she was in love with him when she married him . . .' (Victor Edelstein, couturier)

Diana became an international media star on the day of her wedding, 29 July 1981. In terms of worldwide television, it was the greatest royal event ever staged: three-quarters of a billion people watched as 'Lady Di' became 'Princess Di' and from that moment on she was never to be out of the limelight, becoming an icon of the status of Marilyn Monroe or Jackie Kennedy. The beauty she had become was almost unrecognizable from the shy, chubby girl of engagement day only five months previously. Slim, almost fragile looking, she was radiant in her dress of ivory silk with its huge train, the magnificent Spencer tiara holding her billowing tulle veil. The moment when the passionate bride kissed her not so passionate groom on the lips on the balcony of Buckingham Palace in full view of the watching millions etched itself on the public consciousness as the remembered image of the 'fairy tale' which the Archbishop of Canterbury, presiding at the wedding, had pronounced it to be. Inextricably – and dangerously – the private and public faces of monarchy were seen as intertwined. Prompted by the romance of the 'princely marriage', polls showed the popularity of the monarchy as higher than it had been even at the time of the Queen's Coronation and her Silver Jubilee. It was the apogee of the twentieth-century monarchy. Dangerously too for Diana, the world became involved in what they saw as 'Our Story', when the fairy-tale princess and her dashing prince became *their* property.

Charles and Diana were carried away by the euphoria of the cheering crowds lining the streets, frenetically waving flags and shouting 'I love you'. The sun shone and all doubts and unhappiness seemed forgotten. Despite her sickness the previous evening, Diana had been reassured by Charles's present of the ring. In the run-up to the wedding there had been one of the not infrequent outbreaks of Spencer trouble which had resulted in Barbara Cartland, who was, after all, the bride's step-grandmother, staying away, while Diana had banned both Camilla and Lady Tryon from the guest list for the wedding breakfast. At St Paul's Cathedral, Diana had to concentrate on getting her sick father up the long aisle without mishap. One of the officiating clergy (Dean Webster) told friends how touching it was to see the way she practically carried him, walking painfully slowly, up the aisle. There before the altar, Charles stood waiting for her: 'I remember being so in love with my husband that I couldn't take my eyes off him,' Diana recalled. 'I just absolutely thought I was the luckiest girl in the world.'[1] 'You look beautiful,' he whispered to her. 'Beautiful for you,' she replied.

The feelings of jealousy of Camilla which had haunted her throughout her engagement melted away. Charles was her husband, the 'other woman' just a face in the crowd. As she made her way down the aisle, she spotted Camilla in pale grey with a pillbox hat, her son Tom (Charles's godson) standing on a chair beside her. The image remained with her but at the time, she said, she thought, 'Well, there you are, that's it, let's hope that's over with . . .'[2] As if to emphasize, however, how much the Parker Bowles family was part of the royal circle and inescapably, therefore, of her own future, Camilla's husband Andrew rode beside the Queen's carriage in his role as Commander of the 1st and 2nd divisions of the Sovereign's Escort both to and from St Paul's, and then accompanied Charles and Diana as they drove away from Buckingham Palace en route to the first stage of their honeymoon at Broadlands.

Despite the delirium surrounding her, Diana was alert enough not only to keep a watchful eye on her ailing father but even to notice that one of her bridesmaids, Catherine Cameron, aged only five, who had ridden back from the ceremony in a horse-drawn carriage, had suffered an allergic reaction to the horse and arrived at Buckingham Palace with streaming eyes and swollen face. A shot taken by Patrick Lichfield shows her concern for the little girl as soon as they arrive, bending down to comfort her while the Queen extends a comforting hand. 'I noticed that she was extremely quick to comfort the child,' Lichfield remembered. 'She had a lot of other things to think about: she had to be on the balcony, do the waving, she had to go and do the group photographs again and again and again, you know, so the whole thing was ahead of her, and yet she found time to make this gesture, which was in itself touching . . .'[3] That night she took the time to telephone the people who had helped her, including make-up artist Barbara Daly. 'I thought how remarkable that was,' Daly remembered. 'I can't imagine many people doing that after a day like that. There are many beautiful people in the world, but Diana had that extra thing, which is really a very genuine warmth because she had a very loving and compassionate heart.'[4]

There was a happy family atmosphere about the whole occasion at the Palace epitomized by Lichfield's informal shot of an exhausted Diana collapsed on the floor in a heap of ivory silk and taffeta, surrounded by her giggling bridesmaids, her quizzically smiling husband and two grinning brothers-in-law. At the going away, as the open carriage trailing tin cans and balloons attached by Edward and Andrew pulled away from the portico, the Queen started running behind it waving as everyone threw confetti. 'It felt just like a family wedding,' recalled Mountbatten's granddaughter, India Hicks, one of the bridesmaids, 'until they pulled outside the gates and it changed . . .'[5]

Diana and Charles spent the first two days of their honeymoon at Mountbatten's country home, Broadlands, now the property of Norton and Penny Romsey and the scene of Charles's courtship of Camilla just under ten years earlier. They slept in the same bed the Queen had used on her honeymoon with Prince Philip in November 1947. They then (to the indignation of the Spanish, whose royal family had consequently boycotted the wedding) flew to Gibraltar to join the royal yacht *Britannia*. Honeymooning on a yacht with a crew of two hundred was not a romantic experience. As Charles's official biographer put it, 'even an intimate dinner by candlelight was hardly a private affair, accompanied as it was by the camaraderie of senior officers at the table and a band of Royal Marines playing a romantic medley in the background'.[6] Diana's hopes of romantic bliss had been dashed by the time they left Broadlands: 'Second night, out come the van der Post novels [sic] he hadn't read. Seven of them – they came on our honeymoon. We read them and we had to analyse them over lunch everyday,' she later recalled.[7] A lady-in-waiting at Balmoral discussed the horrors of honeymoons in her day with Diana, who replied, 'Well, I bet your husband didn't read a book by an old boy called Jung the whole time.'[8]

Nor was there any hint of romance in the bridegroom's correspondence: 'All I can say is that marriage is very jolly and it's extremely nice being together in *Britannia*,' he wrote on the second day of their cruise. 'Diana dashes about chatting up all the sailors and the cooks in the galley etc. While I remain hermit-like on the verandah deck, sunk with pure joy into one of Laurens van der Post's books . . .'[9] It sounded as if he drew more 'pure joy' from van der Post's books than from the company of his young bride. He might have been an indulgent father observing the antics of a newly acquired puppy. Moreover, the shadow of Camilla, whom Diana thought she had left behind, hung over the *Britannia* honeymoon. 'She was on the telephone every day,' a friend said. 'And on *Britannia*. I know that's true because the poor girl was so upset that she told lots of people afterwards when she came back . . .'[10] Diana was devastated when Charles opened his wallet one day and two photographs of Camilla fell out. A few days later, as they were about to receive the Egyptian President, Anwar Sadat, and his wife for a banquet on board, Diana noticed that Charles was wearing cufflinks engraved with entwined 'Cs', a present from Camilla. Charles himself admitted that they were and was unable to understand why he shouldn't have worn them on his honeymoon. Years later Diana told friends in crude terms that their physical relationship on board *Britannia* had not been a success.[11] Poor

Diana, for all her youth and beauty, was sexually inexperienced, unable to compete on that level with the women Charles had known before. However honestly he tried, the image of Camilla was hard to erase and the two experiences did not compare.

Not once in his authorized version of the marriage did Dimbleby indicate that Prince Charles loved Diana. In his biography of the Prince, written after the Waleses' separation, he followed the official line which was to demote Diana's importance in Charles's life and to emphasize her difficult behaviour. Yet after Diana's death, Charles was to tell several intimate friends, 'There was a time when we were very much in love.'[12] As a royal relation recalls, 'When he talks about her sometimes, he will say, "You know we did love each other very much." Suddenly out of the blue, "You know there was a time when we did love each other very much." So there was something.'[13] All her life Diana herself always maintained that Charles was in love with her when they married and, so it seems, for a relatively brief time and in a limited way, he was. An eyewitness who was at Balmoral every holiday said that for the first few years 'when they used to arrive at picnics and things hand in hand they really looked devoted'.

Dimbleby's account of the couple's honeymoon, both on *Britannia* and through September at Craigowan Lodge on the Balmoral estate, is limited to biased descriptions of her state of mind. It was, in the Dimbleby version, Diana's failure to understand her husband that cast shadows over the relationship: 'For the Prince it [their stay at Balmoral] was a blissful interlude at his favourite home, complete with his books, his fishing rod, and his friends. He assumed that Diana would share his happiness but . . . she was quite unable to surrender herself to his good humour. So far from being the focus of her husband's attention, he seemed to go out of his way to avoid the moments of intimacy that she craved. Instead – or so it appeared to her – he seemed either to prefer his own company or to have others about him as well as her.'[14] Van der Post also featured at Balmoral: Charles's idea of bliss was to read the sage's books out loud to Diana as they sat on a hilltop. The familiar surroundings brought back to her images of

Camilla who had so often been in attendance at Birkhall. She dreamed of her at night, constantly suspecting Charles of ringing her up to ask her advice about his marriage. It was an obsession: as Dimbleby put it, 'Her insecurity about his feelings for her were fed by the canker of jealousy.' Yet both sides, writing with hindsight, exaggerated the misery of that time: at an informal photo call on the banks of the River Dee, the couple looked fond and Diana radiant. She was already transformed from the mousy girl of a few months previously: her hair was coloured blonde and with bare brown legs and tanned complexion she looked for the first time not just beautiful but glamorous. Sarah McCorquodale told James Whitaker, with whom she was constantly in touch, that Diana had far preferred the time at Balmoral to the days on *Britannia*, that Charles had been sweet to her, leaving loving notes and trinkets under her pillow, 'things which she found enchanting'.[15]

Yet, again with hindsight, that Deeside photo call said it all. While Diana, gazing seductively at the press, her legs adopting a ballet position, draped a possessive arm round his shoulders, Charles looked stiff, nervous and worried, the dead salmon lying as a trophy at his feet. In fact at Balmoral as at Buckingham Palace, Diana was finding it difficult to adapt to life in the Royal Family. She felt hemmed in and isolated, incapable of reaching beyond the invisible barrier which now separated her from the rest of the world. 'All the guests at Balmoral coming to stay just stared at me the whole time, treated me like glass,' she recalled, '[but] as far as I was concerned I was Diana.'[16] She herself had none of the deference which most people felt in the presence of royalty, or even of gratitude that she had been made a member of the exclusive circle. She thought, almost certainly correctly, that her in-laws and their friends and staff were looking at her critically. She thought they were old-fashioned and stuffy, they regarded her as 'a silly girl'. She clung to her sense of herself as 'Diana' which was battered by her perennial feelings of inadequacy; her behaviour, her sulks and bouts of tears, her leaving the table early at dinner or on occasions even refusing to come down, were interpreted as rudeness. The family operated by their own rules and traditions; her refusal to follow or even to try to understand them mystified her in-laws, utterly unused to being confronted by such behaviour. Her upbringing had not taught her to behave 'properly', as her resentment at her husband for always offering a drink to the Queen and the Queen Mother before turning to her showed. Even in ordinary families mother and grandmother would come before wife in such circumstances. 'But I had to be told that that was normal because I always thought it was the wife first,' she complained.[17] A royal relation commented, 'At Balmoral on their honeymoon she started saying that she wouldn't come down to dinner and him being asked by the Queen to go upstairs and persuade her, and then coming down red-faced and saying "I can't". Can you imagine any of us with our mother-in-law, can you imagine anybody, whether they were staying with their mother-in-law in a hovel somewhere, who would actually start to not do what their mother-in-law wanted on their honeymoon?'[18] Diana's defiant behaviour might have been allowed by her indulgent father at Park House: anywhere else, however, it would have been considered unacceptable and at Balmoral in the presence of the Queen it was outrageous.

Unsurprisingly, therefore, her relations with her royal in-laws were not easy. Although she revered the Queen, the aura which surrounded her mother-in-law, coupled with her innate shyness and reserve, precluded intimacy. Diana had once said that she saw her role as building bridges between her husband and his parents. Charles was in awe of his mother and intimidated by his father: it soon became obvious to Diana that no such role was envisaged for her either by her husband or her in-laws. The Duke of Edinburgh, always sympathetic to a pretty young girl, did his best to jolly her along, whirling her into dinner when she hung back overcome with shyness. Prince Andrew she had known and liked since childhood, Prince Edward she simply ignored. Princess Anne, the strongest character of the younger royals, had little time for Diana. Of the older generation, the Queen Mother remained an enigma to Diana herself, although those who knew her well detected she did not like her; that Diana's grandmother, Ruth Fermoy, later joined the ranks of those who denigrated her could be taken as an accurate reflection of her friend and employer's views. Only Princess Margaret was to become Diana's real friend and champion within the family. In her youth she, like Diana, had been the media star of the Royal Family, glamorous, idolized and criticized: no stranger to defiant behaviour herself, she empathized with Diana, seeing in her a reflection of her own rebellious self. Yet a relation denied that the Royal Family was 'cliquey': 'When you're staying there, it's not that they're all very cliquey together, and it's not all in-jokes which you can't join in on . . . they're not really touchy-feely, close-knit – it's not the in-joke that's going on from last night, it's not at all them and us. In a funny sort of way they're quite distant with each other. It doesn't make it too difficult for a stranger coming in, because you're not coming up against a family that is so strongly knit together that you are the object of attention, that you're on the outside and they've all got their in-names and their in-this and you don't know what they're talking about. But,' she added, 'if you don't like the great outdoors, if you don't like getting wet, putting on your gumboots, I can see that it's not the easiest, and I think that in the lead-up to this whole thing, she must have given the impression that she did like the great outdoors . . .'[19]

Part Scottish herself through her grandmother Ruth, Diana always denied disliking Scotland: she loved visiting her mother on the Isle of Seil. 'I was rather surprised that she took so violently against that sort of [Balmoral] life,' said a member of the court, 'because she was really quite keen when she came up for that weekend at Birkhall. They were out on the hills all the time and she appeared to be perfectly happy with it. I think it was the sort of relentlessness of it.'[20] What Diana hated was the regimented life of Balmoral, the emphasis on outdoor activities whatever the weather, the focusing on shooting and stalking and fishing (all sports which she detested) as the *raison d'être* of life there. Despite being on holiday, the Royal Family adhered rigidly to the forms of previous years: women guests would be expected to change their clothes four times a day, from something to wear down to breakfast into sporting clothes for lunch and out with the guns, back to change for tea and then into a long dress for dinner. Courtiers would be in attendance and, to a young girl like Diana, the whole place was oppressive and deadly dull.

It was becoming obvious to perceptive observers that the couple were basically incompatible. Both were psychologically needy, each seeking comfort, devotion and reassurance which the other could not provide (and, in Charles's case, had already found in Camilla). Charles was old for his age, Diana young for hers. Despite his essential kindness, Charles was too spoiled and self-centred to begin to understand Diana, while for her part she was too insecure and blinkered to understand the man he was, or to make allowances for him. The pattern of his life had been set for years and he was not about to change it for anyone. Frustrated, Diana began to play the tricks which she had played on her father to get what she wanted: sulks, tears, withdrawal, utter self-absorption. Perplexed and worried, Charles did what he could to placate her, inviting her flatmates up to stay and summoning 'Uncle Michael' from London to spend the day with her. 'I was summoned to Scotland, rung up on the Saturday night to catch the night sleeper on the Sunday and I spent probably the worst day of my life. I was having my breakfast in the kitchen and then he [Charles] came in and said he was going stalking with Lord Romsey . . . and then the Princess came in and we disappeared into the front room of Craigowan and didn't get out of there until four o'clock. There was a big white clock there and I think it went the slowest it's ever been in its life. At some stage I think it was going backwards. We had tears, we had temper, we had everything that day . . .'[21] Asked what the Prince's particular sin that day had been, the source replied that 'he'd started that attitude of his "You find your enjoyment, I've got mine" – and she didn't like the killing thing, to go stalking up a hill was about the last thing she wanted to do'.[22] Laurens van der Post, whose works had cast a shadow over her honeymoon, was recruited to analyse Diana, the result being mutual incomprehension. 'Laurens didn't understand me,' Diana later recalled. 'Everybody saw I was getting thinner and I was being sicker and sicker.

Basically they thought I could adapt to being Princess of Wales overnight . . .'[23] She was sent down to London to see analysts and psychiatrists and given a Valium prescription in a vain attempt to calm her. Vain because there could be no effective cure for her unhappiness, which was caused by basic insecurity and the tortured fears of unrequited love. The shadow of Camilla had lain over the relationship from the start. According to Dimbleby, Charles's friends with whom he had 'agonized' before ending the relationship with Camilla, considered that Diana had 'already reached the point of obsession'.

Media interest in Diana remained intense to a degree which no one had foreseen. Unworthy and inadequate as she felt herself, Diana somehow managed to cope with being the focus of this huge attention from public and media. On their first public engagement, a three-day tour of Wales in October, the world's press turned up in force, Japanese and American television crews descending on Welsh villages and towns none of them had ever heard of before. Diana was feeling 'ghastly', as one of her staff described it: on the second day of the tour she received confirmation of her pregnancy. She felt sick and apprehensive of people's expectations of her. 'I cried a lot in the car, saying I couldn't get out, couldn't cope with the crowds . . . He [Charles] said, "You've just got to get out and do it" . . . He tried his hardest and he did really well in that department, got me out and once I was out, I was able to do my bit.'[24] She did it superlatively, kneeling to talk to the children, bending down to speak to the elderly in their wheelchairs, exuding sympathy and compassion. 'She was just remarkable,' said a newly appointed member of her staff. 'We set off with no idea what we were really meant to be doing. She immediately saw how to deal with people. She would bend down to children, she got down on her haunches. Talking to very elderly men and holding their hand while they were sitting out in the cold. Probably completely tongue-tied, totally overwhelmed at actually meeting the Prince and Princess of Wales – but she would just talk. It was just that ability to know how to talk to people which was there from day one. She knew instinctively how to react to people, just ordinary people . . . And she had been told that she should make a speech in Welsh, standing up.' Despite her shyness, Diana, who had been coached in the language by an elderly peer, managed it, no easy task for a twenty-year-old.

'This was her first walkabout as such,' remembered Dickie Arbiter, who was, at the time, one of the royal correspondents accompanying the tour, 'and she did it as if she had done it all her life, trying to please everybody, switching from one side of the road to the other, because all people were doing was "We want Di, we want Di, we want Di". And that's something he [Charles] had to get used to . . . the trouble was that he was playing the supporting role, not the starring role. That started almost immediately with the first visit they did . . .'25 'People wanted to see her, not him, and he couldn't stomach it,' said an aide. 'I was with Prince Charles and nobody came to us,' said a former police protection officer on the tour; 'everybody wanted her and that was the start of it really. I think she started thinking and people started looking at her as a divine something . . .'26 Diana was not yet the glamorous being she later became; she was not well dressed and her hair had returned to mouse, yet no one who saw her operating on that first tour could doubt the enormous rapport she had with the crowds. It was a new way of being royal although nobody realized it at the time. Nor did anyone in the Royal Family, not even Prince Charles who had been very supportive and protective of her during the Welsh tour, appreciate what an achievement it had been for the twenty-year-old girl with no training for the role. 'She was amazed,' said one of her staff, 'that after those few days in Wales nobody said anything, that the Queen didn't pick up the telephone and say "Well done". It was the lack of recognition that she got – and the same from Prince Charles – if he had come to her and said well done or a little bit more . . . But again, he had done it all his life: he didn't realize what it would have been like for a relatively shy twenty-year-old.'27

Pregnancy increased Diana's malaise, her sickness and her instability. When they returned to London at the end of October, they had no home of their own, just a relatively cramped apartment on an upper floor of Buckingham Palace: bedroom, sitting room, study, bathroom and two dressing rooms. Diana's dressing room was the only room which was exclusively hers. 'There was no thought,' an aide said, 'as to where she could see her girlfriends, or where she might be able to make a cup of coffee. You know, those silly little things. If she wanted to have a cup of coffee or tea or boil an egg, she had to summon a footman.'[28] Charles was used to it; he had been born and brought up in the Palace. Nonetheless, as one of Diana's aides said, 'It's extraordinary that a man of thirty-two was still living in Mummy's home and it made it very isolating for her . . . if you walk across the courtyard from the gate to the Privy Purse door, the world and his wife are looking at you. And for her friends who were aged nineteen, twenty, it's quite intimidating. And then you have to be escorted upstairs by a footman . . .'[29] 'One or two of Diana's girlfriends were quite worried about her loneliness,' another courtier recalled. 'In the early days when she was pregnant with William, I know she rang one up and said, "Can I come round? I'm so terribly lonely . . ."'[30]

The imbalance between her empty life and Charles's busy one became more marked. He had a programme of official duties, she had none. 'One thing she couldn't accept was this wonderful word called Duty,' a member of Charles's staff said. 'I sat with her one day and she was talking about it and I said, "If you get that diary for next year out, you could write it up: Trooping the Colour, Remembrance Day Service, do a couple of royal tours, you'll go to Balmoral, you'll go to Sandringham, you'll be shooting . . . you could virtually fill half of that up anyway, and you've got to keep on doing it. And unfortunately, your husband, it's his duty. He lives in awe of his mother so you'll never change him."'[31] Diana, besotted with Charles, still failed to comprehend why he could not spend more time with her. Worse still was that no one seemed to take her seriously. 'She was disregarded and that was what probably hurt more than anything else,' said one of her staff. Another recalled that she used to complain 'that there was no equality in the marriage and that the Prince of Wales never for one second considered her to be an equal which was an impossible situation for her'.[32] This royal attitude is common to all the senior members of the family, who never consider other people, their lives, their feelings or opinions. Many of the courtiers share the same view, hard for outsiders to comprehend. For Diana, determined to cling to her sense of self, it was baffling and frustrating to a degree. As one of Diana's staff remarked to Dimbleby, no one had approached her predicament with imagination: 'I don't think they had really thought about her role . . .'

It was not until September, three months after the wedding, that ladies-in-waiting were appointed to her, an indication of the strange lack of foresight and consideration where she was concerned. The ladies-in-waiting included Lavinia Baring, Hazel West and Anne Beckwith Smith. Anne Beckwith Smith was ten years older than Diana but she had been at West Heath and knew Diana's sisters, so there was common ground. Much of their time was taken up with the deluge of presents and correspondence generated by the wedding and then by the announcement of Diana's pregnancy. One 'wonderful' woman who had taken early retirement from Downing Street was there to cope. 'She was just marvellous, she wrote wonderful letters to children and grown-ups, and she kept a record. I think we had something like 28,000 letters, presents and cards, just for William. Every little old lady was knitting beautiful things, a layette and things like that. We always put the things she might like or something that was special aside.'[33]

Away from the gloom of Buckingham Palace, Christmas at Windsor was a rare period of peace and happiness for Charles and Diana. Christmas sees the Royal Family at their jolliest, with silly jokes and clowning, something which Charles greatly enjoys, and an exchange of the most commonplace and utilitarian presents which amazed Diana. Charles wrote to a friend: 'We've had such a lovely Christmas – the two of us. It has been extraordinarily happy and cosy [one of the Prince's highest accolades] being able to share it together . . . Next year will, I feel sure, be even nicer, with a small one to join in as well . . .'[34] Sandringham in January, however, was a different matter. Diana had always disliked going there, even as a child. The proximity of her beloved Park House, now deserted, upset her with its memories of freedom lost and hopes disappointed. As at Balmoral, the focus was on shooting, which she detested and Charles (despite his brief flirtation with Eastern philosophies) greatly enjoyed. Again, it was a source of conflict.

An incident took place there in January which Diana described to Andrew Morton:

I threw myself down the stairs [at Sandringham]. Charles said I was crying wolf and I said I felt so desperate and I was crying my eyes out and he said: 'I'm not going to listen. You're always doing this to me. I'm going riding now.' So I threw myself down the stairs. The Queen comes out, absolutely horrified, shaking – she was so frightened. I knew I wasn't going to lose the baby; quite bruised round the stomach. Charles went out riding and when he came back, you know, it was just dismissal, total dismissal. He just carried on out of the door.[35]

This was a fabrication, a dramatization of an incident which was purely an accident told to Andrew Morton through a desire to dramatize. Diana may well have had a row with Charles beforehand in an effort to prevent him going out riding but, according to eyewitnesses, she did not throw herself down two flights of stairs but tripped as she went down wide, shallow steps at the bottom, landing in front of a member of staff who was talking to the Queen Mother. Diana even rang a member of her staff at the time and told her what had happened: 'I must tell you, you will probably hear about it – I tripped and fell down the stairs. And what luck, what would happen but I had to land at the feet of the Queen Mother. Oh God, if I had to trip why did I have to do it in front of her? . . .'[36] This misrepresentation was typical of much of Diana's dramatic view of her past distorted by the reality of her position ten years later. According to newspaper reports at the time, Charles called a local doctor and sat with Diana until he arrived. When the examination proved that neither she nor the baby had suffered injury, she rested and he took her to a royal barbecue several hours later.

Next month, Charles took Diana off to the Brabournes' house, Windermere, on Eleuthera in the Bahamas, staying with their son Norton and his wife Penny for what he described as 'a second honeymoon'. This time the tabloids excelled themselves: James Whitaker of the *Star* and Harry Arnold of the *Sun* supervised intrusive photographs of Diana, five months pregnant and wearing a bikini, from a nearby beach. 'CAREFREE DI THREW ROYAL CAUTION TO THE WINDS TO WEAR HER REVEALING OUTFIT' ran the *Sun*'s headline. The Queen was outraged, denouncing the tabloids' 'unprecedented . . . breach of privacy'. Just how carefree Diana was is open to question; the Romseys intimated to Dimbleby that she objected when Charles wanted to read or paint and openly expressed her boredom with his conversation. They were also probably among the 'tiny circle of his most trusted friends' with whom Charles discussed Diana's misery and who urged him to tell her to 'pull herself together' and stop indulging in self-pity. Charles apparently insisted that he was to blame and that it was too much to expect anyone to be married to the heir to the throne. While this may well have been true, he would have to have been very obtuse not to realize that the core of his wife's despair was her suspicion that he did not really love her.

Tabloid pressure on Diana increased: media expert Roy Greenslade called the bikini photographs the great turning point in the relationship with the press: 'Here was an intense interest, sexual interest really, in this woman. The press – editors and reporters – were in love with Diana . . . she looked terrific, she sold magazine covers, no one could get enough of her.'[37] Pressure intensified until finally, on 21 June, she gave birth to William Arthur Philip Louis. 'William had to be induced,' she told Morton,[38] 'because I couldn't handle the press pressure any longer, it was becoming unbearable. It was as if everybody was monitoring every day for me . . .' For Diana, guarding her privacy had become an obsession; but courtiers regarded the birth of a son to the Prince and Princess of Wales as an important royal event to be shared with the public, as all births, deaths and marriages have traditionally been. Diana had what was known in her office as a 'foot stamp' when her officials told her that they would come to the hospital to keep the people informed. 'What's that got to do with you?' was her furious response.[39] William's birth came just over a month before their first wedding anniversary: Diana had had little time to accustom herself to being Princess of Wales and now she was a mother; and not just any mother, but the mother of the future King. Charles, who attended the birth, was ecstatic, writing to his godmother Patricia Brabourne: 'I am *so* thankful that I was beside Diana's bedside the whole time because by the end of the day I really felt as though I'd shared deeply in the process of birth and as a result was rewarded by seeing a small creature which belonged to *us* even though he seemed to belong to everyone else as well! I have never seen such scenes as there were outside the hospital when I left that night – everyone had gone berserk with excitement . . .'[40]

When Diana arrived back at their new London home, Kensington Palace, Princess Margaret had organized a welcome reception outside. Everyone waved and cheered. It was perhaps the high point of Diana's life as Princess of Wales. She had fulfilled her duty to the Crown.

7. 'Di-mania'

'In Australia . . . one was aware of little tensions. He [Charles] couldn't
understand that people wanted to see her' (a member of Diana's staff on her
Australian tour, March 1983)

Diana now had a new baby and a new London home: Apartments
8 and 9 in Kensington Palace, the dark, redbrick, seventeenth-
century collection of buildings in Kensington Gardens which had
harboured members of the Royal Family for more than three
hundred years. Queen Mary (wife of William III) and Queen Anne
had died there: Queen Victoria was born and brought up there
before her accession as Queen. George VI, Edward VIII and his
brothers used to refer to it as the 'aunt-heap', an allusion to the
number of elderly royal relations who lived there. In modern
terms, you could call it a royal condominium. The apartments,
however, bear no relation to modern flats: they are attached houses,
comprising several floors with state rooms as well as domestic
offices. When Charles and Diana moved in, Princess Margaret
occupied Apartment 10 where she lived in considerable splendour
attended by numerous staff. Other royal neighbours were the
eighty-one-year-old (born 25 December 1901) Princess Alice,
Duchess of Gloucester, with her son and daughter-in-law, Prince
Richard, Duke of Gloucester, and his wife, Birgitte, and Prince
and Princess Michael of Kent. The Duke and Duchess of Kent
lived nearby at Wren House, Palace Green, while Diana's sister
Jane and brother-in-law Robert Fellowes lived down the drive in
the Old Barracks. All of them were grace-and-favour tenants of
the Queen. There had been a suggestion that Charles and Diana
should occupy the far more splendid Spencer House overlooking
Green Park, left to the younger Spencers under the terms of their

father's will, but the costs of restoration had ruled that out. Perhaps, too, it had been considered unsuitable for the Prince of Wales to live in a house belonging to his wife's family.

Although living in a palace sounds very splendid, there were certain physical drawbacks to 'KP', as it was always known. Behind the splendid south-facing façade is a warren of courtyards and gardens surrounded by blocks of apartments. In fact the Waleses' apartment was far from suitable to the needs of the heir to the throne and his family. 'It was a small apartment,' said one of the staff who worked there. 'It needed to be bigger really. They had a sitting room and a study each, then a drawing room, then a dining room and that was it really as far as reception rooms went. Not a lot of corridor space . . . so it wasn't very comfortable. They needed a second reception room downstairs so that upstairs would be private, but the way it was it was all in together. They should have moved initially to somewhere bigger . . . They were far too important to be in such a small apartment. I think the apartment contributed to certain tensions . . . they were on top of one another as regards what they were supposed to be doing . . .'[1]

Patrick Jephson, who joined the Princess's staff in January 1988, serving first as equerry to the Princess and then as her private secretary, was surprised to find the apartment smaller and gloomier than he had expected. Despite the wide lawns and trees of the surrounding Kensington Gardens, the Waleses' apartment was dark and viewless, tucked away in the heart of the palace complex. There was virtually no privacy: 'Everybody could hear everybody else,' Jephson wrote. 'If you needed to get away from someone there was just not enough space.'[2] Most of the time the house was deathly quiet: the Prince and Princess were usually out and the staff retreated to their places behind the scenes. Outside the sun might be shining, the birds singing and children playing, but inside the apartment there was an historic silence and not enough light. 'If you sent the staff home, closed the curtains and forgot to turn on *all* the lights, no amount of TV channels, loud music or ringing telephones could keep the darkness at bay,' Jephson recalled.[3] For

Diana, despite its convenience in the heart of London, 'KP' was to be less a home than a prison.

She had cooperated over the decoration with Dudley Poplak, who was recommended by her mother and who had also been working with her on the redecoration of Highgrove. The decoration was a mixture of grand and contemporary: the seventeenth-century entrance hall, with its impressive staircase and baroque plaster ceiling (destroyed by a bomb during the Second World War, and subsequently restored), was carpeted in green and grey patterned with the Prince of Wales feathers, a theme emphasized throughout the house. On the first floor the reception rooms, the drawing and dining rooms were furnished either with wedding presents or furniture and paintings, and a tapestry from the Royal Collections, including a Veronese, *The Mystic Marriage of St Catherine*.

Diana and Charles had studies on the same floor. Diana's sitting room was feminine in dusty pink and grey-blue, with a pink sofa and, in a window alcove beside her desk, her school tuck box, stencilled D. Spencer, in which she kept her most private possessions. The room was a grown-up version of a teenager's room, with soft toys and cushions with slogans like 'Good girls go to heaven – bad girls go everywhere', and children's school paintings on the walls. Every surface was crammed with photographs, enamel boxes, porcelain figurines. It was cheerful, girlish and very cluttered, smelling deliciously of her favourite flowers, lilies, potpourri and scented candles.

Charles's more masculine room housed a box-kennel for his cherished yellow Labrador, Harvey, and on his desk a photograph of himself with his father, the Duke of Edinburgh, and the wry, or perhaps even defiant, inscription in Charles's handwriting: 'I was not born to follow in my father's footsteps.' In the master bedroom, the 7-foot 6-inch oak bed from his apartment at Buckingham Palace presented the poignant, even somewhat pathetic spectacle of the couple's toy animals ranged upon it: Charles's worn teddy, which he took everywhere with him and was tucked up in the bed at night by his valet, and Diana's 'family' from Park House, overflowing from the bed to shelves. It would be unkind to put too much emphasis on this attachment to childhood toys but it is hard to imagine such a collection featuring in the bedroom of, say, a Wall Street banker and his socialite wife.

Highgrove had been decorated by Diana and Poplak far more to her taste than Charles's. A royal relation described Diana and Poplak's schemes as 'terrible, like a sort of Trust House Forte idea of a modern princess's drawing room . . . three new magazines on this low table and the day's newspapers on that, I mean awful'.[4] It was to Highgrove (Kensington Palace was not yet ready) that Charles and Diana had returned after their Balmoral honeymoon. According to Stephen Barry, Charles had not seen the house since before the wedding: now the Princess, 'very excited, led him round, showing him every room. "Are you pleased?" she kept asking him. You could tell from his expression that he was. "He likes it," she said to me triumphantly. "And it's my dream house now."'[5] Yet Diana came to hate Highgrove, which became more Charles's house than hers; where he spent days hunting in the winter, playing polo in the summer and mixing with his horsey friends, while Bolehyde Manor, the Parker Bowleses' house, was in menacing proximity. Immediately after the separation, Charles, whose taste was more discriminating than Diana's, substituted his own style and that of his chosen decorator, Robert Kime, for hers. Although it had been their first shared home, Diana used to say that it was never her 'cup of tea'. For Charles it had always been his ideal house; he had chosen it himself instead of Chevening, the splendid eighteenth-century house in Kent which had been allotted as his official residence. His excuse to the then Prime Minister, Margaret Thatcher, for abandoning Chevening was that it was too far away from his properties in the Duchy of Cornwall. The real reason, however, was that Highgrove was in the heart of 'horse country' and convenient for the Prince's two favourite sporting activities, polo and hunting. It was also conveniently close to the home of Andrew and Camilla Parker Bowles. At Highgrove Charles could fulfil his cherished dream of creating a splendid garden which he had begun with the expert advice of a circle of grand gardening ladies including Molly, Marchioness of Salisbury, and Rosemary Verey.

'Horsey' people were anathema to Diana, who was spiralling into deep post-natal depression after the birth of William. She was twenty-one that July but no one – not even her family – thought to give her a twenty-first birthday party. A new friend came to lunch, Sarah Ferguson, whom Diana had met at the Cowdray Park polo two years before when Charles first made his advances and who was soon to become very much a part of Diana's life when she married Prince Andrew four years later. Charles, however, did arrange a candlelit picnic dinner at the Queen's House at Kew for their first wedding anniversary. At Balmoral that autumn, she became sicker and thinner, the scenes of screaming, crying and throwing things more frequent. Charles worried but he did not understand post-natal depression. No one in the Royal Family recognized either that or her bulimia.

Bulimia nervosa, as it is called, is an eating disorder where people have a cycle of binge eating and purging by vomiting; they can have a binge–purge cycle which occurs at least twice a week for three months or more. Its cause is not fully understood but it may develop owing to a combination of emotional, physical and social triggers. It can be caused by low self-esteem, which certainly characterized Diana, or mood problems, especially depression, from which she was suffering after the birth of William. Finally, it can be due to a specific emotionally upsetting event such as abusive family relationships. Later, the doctor who treated Diana attributed her bulimia directly to her problems with Charles and it became noticeably worse in surroundings with unhappy memories or in difficult situations, such as family gatherings at Sandringham and Balmoral. The general feeling in the royal circle was that Diana was 'an extremely tiresome girl', 'basically a bad character . . . [with] flaws in her character' and that they had 'no patience with all this about being sick'.[6] Diana in her desperate depression became, as even her own staff admitted, 'very unpredictable'. By her own account she began to mutilate herself in an attempt to focus Charles's attention on her: the 'cutting' cannot have been very severe as she was so often seen wearing low-cut, sleeveless evening dresses and no scars were ever evident. But, as a result of these episodes, in mid-October he took her down to London again for psychiatric treatment. The analysts, as is their wont, probed Diana's family background, blaming everything on her 'broken home', which was hardly helpful in the circumstances.[7] While the Prince ordered his friends to say nothing (despite writing letters in which he told of his difficulties with his wife), the public nature of some of Diana's erratic behaviour made it inevitable that the rumour machine would start up. The most glaring instance came at a major royal public occasion, the British Legion Festival of Remembrance at the Albert Hall on 13 November 1982, always attended by the senior members of the Royal Family.

That evening, before leaving, Charles and Diana had a major row which resulted in Diana's refusing to go. He left without her but she then had a change of heart and determined to go after all, despite her staff warning her that it was now too late and she would arrive at the Albert Hall after the Queen, an unpardonable breach of protocol. Diana paid no attention and turned up, causing a commotion as a seat had to be found for her, and there she sat, clearly continuing the row with Charles in public view. Anne Robinson, editing the *Sunday Mirror* that weekend, put James Whitaker on to the story – 'James, I want you to find out why Princess Diana is looking as awful as she is. She behaved awfully at the Albert Hall and she looks f------- awful. She's so thin. Go and find out.' Whitaker rang his main contact, Sarah McCorquo-dale, who confirmed that the family were very concerned over Diana's loss of weight. 'We think she could be anorexic . . .' Robinson ran the story, and the result was a major complaint from the Palace which cost her her job.

Among the media curiosity to know the truth of what was going on was at fever pitch. Nigel Dempster, probably the best connected of the gossip-columnist diarists to the circles in which Charles's friends moved, having at first rubbished the rival journalist's report, then appeared on US television to denounce Diana as a 'fiend' and a 'monster', claiming that she was 'very much ruling the roost' and that Charles was 'desperately unhappy'. He later asserted that he had the information 'straight from one of Prince Charles's staff'. With tongue firmly in cheek, Auberon Waugh headlined a piece 'GOSSIP COLUMNIST ATTACKS PRINCESS FAIRYTALE. NATION RISES IN ANGER'. Cracking the crystal through which an adoring public gazed at the fairy-tale couple was not welcomed. Just after the birth of Prince William, Victoria Glendinning, reviewing a selection of royal books, quoted Robert Lacey as saying, 'it is important to us that the magic does not die', adding, 'and that is why we hope the fairy story will end in the proper way and that the Princess of Wales and her Prince and their son will live happily ever after'. The trouble, however, as the acute Lacey pointed out, was that Charles got 'the woman "we" wanted'. As far as the press was concerned, however, though no one wanted to believe the reports of cracks in the marriage, the 'fairy tale', which was still the image the general public cherished, had turned into a soap opera which was more like the current American favourites *Dynasty* and *Dallas* in which skulduggery, infidelity and double-dealing were the norm.

'At the point at which there began to be more hard and fast evidence, her weeping in public, that kind of incident, cancelling going places at the last minute, him turning up alone when she had been expected . . . the whispers became more insistent that it [the marriage] was indeed going down,' said a well-known media analyst. 'And the press loved this because it was a drama, and it was a drama in which . . . because of the nature of the Palace's press relations which is "never admit, never deny", you more or less could get away with anything . . . You could actually schedule a news story on Di which would be inevitably a story about some difficulty in the marriage – some hint at what's been happening this weekend, he's been at Highgrove or she's been at Highgrove and he hasn't or she hasn't . . . the royal rat pack began to feed off each other [as to] who could outdo the next one with a more outrageous claim . . .'[8]

Media comment only increased Diana's unhappiness and the

pressure on her. She devoured the news, almost living her life by proxy through the press. *The Times* and *Telegraph* were the papers officially delivered to her but copies of the tabloids found their way to her via the back stairs. Consciousness of growing criticism of her within royal circles and especially from Charles's friends, added to the hostile comment in some of the newspapers, drove her to despair. Ruth Fermoy, always reflecting court opinions, told Roy Strong in March 1982 that Diana 'had a lot to learn' about royal life,[9] opening herself further to Archbishop Runcie: 'Ruth was very distressed with Diana's behaviour,' the Archbishop recalled. 'She [Ruth] was totally and wholly a Charles person, because she'd seen him grow up, loved him like all the women of the court do, and regarded Diana as an actress, a schemer.'[10] Charles, while still sympathetic, remained baffled by Diana's illness. Out hunting in March 1983, he turned to two lady companions and asked them: 'Have you ever been very, very sick? I don't understand it and my mother doesn't either . . .'[11]

One might wonder why – considering Diana's family were worried about her weight loss and that Sarah and her mother had had first-hand experience of Sarah's eating disorder – none of her family came forward to help her. Frances Shand Kydd had been curiously absent from her daughter's life for two years following the wedding. Diana had been upset by Frances's disclosures about her marriage break-up to the author Gordon Honeycombe, and Frances had made some curious statements to the *Daily Mail*, putting a favourable spin on her absence from her daughter's life: 'I am a firm believer in maternal redundancy,' she said. 'When daughters marry they set up a new home and they don't want mother-in-law hanging around. They should be free to make their own decisions and maybe to make their own mistakes.' This begged the question: Frances was Diana's mother, not her mother-in-law, but her absence from her daughter's life was confirmed by one of the Waleses' officials: 'After the wedding, she sort of disappeared,' he said. Diana's sister Jane was in the awkward position of being married to the Queen's assistant private secretary, which involved having to tread carefully where the

Waleses were concerned; she was a level-headed woman who was not much moved by Diana's more dramatic performances. She went round to check on Diana and found marks on her chest. Sarah, who was closer to Diana, had her own married life on a farm in Lincolnshire and, in any case, often found it wiser to keep her distance from Diana. Her brother Charles was away most of the time, at Eton and then Oxford. Johnnie Spencer, according to an entry in the visitors' book, had been one of the first visitors to the new apartment at Kensington Palace, but the sales of Althorp treasures which had begun shortly after Johnnie's recovery from illness were a further source of controversy between Raine and his children. News of the sales had led to much criticism in the press. According to *The Times* in December 1982 the Spencers had sold £2 million worth of art which they claimed was to pay the costs of refurbishing Althorp, but in September of that year they had bought three houses in Bognor Regis, which cast some doubt on their claim.

Yet, as with all depressive illnesses, there were periods of light among the clouds: in September, Diana had been well enough to attend the funeral of Princess Grace of Monaco who had died of injuries sustained in a car crash. Diana had greatly admired Grace, feeling a sense of empathy with her as another outsider who had married into a ruling family, and whose marriage also had not turned out the fairy tale it had initially been thought to be. 'I remember meeting Princess Grace and how wonderful and serene she was,' Diana recalled of the evening she had worn '*that* dress', 'but there was troubled water under her, I saw that.'[12] Charles's initial reaction when told she had wanted to go to the funeral in Monaco had been negative: it would be the first time she officially represented the Royal Family on a solo engagement. Diana, however, had been determined to go and on her own initiative written to the Queen about it and obtained her agreement. One of Diana's staff who accompanied her to Monaco later told a television programme, 'She was absolutely brilliant. She came into her own. And on the aircraft back she burst into tears with exhaustion. She asked "Will Charles be there to meet us?" We looked at her big eyes looking out of the window in expectation. She said, "There's one police car." That meant Charles wasn't coming.' Another remembered, 'She rang up and asked me "Have you seen the papers?" I said, "You were absolutely brilliant, Ma'am." She said, "Thanks for saying that because nobody at Balmoral has mentioned it." '[13] 'It was always important to Diana to feel appreciated from an early age,' her brother Charles said in a television interview after her death; 'she was childlike, wanting approval – "Am I doing OK?" '

The couple's joint tour of Australia in March 1983, accompanied by William, and New Zealand, was a pivotal moment in the marriage. Outwardly it was a glorious success but behind the scenes people travelling on the tour noticed 'little tensions' between them. It was the beginning of worldwide 'Di-mania'. Instead of seven photographers being there, there were seventy. Before there was one from each paper and a couple of freelances. Now they were coming from France, Germany, America and Japan. One hundred thousand people turned out to see them in Brisbane. 'The police are concerned about an element of hysteria that has become evident among the huge crowds that have turned out to see the Royal couple in the New South Wales cities of Sydney, Newcastle and Maitland over the past 48 hours,' a newspaper reported. A security officer told the reporter: 'We haven't seen this in royal tours here before. It is more akin to Beatlemania.' The adulation of the crowds at first terrified and then empowered Diana. This was something she could do, and do well. It was a part she was born to play.

It was the first time a hint was seen of Prince Charles's jealousy of Diana's huge appeal to the crowds, which was to be an increasingly divisive factor in the couple's relationship. Although he concealed it nobly and even joked about it, it was nonetheless humiliating for a man who since childhood had been the centre of attention wherever he went, to be upstaged by his wife, a novice on royal occasions. It was not pleasant to hear the crowds groaning, 'Oh, we've got old Big Ears', when they saw he was going to be on their side of the walkabout, or to hear the hysterical screams for

'Lady Di'. The scale of the adulation of his wife worried him. 'How can anyone, let alone a twenty-one-year-old, be expected to come out of all this obsessed and crazed attention unscathed?' he wrote to a friend.[14] Diana, according to a letter seen by Dimbleby, wrote that her black moods had vanished and that she felt ashamed of the way she had been behaving in the past. Now, she said, she only thought of Charles and the job. Alone together with William at the sheep station where they left him with his nanny, Charles wrote to Hugh and Emilie van Cutsem, '. . . we were extremely happy there whenever we were allowed to escape. The great joy is that we were totally alone together . . .'[15] At the same time he pondered glumly on the nature of the public's reaction to them, which was unlike anything he had ever experienced before. 'Maybe the wedding, because it was so well done and because it made such a wonderful, almost Hollywood-style film, has distorted people's view of things? Whatever the case it frightens me and I know for a fact that it petrifies Diana.'[16] Petrified at times, maybe, but also excited by the scale of the public's approval of her: Diana had discovered her great gift for satisfying people's expectations, communicating with them, lifting their spirits. Her rapport with ordinary people in public and in private was to be an enormous source of strength and comfort to her. There was no doubt about her media status: a Spanish magazine covered the tour under the headline 'THE FRONT PAGE GIRL', while *Tatler* dubbed her 'Number one, indisputable brand leader'. Their subsequent seventeen-day tour of Canada was also a huge media success, particularly for Diana: one newspaper described how journalists lavished particular attention on Diana, 'gorging themselves on her fresh good looks and her fetching ways'. Another paper, the *Ottawa Citizen*, referred to Charles as an 'also-ran'.

'I think they were happy, they had William out there, a sort of family enclave,' a member of staff recalled. 'But one was aware of little tensions. He couldn't understand that people wanted to see her. He couldn't understand that they wanted to see a beautiful woman rather than a man in a suit. And that was really sad, actually. It was so unnecessary because together they were absolute dynamite. But one was just aware of a sort of petulance in him and she, I think, found it very difficult, knowing how to cope with that. And she was quite emotional at that time, there were tears . . . she didn't understand and it was all very stressful . . .'[17] Things, however, were to go from bad to worse, and Charles's resentment at his wife's popularity began to poison their relationship. His puzzlement at people's reaction to her was palpable, as he once said to a friend: 'Why do they love her so much? All she ever did was to say "yes" to me . . .'[18]

Consciousness that she was a real success boosted Diana's still fragile confidence. While she had confessed to the wife of a Nova Scotia editor that 'the wolf-pack-like British tabloid press' still upset her – 'When they write something horrible I get a horrible feeling right here,' she said, pointing to her chest, 'and I don't want to go outside' – she told the Premier of Newfoundland that she felt she was doing her job as Princess of Wales 'better now than I previously did'. Like many others before him, Premier Peckford was struck by 'her really soft spot for people who are sick and disabled,' he said. 'She almost cried when she was told that little boy who had presented her with a bouquet was blind.' Worldwide adulation for Diana continued to grow: one British magazine dubbed her 'Royal Superstar': according to a recent American poll she was 'the most popular woman in the world'. *Paris-Match* said that she was more popular in France than even Brigitte Bardot, while the editor of *Ladies Home Journal* proclaimed, 'without a doubt she is the greatest media personality of the decade. One comes along every ten years – Jackie, Liz Taylor and now Diana.' Excessive press attention was by now inevitable: pictures of Diana sold newspapers and magazines. Popular women's magazines such as *Woman* and *Woman's Own* reported sales increased by up to forty thousand in weeks when Diana featured on the cover. One editor said that his sales dropped by 15 per cent when she was not on the cover. 'She's the one that's news, the one they want to see. We often think, for heaven's sake we've had her on for the last seven months, let's try someone else. It doesn't work.'

Between the two tours the couple had travelled on 30 April via private jet, lent them by Armand Hammer, from Los Angeles to the Bahamas to spend ten days at the Romseys' villa. Long-lens photographs published in a Spanish magazine showed Charles and Diana on a beach – happy and playful with each other, walking hand in hand: on one occasion the Prince hefted her over his shoulder to dump her in the water. 'The Prince, away from protocol, reveals himself as truly in love with Diana' the caption ran. Back in England for their second wedding anniversary, the couple publicly demonstrated their affection: 'They looked more like they were on honeymoon,' said a spectator.

But there was a downside to this public success and apparent happiness – the private difficulties. Prince Charles's friends lined up to denigrate Diana. While they were not aware, or did not recognize, that the marriage still had a chance, they seemed to think they should encourage the Prince to regret it. Charles's complaining letters had their effect. None of them, however, appeared to realize that, in encouraging Charles to feel that his marriage was hopeless, they were setting him on a course which might endanger the monarchy. It now seems incredible that these people, in order to curry favour or to maintain their influence with the Prince, should have actually attempted to undermine his marriage. One might ask oneself what they were trying to achieve.

Leaked stories began to appear, bolstering Dempster's claim that Diana was a 'fiend' and a 'monster'. Diana, according to the stories, was responsible for an exodus of staff and a dog. The first to go was Stephen Barry, the much indulged valet, who was intuitive enough to recognize that his reign and influence over Charles would end with the Prince's marriage. Most of the staff believed that she did 'winkle' Barry out of his position: 'he was keeping the Prince way back in the Dark Ages,' said one, 'she wanted to drift him into the present. Stephen . . . one of his great claims to fame was that he kept the Prince of Wales in the top worst dressed list for years and kept himself in the best . . .' On the honeymoon at Craigowan, Barry was completely insouciant as far as his duties were concerned. 'There's Stephen, Sunday morning, whacking great gin and tonic, radio under one arm, all the papers under the other. "Darling, I'm just off to do a little heavy pressing . . ." Three hours later he's snoring his head off,' one member of staff remembered.[19] Diana was no fool where domestic staff were concerned and Barry himself recognized that his happy years of getting away with everything with the indulgence of the Prince of Wales would soon be over. He jumped before he was pushed.

Alan Fisher, whom Charles and Diana had met at Althorp where he was acting as extra butler when they were staying there for a big party, also left. It was rumoured that he did not like Diana, but it was also said that, having worked in the past for people like the Windsors and Bing Crosby, he did not like the way things were done at Highgrove and Kensington Palace. The unkindest accusation concerned Harvey, the Prince's beloved yellow Labrador, who had been bred by the Queen and accompanied Charles everywhere. The rumour ran that Diana had banished Harvey as she had some of Charles's friends. In fact, Harvey was old and incontinent, his hind legs dragged behind him and he was no longer capable of getting up the stairs. He was given to the Prince's comptroller, Colonel Creasy, to look after.

The saddest departure was that of Oliver Everett, who had acted as the Princess's private secretary and aide from before her wedding. Charming, highly educated and a skilful polo player, Everett had given up a promising diplomatic career to answer the Prince's call 'to look after Diana'. At first they had got on well, joking and chatting in the light-hearted manner which Diana enjoyed in her relations with her staff. Suddenly, in a way which was, sadly, to become characteristic of her, she turned against him for some perceived although totally minor offence. She demanded that Charles tell him to go, and go he did at the end of 1983. It was evident that the Royal Family and household thought he had been badly treated, since he was subsequently given the desirable post of royal librarian at Windsor.

The resignations of Edward Adeane and Michael Colborne were both unfairly attributed to Diana. Adeane, a top libel lawyer with a first-class brain and a dry wit, managed to get on with Diana although as personalities they were worlds apart. He was shocked when, working on the preparations for the Australian tour, he discovered that the future Queen of England did not know the name of the capital of Australia.[20] Adeane was seriously taken aback when, after the birth of William, he was told to give up his early morning meeting with Charles because Diana insisted that William's father should spend some time in the nursery with his son. That was not at all how things had been in Adeane's father's time.

Yet it was the Prince, not the Princess, who prompted Adeane's departure. Adeane appreciated the conscientious way Diana dealt with her paperwork, in contrast to the confusion of her husband's handling of his office affairs. The Prince, said a former member of his staff, 'was a muddler and liked it like that so that he could blame other people, throw up his hands and say "Oh, the office!"' Edward Adeane, who had been brought up in the tradition of his father, the Queen's private secretary, had become increasingly annoyed with the confusion, the Prince's habit of taking the advice of the last person he had seen, of refusing to listen to Adeane's and taking private initiatives of which his private secretary was unaware until it was too late to stop him. The last straw for the private secretary was the Prince's notorious speech on 30 May 1984 given at Hampton Court Palace at a dinner in honour of the 150th anniversary of the Royal Institute of British Architects, when he compared the new design for the wing of the National Gallery in Trafalgar Square to 'a monstrous carbuncle on the face of a much-loved and elegant friend', and launched an attack on modern architecture and architects. Edward Adeane had vehemently opposed the Prince's plan for his speech: it was not only insulting to his hosts, the architectural profession, but pre-empted the judgement of the public inquiry on the development which was then in progress. While he attempted to persuade the Prince against the speech even in the car going down to Hampton Court, he did not know that Charles had already leaked the text to *The Times* and the *Guardian* for publication the next day.[21] Adeane resigned six months later after yet another row.

Michael Colborne's resignation was partly prompted, it was

rumoured, by the snobbery of the household, who could not envisage a grammar school boy with the title of Comptroller of the Prince's Household. Whatever the truth of that, a root cause of Colborne's going was the increasing difficulty he experienced in treading the tightrope between Prince and Princess. 'I couldn't look after two,' he said. 'I mean, he wanted me to do one thing and she wanted me to do another so I thought the best thing was to get out while the going was good. And I resigned in the April [1984] but didn't get out till the December because they kept asking me to change my mind, to stay on and do this and that.' The last straw for Colborne, as it had been for Adeane, was the behaviour of the increasingly edgy and jealous Prince on the April trip to Canada which followed the couple's Australian tour in 1983. Colborne had spent the afternoon with Diana at her request while Charles went about his official business. When Charles returned, he flew into one of his towering, shouting rages, accusing Colborne of neglecting him for Diana. Outside the door, hearing everything that had gone on, was a sobbing Diana. The Prince took her in his arms, but the damage had been done. Diana was aware of the resentment eating away at her husband, but there was nothing she could do about it.

For Colborne, who had borne the brunt of the Prince's tirades many times before, this was a row too far. 'I get an inner gut feeling when things are going to change,' Colborne said. 'I had ten wonderful years.' Members of the Queen's household, aware that Colborne was one of the few people whom Diana listened to and trusted, attempted to dissuade him. The effect of the resignations of both Adeane and Colborne was to diminish the numbers of people who could genuinely be called impartial in the Prince's office.

Diana's unattainable desire to have her husband all to herself, and his early willingness to do anything to please her and to avoid the constant rows, did result in the distancing of some of Charles's closest friends. Nicholas Soames, who for years had been accustomed to speak to him on the telephone at least once a week, heard nothing from the Prince for two and a half years. It goes without saying that the Parker Bowleses' and the Tryons did not receive invitations, a point which Diana had made very clear by crossing them off the list for the wedding breakfast in 1981. The Romseys, Brabournes and Palmer-Tomkinsons also found themselves blacklisted: Charles had let drop during one of their rows that Norton Romsey had advised him not to marry Diana. According to a royal relation, Diana crossed every single woman of Charles's previous acquaintance off their mutual Christmas card list.

Camilla's family and Charles's close friends were very upset when he ceased to get in touch with them. Not only were they genuinely fond of him but they also basked in the glow which surrounds royal access. 'I think they were a little put out that they didn't see him and gone were the close contacts and everything else,' a neighbour said.[22] Charles's friends – and Camilla's – were the country house set, the owners of great houses like Bowood in Wiltshire, Chatsworth in Derbyshire, families with resonant names like Shelburne and Willoughby de Broke. Diana was offending a powerful network reaching from the country to the court and she would not easily be forgiven. In social terms, despite being Princess of Wales and a Spencer, she had no comparable network of her own. Stories of her possessiveness were bandied round by the exiles, no doubt giving rise to the 'fiend' and 'monster' accusations. The mantra was that Diana was a scheming girl who had set her cap at Charles and got him, that she was 'a really nasty person', or at best an unhappy one. She was 'impossible to live with – the reason why so many staff had left'. Her treatment of Prince Charles had been cruel and domineering from the start. One friend recalled when the couple came to have a drink during their engagement period: Diana had left her engagement ring in another room and peremptorily ordered Charles to go and fetch it. The visiting couple had initially applauded her firmness with the Prince: 'at the time I thought this was good news but later it turned out not to be at all . . .' Diana, they said, 'tortured' Prince Charles, saying, 'No one wants to see you, they all want to see me', and, 'You'll never be King, no one wants you to be King.' Charles's riposte, according to Diana, would be, 'They only come to see you because you're married to me.'[23] When Diana's uncle Lord Fermoy, of whom she was very fond, shot himself in August 1984 after a long struggle against depression, the tragedy strengthened comments about 'bad Fermoy blood': Frances was a bolter, her sister Mary a recluse and Fermoy himself a depressive. Diana was, therefore, 'tainted'. Much was made of Ruth Fermoy quoting a school report on Diana describing her as 'the most scheming little girl I have ever met'.

While this last may have carried an element of truth, and it could indeed be said that Diana's desire that Charles 'should give up everything' for her was totally unrealistic, considering that he had official duties and responsibilities as Prince of Wales and was a spoilt bachelor already set in his ways to boot, the evidence is that, although she undoubtedly treated him badly when in one of her moods, she still loved him far more than he ever loved her. 'Prince Charles was so self-centred that he couldn't handle the situation with Diana when she behaved erratically [but] she was besotted with him and always put him first,' a member of their staff said. 'The Princess was very much in love with him – romantically so and at the same time rather afraid of him.'[24] The irony of the situation was that she was terrified of losing Charles and, above all, of his going back to Camilla, but her tormented behaviour only succeeded in turning him away from her. At some point, probably in 1983, Charles and Camilla began to get in touch again. Diana believed that Camilla had never gone away and that she had always kept in touch.

The allegation that Diana 'dominated' Charles was described as nonsense by Andrew Neil, then editor of the *Sunday Times*, who, with Charles Douglas-Home, editor of *The Times* and Diana's first cousin, lunched with the couple at Kensington Palace in April 1984. 'It was clear the royal couple had very little in common,' wrote Neil. 'Charles roamed far and wide on the issues of the day . . . Diana played little part in the conversation . . . Charles made no attempt to involve her.'[25] 'The Princess would consult Prince Charles on everything and he liked that,' a member of staff said. 'She was very anxious to get everything right.'[26]

At this point there was still intimacy between them. On Valentine's Day 1984 Diana's second pregnancy was announced. As Diana recalled it:

then between William and Harry being born it is total darkness. I can't remember much, I've blotted it out, it was such pain. However, Harry appeared by a miracle. We were very, very close to each other the six weeks before Harry was born, the closest we've ever, ever been and ever will be. Then suddenly as Harry was born it just went bang, our marriage, the whole thing went down the drain. I knew Harry was going to be a boy because I saw the scan. Charles always wanted a girl. I knew Harry was a boy and I didn't tell him. Harry arrived, Harry had red hair, Harry was a boy. [His] first comment was 'Oh God, it's a boy', second comment, 'and he's even got red hair'. Something inside me closed off. By then I knew he had gone back to his lady . . .[27]

Prince Henry Charles Albert David, always known as Harry, was born on 15 September 1984.

8. 'The Best Double Act in the World'

'How awful incompatibility is, and how dreadfully destructive it can be for the players in this extraordinary drama. It has all the ingredients of a Greek tragedy' (Prince Charles to a friend[1])

'I think she was happiest almost when they were expecting Harry and soon after,' a close aide said. 'Again, I don't believe Prince Charles was upset that it was another boy. I think that was a complete fallacy [which took root] in her life later on . . . He was delighted with Harry.'[2] Both Charles and Diana enjoyed being parents: Charles in his Buckingham Palace days used to love going up to the nursery when Andrew and Edward were young, playing with them and talking to them while they were being bathed. With Harry, as with William, he took his fatherly duties seriously, even to changing nappies. He cut down on his engagements to the extent that it was publicly noticed, so that he could be at home more with the children. Shortly after Harry's birth, Diana wrote describing William's reaction to his new brother: 'William has totally taken over his brother and Charles and I are hardly allowed near as he covers Harry in an endless supply of hugs and kisses.' They had been deluged with baby clothes by the public: 'The reaction to our small son's arrival has been totally overwhelming – having been sent millions of pink (!) clothes for the last nine months.'[3]

Harry had been christened on 21 December 1984 in St George's Chapel, Windsor. The godparents were Lady Sarah Armstrong-Jones, the painter Bryan Organ, Gerald Ward, Prince Andrew, Lady Vestey (a friend of both Charles and Diana) and Diana's former flatmate Carolyn Bartholomew. Princess Anne was the only one of Charles's siblings not to attend the christening; it was announced that she and her husband were unable to attend owing to 'a long-standing private engagement that had been fixed far in advance of the christening'. When it turned out that the long-standing engagement was nothing more crucial than shooting with Mark Phillips's father, the press mischievously intimated that Princess Anne had 'snubbed' Diana who had not invited her to be a godparent. The outstanding beauty of the three generations – Diana, her mother and her grandmother – was evident in the formal photographs of the occasion taken by Snowdon, but while Diana looked radiant and Ruth Fermoy serene, poor Frances Shand Kydd, unnerved by the presence of Raine and Johnnie, and aware that the Royal Family neither liked nor approved of her, looked tense, sad and isolated. Her husband, Peter Shand Kydd, was not, apparently, present, although Diana's brother and sisters were.

In theory, Diana now had what she had always wanted: a home and children, and a husband whom she loved. At Christmas she would attach loving notes to her presents to him: 'to my adorable, wonderful hubby with special love at Christmas . . .'. 'My boys' in particular were the centre of her world and her life revolved around them, more so as she became lonelier in her later years. She would stick notes on a door: 'I love William and Harry'. She organized children's parties for them when the chef, Mervyn Wycherley, baked cakes shaped as Thomas the Tank Engine or some other popular toy. 'Everything was done for the boys,' a member of staff recalled. 'She took a lot of trouble. One birthday party she organized a bouncy castle in the middle of the quadrangle at Kensington Palace and we hired bear suits and raided their birthday party . . . William was very smart, he could recognize people by their shoes.'[4] William was christened the Wombat and Harry was Harry Snail. She was strict with them, rationing their chocolate allowance and insisting that they pick things up after them.

Diana was a modern mother, absolutely devoted to her children and dedicated to putting them first and arranging her life round them. 'The thing that mattered most to her was her sons,' said Sam McKnight, her friend and hairdresser, who saw a good deal of her in the family setting at Kensington Palace. 'They were at the heart

of her life and her absolute preoccupation was to give them as
normal a life as possible. She saw her whole mission as being to
prepare them for their future roles but she wanted that to be based
on as normal a life as possible.'[5] Diana is often depicted as a rebel
but she was committed to the monarchy and to her sons' roles
in its future. It was the monarchy as she saw it, popular and
communicating with the people, doing good in a heartfelt rather
than distant and dutiful way. She wanted 'her boys' to know how
other people lived and insisted that they should go to ordinary
little schools with other children, first, Mrs Jane Mynors' nursery
school and then Wetherby School. Her protection officer, Ken
Wharfe, who had guarded the boys before being transferred to
Diana, if asked what he would remember best about the Princess
said: 'I always say that it would be my memory of her influence
over the children as a mother and her care of them, because it was
one arena that she felt totally confident in. I suspect, right from
the day they were born she knew "this is the way I want these
children to grow up". They were still in a very privileged, fortunate
position, they were not going to be re-housed in any local funded
programme, but given that, she did everything she could to give
them a normal upbringing.'[6]

'The days were always set around taking William and Harry to
school and, wherever possible, being home to pick them up. Or
at least be in the house when they got back . . . She'd arrive at
school in the morning in a tracksuit, no make-up, drop the kid
off, say "hello" to the other children . . . One of the other parents
would say, "Oh, William's coming round to us tomorrow night."
"Oh, that's fine," she'd say. So they would go off to his friend's.'
She would invite them back and 'they'd all come back to the
nursery at some point, throw jelly at each other and have a fight
behind the garden . . . So there was this natural interchange of
friends that was approved in its entirety by the princess because
the prince chose to be elsewhere . . . And I think that the success
of that is what we see in William and Harry . . . I'm absolutely
certain that that is why a lot of their friends now are the friends
they met at prep school, through Eton and so forth . . .

'The reality of her life was so much more than this image of somebody performing on the royal circuit, shaking hands and taking bunches of flowers. Here was somebody with this incredibly complex life, able to find time, with all these pressures, to take her children to school and be there for them. But also educate them in a way that was going to be of value to them in later life. For example there weren't any grand teas . . . butlers laying tables . . . neatly cut fingers of tomato sandwiches. They'd sit with their mother in front of the television with a bowl of beans on toast . . . or we'd go into the kitchen and just sit there and knock up something together. So the children would have this interaction with normal people. And so it was a great education to them, frowned upon, I might add, by the prince, I think, in those early stages. I don't think he'd like what he deemed familiarity. I think it was crucial to William and Harry for where they now find themselves.'[7]

Diana was obsessed with protecting them from the press, arranging things through her excellent press secretary, Vic Chapman, so that they were not overwhelmed and yet would become used to the odd photo opportunity. She was determined that they would never suffer what amounted to the press persecution she experienced.

'I do remember one day at school,' a friend said,

when William was in the school play. He was very little, probably three and a half – and he came out with his school friends, all dressed up in their little nativity outfits. And there was this huge bank of photographers all on ladders. They've even got big coats and woolly hats. They look like a rabble and they've all got these big cameras. It's terrifying, anyway, let alone if you're a little tiny boy. And, everyone was shouting out, 'William, William, William!' It must have been incredibly difficult for a child that age to understand why they were all calling for him. I asked her once, 'What do you do about that?' Because she was very, very aware of this and was very worried about this with him. And she said she had had to say to him, 'You're going to go to school today, there's going to be all of these people who want to take your picture, and if you're a good boy and you let them take your picture, then I'll take you to Thorpe Park next week.'[8]

Shortly after Harry's birth, Diana began to involve herself in charity work, replacing Princess Margaret, at the Princess's own suggestion, as president of Barnardo's, the children's charity. In 1984 with Barnardo's, Diana, still only twenty-three, embarked on the course which, after motherhood, was to give her increasingly difficult life meaning. Roger Singleton, the chief executive, was amazed that so young a woman could have such rapport with people of all ages at Barnardo's projects round the country.

Her capacity to make people feel good was really quite exceptional and I've seen her sit in a group of young mums struggling to bring up a handful of children, very often on their own, almost choking with cigarette smoke. Perhaps some of them themselves were in the care of public authorities when they were children. She would just sit and listen to what their everyday lives were like. Very often she didn't say a great deal in response although she would always answer questions about herself and her own children. But after she'd gone . . . that group of people would feel sheer exhilaration about the fact that they'd been able to talk to a senior person in public life . . . She left them with the very full impression that she understood what they were talking about and she knew what it was like . . . That was a particular skill and I would say that her biggest single contribution to Barnardo's was the difference she was able to make by dint of those visits to people's lives. I can visit those same projects five or ten years later and if some of the same people are involved they will almost invariably bring out the photographs and say 'Do you remember?'[9]

Despite her young age, Diana was a professional in her private life as well as professional duties. 'She took being mistress of the house very seriously,' a member of staff said. 'And she would do the menus for both [houses] in the menu book each week. She knew what she had to do and she did it.'[10] Each day she would see the butler and give him a list of what needed doing, who was coming to lunch or tea, or what appointments she or the Prince might have. However much she might complain that she didn't understand what being the Princess of Wales entailed, she was very domesticated and her Althorp background had taught her how the household should be run.

Similarly, she was considerably more professional than her husband when it came to dealing with her public life. While Prince Charles's secretaries might compare getting him to work on a regular basis to 'nailing jelly to a wall', Diana, even in these first years, was direct and competent in her attitude to paperwork and to her staff. Her principal aide in her early years was Anne Beckwith Smith who acted as private-secretary cum lady-in-waiting. One observer paid tribute to Anne's importance in Diana's professional life. 'Anne would be the last person to say it, but she was an excellent source of support and guidance to someone who was new to the Royal Family, very much in the public gaze and having to cope with public embarrassments especially around the patently obvious fact that she was more popular than her husband . . . in the full glare of publicity with people drawing attention to it, it couldn't have been easy.'[11]

From the beginning, only a few months after the wedding, Beckwith Smith had been impressed by how Diana handled a first meeting, and subsequently by a thoughtful note from Balmoral welcoming her to the staff on her first morning at Buckingham Palace. No one, Diana intimated, knew what precisely they were going to do, but they would muddle through together. As she developed, Diana emphasized 'her team' which she named the 'A-team', after the American TV series. In future no one would be in any doubt as to which was the 'B-team'. 'She was efficient,' said a member of the team, 'she turned things round quickly, you sent her things and she turned them round. On the whole she was extremely conscientious professionally.' As she matured and the demands of her public life multiplied, she became even more so. Patrick Jephson, who became her private secretary in 1988, described her as 'quick and decisive', and she expected him to be the same.[12] 'This,' he added waspishly, 'was at least partly to draw a distinction between herself and the Prince, whose capacity to sit on paperwork was legendary.' Diana's *modus operandi* in opening the 'Bag', which contained all correspondence, memoranda and other paperwork from the joint office at St James's Palace forwarded to Kensington Palace, was described by Jephson:

She would snap the little plastic seal [of the large red plastic envelope], pull back the heavy zip and delve inside. Balancing the inner cardboard file on her lap, she quickly sorted the papers into piles. Fashion catalogues or designers' bills were dealt with first; then loose minutes from the secretaries about things like therapists' appointments or school events for the boys; the personal mail – some of it saved for private reading later; then real work – memos that required a decision, outline programmes, draft speeches, invitations, suggested letters . . .'[13]

She would leave notes for members of staff in her round girlish handwriting, sometimes even notes for herself. She had a compulsive desire to communicate, to reach out to people, even if she hardly knew them, people like the manager of the shoe shop she patronized, Charles Jourdan, to whom she wrote a sympathetic letter when she heard he had lost his job. She also wrote to staff from her past life, like Mrs Pendrey, wife of the butler at Althorp; one such letter, written three months after William's birth, read poignantly: 'William has brought us such happiness and contentment & consequently I can't wait for masses more . . .'[14]

But, according to Diana, Charles no longer shared her bed after William was born and she never had 'masses more' children or the daughter she longed for. Whether he did 'go back to his lady' in 1983/4, as Diana alleged, or, as Jonathan Dimbleby affirmed in a statement passed by Charles, only in 1986, 'after the irretrievable breakdown of the marriage', Camilla remained present in Diana's mind and no doubt in Charles's mind also. Diana's continuing jealousy and neediness made Camilla all the more attractive in contrast. A mutual friend said of Camilla and her undoubted attraction: 'It's hard to describe. She's got laughing eyes, she's full of fun and she's rather motherly and I can see what it is – what Charles must love in her. At the time I remember thinking "Oh God, she's got something Diana hasn't got" which is a sort of warmth . . . I mean my children adore her. She's warm and motherly. At the same time she must have known what she was doing then. There's no question . . . She must have been just as jealous [of Diana, as Diana of her]. How must she have felt when she saw this young girl – I know she contrived it, she obviously manipulated it a bit, but how must she have felt when this beautiful young girl married him? It must have been awful . . . knowing he had to marry. How could she possibly have lived with that?'[15]

The answer is that, as Princess Margaret had foreseen, Camilla never gave up on Prince Charles. Although Jonathan Dimbleby asserted that, apart from 'a few telephone conversations during the four months of his engagement and only one after his marriage (when he rang to report that the Princess was pregnant with William) they had not talked to each other at all', Camilla was interested enough in the whole scenario form a close [telephonic] relationship with a powerful tabloid journalist which lasted from 1982 to 1992. 'I mean here was the unique example, surely unprecedented,' a well-informed observer commented, '. . . here was a woman who was as close as it is possible to be to the Prince of Wales, a man of supposed rectitude in his dealings with the press. And yet she is talking to the editor [sic] of the most popular paper in the country, and the most scurrilous, and the most intrusive and the one that's been most hostile to him . . .' Stuart Higgins told Sally Bedell Smith, an early and authoritative biographer of Diana:

I talked to her once a week for ten years . . . I talked to her about Diana and Charles. She guided me on things that were not true or things that were off the beam. Everything was behind closed doors, and I didn't write about her, although I spoke to her all the time during that period. I didn't sense that she and Charles were out of touch. I felt she was involved, but not necessarily in a romance or affair with Charles. I never sensed that she was out of contact, though I definitely believe there was

a cessation in the relationship and that Charles put an effort into the
marriage . . . Our relationship was two ways. We had some long conversations. She was really trying to gauge whether the press was on to her
[and Charles] so it was a question of keeping her in touch, too.[16]

It was a curious relationship which illustrated the web of understanding and complicity in the circle around Charles. 'She was
always trying to find out what he [Stuart Higgins] knew . . . why
was she doing that? There were extraordinary things on the phone
. . . he'd ring her and say "they say you're about to do this" and
she'd half cup the phone, not properly cup it and say "Andrew,
guess what they're saying about us now" . . . and even Stuart
was utterly baffled by how incredibly open this whole thing was
between her and Parker Bowles and – obviously – between her
and Charles . . . He [Higgins] could run stories past her.'

While Camilla was the shadow over the marriage, another factor
was driving the couple apart: the way in which Diana, through no
fault of her own, outshone her husband in their public lives. It
cannot be denied that Diana had a mischievous desire to annoy
and an apparently endless capacity to do so. That past November
she had even gone so far as to upstage the Queen in public at the
State Opening of Parliament. It was typical of her to do it with a
fashion statement – in this case an entirely new upswept style with
a chignon – which made her look regal – and older. Her new style
was widely criticized by admirers and enemies alike. *Daily Express*
fashion editor Jackie Modlinger wailed, unfairly as it happened,
'They've made her into a right royal clone . . .' 'Is she still our
Princess Di?' the newspaper asked. Diana's coiffure generated far
greater column inches than the government's programme for the
new session of Parliament: 'The entire popular press without
exception abandoned the attempt to squeeze excitement out of the
Government's legislative programme and devoted several columns
each to the most radical and contentious item revealed there,
Princess Diana's new hairstyle.' Diana had ridden to the Palace of
Westminster in a carriage with the Queen, who, as usual, gave no
hint of her feelings, but Prince Philip was said to have been enraged

that press coverage of the day both in photographs and comment had elevated the Princess's image to the detriment of the Queen's on what should have been a solemn state occasion. Once again the newspapers reflected the nation's possessive obsession with 'our Princess Di'. Not long afterwards, on 21 November, Diana chose to exhibit another new hairstyle, dubbed by the papers 'the Vera Lynn style of the 1940s', at the Remembrance Day Service to the dead of two world wars at the Cenotaph in Whitehall, when she shared a balcony with the Queen Mother, Princess Alice, the Duchess of Gloucester, Princess Anne and King Olaf of Norway.

The two important tours the couple undertook in 1985, for all their success, brought the problem into high relief. Their joint seventeen-day tour of Italy in April 1985 was one of those times, even though staff who accompanied them remembered it as a 'very happy' trip. At Milan, in a borrowed palace, one of the staff, engaged in moving round the furniture to give the huge room a more lived-in air, found the couple waltzing round him. Prince Charles had been hugely looking forward to this, his second visit to Italy, but once again he found himself taking a back seat to his wife and her wardrobe. 'They were both popular,' a member of staff recalled, 'but even then the Prince of Wales couldn't cope with his wife's popularity.'[17] The couple stayed with the renowned aesthete Sir Harold Acton at his magnificent villa, La Pietra, on the outskirts of Florence. Diana was fascinated by Sir Harold who, an observer said, 'made up to her in his mandarin way'. At the Uffizi Diana stood amazed in front of Rubens' huge masterpiece, *The Horrors of War* – 'Did one man really paint all that?' she asked Sir Harold. As Charles praised Brunelleschi's great dome standing majestically above the Duomo, the newspapers commented: 'the Church could have been in the Mile End Road for all anyone cared. What really mattered, the pictures which would be carried by virtually every TV station and newspaper in the Western world, was Princess Diana's latest outfit.' The Waleses' press secretary, Vic Chapman, briefed the four-hundred-strong press contingent each day with details of the Princess's wardrobe. In Rome, they had a private audience with Pope John Paul II, which awed Diana;

Charles had wanted to attend a private mass with the Pope but Buckingham Palace, with its customary caution, headed him off. They lunched with President Pertini and dined at the smartest club in Rome, the Circolo della Caccia.

To make things worse, the British press lectured Charles on his duty to Diana: 'Charles must – and does – look at his life long-term. And at the moment it is Diana who is important,' the *Mail on Sunday* representative in Rome declared. 'The Italian tour has seen a new phase in their relationship,' he wrote. 'Few in the Palace entourage now deny that the marriage did go through an awkward stage when the Princess was pregnant with Prince Harry . . . some reporters who follow the Princess around the world full-time believe his coolness has continued. At the start of their marriage, Prince Charles was constantly seen to be taking his wife by the hand or the elbow.

'It happens less these days but two small incidents summed up for me how Charles and Diana feel about each other now. The first happened at Florence Town Hall when the Prince gave a speech in Italian. He obviously found the moment a strain. As he finished the speech the Princess leaned over and said "Well done, darling". Her eyes shone and he smiled warmly back.

'The second came when the Prince stopped opposite a self-portrait of the artist Filippo Lippi. It obviously reminded him of someone. He put his arm around Diana's shoulder and whispered something in her ear. She burst into a fit of giggles.

'*Such intimate moments show a man and a woman deeply in love.*'

At times like these, when the Charles–Diana partnership was acclaimed as the best double act in the world, the general enthusiasm carried them through. Unfortunately, the enthusiasm was largely for Diana's beauty and the glamour of the fairy-tale romance in which everyone still wanted to believe and in which the vast majority of those who did not pick up the media's hints still did. From the Palace point of view, however, such headlines as 'PRINCE HAS SECOND BILLING TO TRIVIA' were deeply disappointing.

A new international tour was planned for the couple – their first joint visit to the United States preceded by yet another tour of

Australia. By this time rumours of the couple's marital difficulties were common currency in media circles. Tina Brown, the Oxford-educated British journalist who was then editing the American magazine *Vanity Fair*, wove them together in a piece published in advance of their US visit, which underlined their differences: 'Diana is a very young twenty-four, he is a very old thirty-six'; in taste in music (Diana was unfairly pictured as glued to her Walkman and pop music while Charles organized musical evenings with the Royal Philharmonic); their differences over friends – he bored with her Sloanes and Hooray Henrys, she with his intellectual gurus and horsey couples from Gloucestershire – which was true. Both, she claimed, had lost touch with reality but, she finished somewhat improbably, reality was still there if they looked for it. 'He's in just the kind of mood to fall in love with a nursery school teacher in flat shoes who's kind to guinea pigs and babies. If he looks hard enough, she's still there . . .' the piece ended. The fairy tale was not yet doomed; there could still be a happy ending.

Fortunately for Buckingham Palace a timely interview with the couple designed to counteract the marriage rumours was ready for transmission. With skill and considerable self-control Charles and Diana put across the image of a diverse but essentially united couple. Diana, who had been coached by Sir Richard Attenborough, displayed confidence as she spoke of her role as 'supporting my husband whenever I can . . . and, also most important, being a mother and wife'. Only the sly upwards look from under her eyelashes gave any clue that she might have been playing a part, tongue in cheek. Charles admitted to 'becoming more eccentric as I grow older', defending his interests in alternative medicine and his criticism of modern architecture on the grounds that he hoped occasionally to 'throw a rock into the pond and watch the ripples create a certain amount of discussion and hopefully to see whether something better can come out . . .' Tina Brown's views were largely condemned; even the *Sun* declared that 'Di and Charles are so very much in love'.

On tour in Australia and the United States that autumn, Charles and Diana kept up the façade of a relaxed, happy couple with consummate ease, even in the presence of Mary Robertson, Diana's old employer, who visited them at the British Embassy in Washington on 8 November after their arrival from Australia. She was immediately struck by the change in Diana, blossoming from 'a naïve, unaffected teenager into a stunning, poised, adult', and particularly by how 'chatty and outgoing she had become . . . no trace of shyness left'.[18] Charles and Diana, she recalled, 'seemed very amicable together, even joking mildly about wanting a girl "the next time"'.[19] At the banquet and ball given by President and Mrs Reagan for eighty select guests, Diana looked stunning in an eight-strand pearl choker and an off-the-shoulder black dress by Victor Edelstein, and her dance with John Travolta was the star turn of the evening. She shone in a crew-necked white lace and satin gown at the British Embassy dinner and in an off-the-shoulder silver embroidered sheath at the dinner at the National Gallery of Art. Smiling, radiant, slim but not skeletal, she looked the picture of health and happiness. Photographs of the same occasions showed a less than radiant Charles, although, as previously in Australia when he had danced with Diana who was wearing an astounding emerald necklace as a headband, he put on a good show of affection and harmony when he took to the floor with her at the White House.

He was still smarting with resentment at the treatment he had received from certain sections of the press and public in Australia where it had become all too obvious that Diana was the draw for the vast crowds. 'So infatuated was the throng at every walkabout,' Dimbleby wrote, 'that as they got out to "work" the crowd, an involuntary moan of disappointment would rise from that part of the crowd which turned out to be nearest to the Prince and furthest from the Princess. Even as they drove through the streets, the Prince could hear the cries of disappointment, "Oh no, she's on the wrong side." '[20] Worse, sections of the crowd held up placards caricaturing his sticking-out ears; it was agony for him to have to confront 'the fatuous remarks and insults made to me; rude things shouted out, gestures made, plastic masks waved about, wound-ingly unnecessary things written in the papers about me etc,' he told a friend.[21] Not surprisingly, it sapped his confidence and made him long to escape the ordeal.

The Prince was happier in surroundings where he was appreciated, like 'Bunny' Mellon's estate, Upperville in Virginia, where the hostess, one of America's *grandes dames*, was a renowned gardener who also owned a superb stud. He was more relaxed too when they reached Florida for a polo match, exchanging a suitably sweet kiss with Diana as she presented the trophies. The principal reason for the visit to Palm Beach was a fund-raising dinner for one of the Prince's young people's charities hosted by the social-climbing and deeply controversial octogenarian chairman of Occidental Petroleum, Armand Hammer. Hammer had been wooing the Prince since 1977 when he had opened an exhibition of Sir Winston Churchill's watercolours and Hammer gave him one of the paintings as a contribution to the Queen's Silver Jubilee Appeal, of which Charles was chairman. Since then Charles, who seemed to have no qualms about accepting largesse from millionaires like Hammer and John Latsis, the Greek shipping magnate, had frequently been the beneficiary of favours from Hammer, including use of the private jet that had flown him and Diana from Los Angeles to the Bahamas after their previous visit to Australia. To be fair to Charles, the shadowy rumours surrounding Hammer – of his being a KGB stooge helping money-laundering to finance Soviet espionage activities, of bribing middlemen to arrange his oil concession in Libya, and misappropriating Occidental funds for his own use – had not yet been brought into the open. In pursuit of funds for his favourite charities Charles was prepared to overlook their source. Since the money was not for him, it never seemed to occur to him that renting out himself – and his wife – was undignified and unworthy of his royal position. One Palm Beach resident had written to the Prince's new private secretary, Sir John Riddell: 'We would like His Royal Highness to know that many loyal Americans would be offended if they looked upon a scenario in which one saw the Heir to the British Throne in any way to be in the pocket of a man they regard as a friend and ally of the Soviet Union and who seems to betray the best interests of the United

States, and therefore, of Britain.' Another anti-Communist described Hammer as 'a Soviet-sympathising slicker of dubious character and integrity . . . [who] has used guile, gold and gall to rope in a lot of good, well-meaning people, including British royalty, to help him organise a testimonial to himself'.[22] Ignoring all advice, the Prince went ahead, flying down to Palm Beach with Diana in Hammer's jet and making a well-received speech at the dinner where he had the much-appreciated pleasure of dancing with Joan Collins whose wit did not distract him from her eye-catching cleavage.

Diana, it seems, had sharper antennae where people were con-cerned. According to Charles's biographer, Anthony Holden, she had vetoed his suggestion that Hammer should be invited to be a godfather to William, describing him as this 'rather reptilian old man'. On the occasion of the Florida dinner, apparently, she made her distaste for Hammer apparent, as she towered over him on the dance floor. 'The Princess's instinct for people was spot on until the later years when it deserted her,' a member of her staff said. 'She used to say to Charles "Why are we having these people to dinner?", i.e. she knew they had ulterior motives for sucking up like being invited to shoot at Sandringham. He never seemed to realize that if he wasn't the Prince of Wales, they wouldn't give him the time of day . . .'[23]

Diana's success on these tours, instead of gratifying her hus-band, had only resulted in increasing his jealousy of her. 'He didn't understand her appeal and resented it,' a member of the Waleses' staff said. 'He didn't understand that people don't get excited by a man in a suit.' 'There was no way anyone could compete with that, the beautiful clothes, and then she was tall, slim and getting educated about dress sense and it worked beautifully. It's a per-fect recipe, isn't it? It's a young woman becoming a woman, maturing, learning how to wear things, but always that freshness. I think that was her secret. She could be dressed in the most fantastic thing but she could walk up to someone, smile at them – no shyness – no one's going to resist that.' 'She had a great gift for people, perhaps too much so, she could go into a room and go directly to someone – people fell in love with her – men and women too.'[24]

One important person did appreciate Diana's public success – the Queen, to whom the prestige of the monarchy was always all-important. 'The Queen liked her success – the glamour she brought to the monarchy,' a member of staff said. 'Diana always said she had immediate access to the Queen and it helped.' Although the Queen took no positive action as far as the Waleses' marriage was concerned, whenever the subject was raised Diana described her as looking worried and twiddling her glasses in her hands. She was, of course, anxious that the marriage should work and indulged Diana. 'Diana could do what she liked,' a member of the Royal Family said. 'Absolutely what she liked. She realized quite early on that there was nobody, not even the Queen, who would stand in her way. Because they were worried about her. Mustn't upset Diana . . .'[25]

As *Time* magazine put it in its cover story for the US visit of Charles and Diana, their storybook marriage had become a night-time soap opera, 'Palace Dallas', behind the imperturbable Windsor front. 'The Princess, once known as Shy Di, has been transformed as "Dynasty Di"; and Prince Charles, once dubbed Action Man for his intrepid sky- and skin-diving, has become a hermetic, mystical crank.' But, the magazine concluded, 'if "The Windsors" is like a primetime serial, it is one that, before Lady Diana Spencer joined the cast, was having ratings problems . . . Then, like an inspired casting director, Charles picked an unlikely *ingénue* for the role of Princess: the girl next door. *Voilà!* She became the biggest star of all and made "The Windsors" the most watched show of all time.'[26] But if the Queen was alleged to have appreciated what Diana's success contributed to the monarchy (and it is hard to believe that anyone could have known the Queen's feelings on that subject), a powerful section of her courtiers took the view that Diana was upstaging not only Charles but their illustrious employer and took umbrage on her behalf.

'To be perfectly honest,' said a member of staff, 'you wouldn't know what the Queen felt. And I think anybody who says they do know is absolutely wrong because she would never say. What I think is the case is that a lot of her household were very jealous of Diana – and I'm talking about earlier rather than later. And they saw that as threatening their Queen. There is terrible rivalry between all the different [royal] households. It's very difficult to get it across to anybody who has never worked there that it's not like a company, you are not working for the monarchy or the Royal Family. You are working for your individual and that is the difference.' Between Charles's friends and some of the Queen's people, a venomous attitude towards Diana was developing. '[One of Diana's friends] happened to be at a dinner party with a member of the Queen's household and they were slating Diana and this person said, "I don't think you should be doing that", and reported it back to Diana and Diana reported it to the Queen. The Queen remonstrated with them.'[27]

Increasingly, however, the couple's different approach to their royal duties was becoming a debate as to the nature of a modern monarchy. Charles, heir to the throne from the age of three, regarded the attention of the populace as a God-given right to which he was by birth entitled, which he could ennoble by his humane interest and his genuine attempts to communicate with people, while inwardly bemoaning his lot. He worried about issues, was concerned about people and did his best, usually successfully, to communicate that concern. In his own view he was the human face of the monarchy whose ceremonial aspects his mother represented. Hitherto, the monarchy had been supposed to be popular without doing much about it, certainly not descending to crowd level. Diana changed all that. Her glamour, her ability to communicate, her genuine rapport with the elderly, the sick and the young, her empathy which enabled her to guide the hand of an old blind man to touch her face when he was in tears because he could not see her, the witty repartee which lightened her dialogue with officials, combined to present a vision of the role of a member of the Royal Family which was utterly new and, to royal officialdom, confusing and in some way challenging to royal dignity. Charles felt unfairly outshone; Diana, with some reason, felt that her efforts to enhance the couple's public image were unappreciated. She enjoyed being regarded as a superstar but behind the walls of Kensington Palace and Highgrove she wanted the Barbara Cartland cliché of loving wife and husband, with adorable children. Increasingly the public success made private harmony more difficult. Caught between the radiant public image of herself and her own insecurities and longing for love and appreciation, she made demands on Charles to which he could not and would not respond.

Diana still hoped for Charles's love and approbation. Much as she loved him, she showed little real understanding of the kind of man he was: bred into him was a horror of public exhibitionism or displays of emotion. Secretly she prepared a surprise for Charles; whether she thought it was something he would appreciate or whether she wanted to show him what a desirable woman she was, underlining what he was missing, is impossible to guess. Charles's thirty-seventh birthday was to be celebrated at a gala evening at the Royal Opera House, Covent Garden. At the end of the performance Diana slipped out of the royal box to change into a slinky, body-hugging, silver dress, to perform something she had been secretly rehearsing with the Royal Ballet star Wayne Sleep, a dance routine to Billy Joel's 'Uptown Girl'. To see the Princess of Wales cavorting in a sexy number on a public stage was a severe shock to Charles's sense of royal propriety: how Diana could ever have thought otherwise is a measure of the distance between them and between her way of thinking and the inbred royal mind. She received eight curtain calls and a standing ovation, then dropped a curtsey to her husband in the royal box. 'Look what you're missing' did indeed seem to be her message: it fell on deaf ears. Charles was horrified. He saw the episode not as a gesture of love towards him but as yet another example of Diana courting the public eye.

The stage was set for another downturn in their private relationship.

9. 'Charles has gone back to his Lady'

'You know about Camilla, don't you? . . . I don't know how to deal with it. It's there and I can't do anything about it . . .' (Diana to Ken Wharfe, 1986[1])

The couple's sex life was virtually non-existent by then. Diana was only twenty-four: the contrast between the adulation she received in public and the total lack of appreciation she found when she returned home was hard to take. When asked by Peter Settelen, her voice coach, who taped their sessions, 'There's virtually no sexual relations between the two of you? . . .' she replied, 'Well, there was. There was, there was. But it was odd, very odd. But it was there, it was there and then it fizzled out about seven years ago . . . Well, seven was Harry. It was eight . . .' Asked how she knew it was odd, she replied, 'Instinct told me. It was just so odd. I just don't know. There was never a requirement for it from [sic] his case. Sort of once every three weeks, and I kept thinking, and then I followed a pattern; he used to see his lady once every three weeks before we got married . . .'[2] It seems that sex never mattered very much to Diana, certainly not as much as expressions of love and appreciation. Her careful preservation of her virginity − 'keeping myself tidy' − hardly indicated a passionately sexual temperament. With the consciousness of Camilla in the background and her husband's infrequent sexual advances, she was probably, like many beautiful and inexperienced women, insecure about her own sexual attraction. She liked to flirt and was immensely successful at it: men of all ages would go weak at the knees when she fluttered her eyelashes at them, focusing on them with her amazing blue eyes. Her lavatorial sense of humour, fondness for coarse jokes and fascination with other people's sexual behaviour indicated a vicarious rather than a practical interest in sex.

The role of the Royalty and Diplomatic Protection Department officers in the life of the 'principal' they are entrusted to protect is a curious one. The men are SAS-trained in threat avoidance while driving, the use of a gun, fitness and awareness, regularly tested and expected to keep up with the latest intelligence. 'From '72 until recently the IRA was the biggest threat,' one said. 'You get the nutters, you always got the nutters, but your main intelligence was that the IRA said that members of the Royal Family, while working and representing the Royal Family, were a legitimate target.' From the moment Diana symbolically entered the Royal Family on the night she went to stay at Clarence House, she became used to the presence of policemen dedicated to her protection.

Her private protection officer became part of her life: with her when she walked in the park, with her when she went shopping; wearing black tie he shadowed her at evening events, played informally with the children at home. One of Diana's first protection officers, Graham Smith, who was on *Britannia* for the honeymoon, became a father figure to her; she visited him in hospital just before he died of cancer. Diana was absolutely open with her protection officers, almost to the point of embarrassing them. It was Graham Smith who warned one of his successors of the frankness he could expect. 'He said, "Look, Ken, whatever I say it's going to be confirmed by her because you'll be a part of it."' 'In a way,' Wharfe said, 'this was probably one of Diana's strengths but it was also a weakness. I'm not so certain it's a good idea to keep telling people everything.'[3] Naturally the 'principal' and the policeman would become close. In 1985 Diana, in her loneliness and longing for love, comfort and appreciation, became close, perhaps too close, to her protection officer Barry Mannakee. When asked about Mannakee, a member of staff recalled him as 'Really a very nice man, very down to earth . . . genuine . . . a nice person to have around. He came across as being someone you thought "if there was a crisis, I'd be glad to have him standing next to me".'[4] There has been much gossip and rumour about Diana's relations with Barry Mannakee. Diana, in the tapes she made with Peter Settelen, recorded in 1992 but broadcast on NBC, one of the major US networks, after her death, in the autumn of 2004, admitted to a crush on him: 'I fell deeply in love with someone who worked in this environment. And he was the greatest fella I've ever had.' 'I was always walking around trying to see him . . . I just wore my heart on my sleeve and was only happy when he was around . . . I was like a little girl in front of him the whole time. Desperate for praise. Desperate.' She even half-joked about running away with him (although he had a wife and children). When asked by Settelen, 'What you're saying is that there had been sexual . . . ?' Diana replied 'No'.[5] A later lover, James Hewitt, claimed that she told him that a teddy bear on her bed had been given her by Mannakee, and that he had been her lover. Hewitt's testimony, given in his second book about his affair with Diana, cannot be corroborated but any sexual affair was denied to Mannakee's successor, Ken Wharfe, by the house staff who would have known of it had it happened. This may have been out of a loyal desire to protect Diana: the rumour in the Kensington Palace village alleged that Mannakee used to go and see Diana when Charles was not there, and that he really cared for her, comforting her and fulfilling her needs.

What had happened, or was witnessed on one occasion, was Mannakee in Diana's sitting room, jacket off, having a cup of tea, laughing and joking and giving her a cuddle before he left. That was his downfall. As Diana told Settelen, '. . . it all got so difficult. And people got so jealous. Bitchy in this house [Kensington Palace]. And eventually he had to go . . . it was all found out and he was chucked out.'[6] Word from the staff got to the chief protection officer, Colin Trimming, who worked principally for the Prince of Wales. Mannakee was removed from his post overnight and sacked from royal service a few months later. Not one of Diana's staff believed Mannakee had slept with the Princess: 'He was just stupid . . . familiar and arrogant' was the general opinion. Did Charles know of it? Trimming was very much the Prince's creature and recipient of his favours; it seems likely that, if asked why Mannakee had left so suddenly, he would have given 'overfamiliarity' as the reason. Certainly Charles knew enough about Mannakee to inform Diana when he was killed in a motorcycle accident two years later. He told her when they were travelling together in the back of a limousine en route to RAF Northolt to catch a plane to the Cannes Film Festival. Diana thought he had done it with deliberate cruelty. She fantasized about Mannakee, consulting clairvoyants in an attempt to contact him, having disturbing dreams about him, that 'he was very unhappy wherever he's gone to'. She found out where he had been buried (he had been cremated and his ashes scattered), and laid flowers for him. The dreams stopped.

The death of Mannakee has been resurrected as part of the investigation into Diana's own death. Mannakee believed that he was in danger: 'He thought that if ever anything happened [between him and Diana], something would happen [to him] and he was terrified.'[7] Diana, always a fan of conspiracy theories, believed it too. She asked Andrew Morton to find out the truth. In fact, it had been a simple, tragic road accident: Mannakee had been riding pillion on a friend's motorcycle, when an inexperienced woman driver pulled out of a side road, turning right across their path. Mannakee was thrown off, went through the car's rear window and was killed instantly. It was not the type of 'accident' which could have been set up beforehand.

If Charles had indeed known of his wife's affection for her detective, there is little reason to suppose that he cared. In court circles, where it was known, it would have been regarded as yet another instance of Diana's 'not knowing how to behave'.

Into Diana's life at this critical point, eager to be her new best friend, came 'Fergie' – Sarah Ferguson, the bouncing, cheerful and loud daughter of Prince Charles's polo manager, Ronald Ferguson, always known by Sarah as 'Dads'. Fergie muscled her way into Diana's life: 'I met Fergie when Charles was getting near me,' Diana told Morton, 'and she kept rearing her head for some reason, and she seemed to know all about the royal set-up, things like that.

DIANA . . . I said: 'I'm just myself.'

JG They can't get to grips that, underneath there is such a beautiful person in you . . . They can't think that it isn't cluttered up by this idea of untold riches.

DIANA I know. He kept wittering on about how one must never think how good one is at one's job. There's always something you can learn round the next corner. I said: 'Well, if people know me, they know I'm not like that.'

JG Yes. Absolutely right. So did you give him a hard time?

DIANA I did, actually, in the end. I said: 'I know this sounds crazy, but I've lived before.' He said: 'How do you know?' I said: 'Because I'm a wise old thing.'

JG Oh, darling Squidge, did you? Very brave thing to say, actually . . .

DIANA It was, wasn't it?

JG Very. Full marks. Ninety-nine out of 100.

DIANA I said: 'Also I'm aware that people I have loved and have died and are in the spirit world look after me.' He looked horrified. I thought, 'If he's the bishop HE should say that sort of thing' . . .

DIANA . . . with that bishop. I said: 'I understand people's suffering, people's pain, more than you will ever know', and he said: 'That's obvious by what you're doing for the AIDS.' I said: 'It's not only people with AIDS, it's anyone who suffers. I can smell them a mile away.'

After this exchange, the flummoxed bishop turned the conversation to children's toys. Triumphant Diana, she told Gilbey, thought, 'Ah! Defeated you.'

Diana was not being unfair when she described Charles as making her life 'absolute torture'. His jealousy and resentment of her had led him to treat her with what amounted to emotional cruelty. Aware as he was of her vulnerability, he could not refrain from constant pinpricks to her already low self-esteem, putting her down in public in the most humiliating way. Patrick Jephson witnessed an incident on the royal couple's tour of the Gulf States earlier that year, in March 1989. The royal host was offering his visitors coffee:

The royal host and his senior guest [the Prince of Wales] were sticking manfully to their scripts . . . Plainly uncomfortable, the Princess was not joining in either, nor was she invited to by the Prince or her host.

She seemed to have created an invisible barrier round herself, as if to say that she was apart from the polite charade going on around her. To me she looked excluded and vulnerable. To the host as well, presumably, because eventually he leaned across the Prince to ask her politely what she was going to do during her visit. Under the unexpected attention she visibly brightened, perhaps thinking – as I was – of the serious programme we had arranged: visits to a day centre for mentally handi-capped children, a clinic for immigrant women and a girls' business studies class.

The Prince also turned towards her, looking as if he were seeing her for the first time, ruefully indulgent, patronising. There was an expectant hush. Before she could reply, he said with studied innocence, 'Shopping, isn't it, darling?'

The words dropped into the marble stillness like bricks into plate glass. The Princess coloured, mumbled something inaudible and lapsed into silence. There was an awkward pause, broken by the Prince pointedly resuming his conversation with a host whose aquiline features now registered a politer version of the disbelief I felt.

When we were outside again I cornered John Riddell [former private secretary to the Prince and Princess of Wales]. 'Did I see what I thought I saw in there?' I asked him.

He looked at me pityingly. 'Oh yes, Patrick. Indeed you did. That is the world we have to live in.'[21]

It was a world in which Diana would find it increasingly hard to live.

12. The War of the Waleses

'Diana was obsessed with Charles. And I think that all the wrong steps she took in life were because of him . . . either to hurt him or show off to him' (a close friend of Diana[1])

In June 1990 Prince Charles broke his right arm falling from a horse during a polo match at Cirencester. The accident marked a distinct stage in the downward spiral of his marriage. To Diana's anguish and humiliation he made it quite clear that her attention was unwanted, and that the only person he required in charge of his convalescence was Camilla. While Diana visited him publicly during the two hospital stays needed for operations on his arm, in private Camilla was by his side at Highgrove where he now spent most of his time.

By now, editors were aware of Camilla's role in Charles's life. Max Hastings, then editor of the *Daily Telegraph*, recalled being told by 'a friend of the Prince's': 'You have got to get your mind round the fact that there is only one woman in the Prince's life, and that is Camilla.' 'This,' he told Diana's biographer, Sally Bedell Smith, 'was in 1990, when everyone knew there was trouble, but there was still no idea of a divorce.'[2] The closeness of the relationship, however, only became public knowledge with the publication just over three years later of the infamous Camillagate tapes, originally recorded in December 1989 shortly before Diana's New Year's Eve conversations with James Gilbey.

These revealed a couple totally in love, emotionally and sexually, consumed with longing for each other. Charles's puerile dirty talk about being reincarnated as a Tampax inside Camilla's trousers and her eager responses – '. . . Just what I need at the moment . . . I can't bear a Sunday night without you . . .' – demonstrated their physical need for each other. Camilla's role in Charles's life as principal comforter and soul mate was clearly revealed: 'You're a clever old thing. An awfully good brain lurking there, isn't there,' she told him. 'Your great achievement is to love me,' Charles said. 'Oh darling, easier than falling off a chair,' Camilla replied. 'You suffer all those indignities and tortures and calumnies,' he responded. 'I'd suffer anything for you. That's love. It's the strength of love,' she told him. Fortunately for Diana's peace of mind, the contents of the tape were not revealed until January 1993 when the full extent of the conspiracy of Charles's friends to provide rendezvous for the lovers came to light. A web of deception surrounded the affair, from people whom she had thought of as mutual friends, who provided safe houses where Charles and Camilla could spend the night, to loyal Highgrove staff who had no alternative but to cover up for the Prince both to ingratiate themselves with their principal employer and to spare her pain. Long before the eventual separation, the Waleses' staff had divided into two camps. Most of them did not enjoy being used in the deception of Diana, even to the extent of the butler being asked to wrap a sapphire and diamond brooch as a present to Camilla from Charles, while the Prince's gift to Diana was a paltry souvenir straw hat decorated with fruit, acquired during a trip to Cornwall.

Unlike many unfaithful husbands who are kinder to their wives as a result of their adultery, Charles by now seemed almost to hate his wife. And despite her declarations of love for Charles, Diana's screaming scenes only succeeded in alienating him further. While their disharmony was concealed from outsiders, the un-happy relationship created tensions within the family. At Balmoral later that summer, with problems in both the Wales and the York marriages, the atmosphere was noticeably difficult. The Queen, unusually, expressed her frustration at Prince Charles, his arm in a sling, who had chosen to take the van Cutsems' choice of doctor rather than hers. It was a celebration of Princess Margaret's sixtieth birthday but the atmosphere was far from cordial – there were endless evening picnics at which Prince Charles appeared 'in a very cross mood'. Colin Glenconner 'did some silly things with napkins to amuse Fergie and Di, when they all did a number and everybody laughed except Prince Charles'. Asked if he found it amusing he said icily, clearly referring to his wife and sister-in-law, 'Little things please little minds.'[3]

At Balmoral, Fergie and Diana appeared as allies once again but, as Diana's secretary Patrick Jephson pointed out, 'running through it all was her mistrust of Fergie'.[4] In her Squidgygate conversation with James Gilbey on New Year's Eve 1989, Diana had referred cautiously to Fergie: 'The redhead is being actually quite supportive . . .' Gilbey had warned her that Sarah was not to be trusted, that she had her own agenda and was trying to hang on to Diana's coat-tails. Her former popularity with the public had disappeared, after the Australia visit when she had been severely criticized for leaving the baby Beatrice behind for six weeks. She was slated for her weight, her dress, her penchant for free holidays, and she was becoming increasingly unpopular at court. 'I just worry that she's desperately trying to get back in. She's trying to tag on . . . She knows that your PR is so good, she's trying to tag on to that.' Charles, Diana told Gilbey, had been trying to help Fergie, calling on a Royal Family favourite, the broadcaster Sir Jimmy Savile, to advise her on improving her image. Diana, more cautious and instinctive than Sarah, watched 'the redhead's' head-long rush towards destruction with more than a little Schaden-freude. Always sensitive of her public image, she was well aware that Fergie's infatuation with an American, which she made little effort to conceal, and her open defiance of the Queen's senior courtiers, including her cousin and particular *bête noire*, Sir Robert Fellowes, was not the way to proceed. Fergie, as has often been said, was indeed the 'yellow canary' used by miners to test for dangerous gases underground.

There is little evidence that Sarah listened to Savile's advice any more than she did to anyone else's. By August 1990 her marriage was in trouble. Sarah was evidently bored with her husband whose frequent absences on naval duty left her at a loose end. Sarah told a friend that in 1988 Andrew had spent only forty-two nights at home out of a year. Once the Yorks' controversial home,

Sunninghill Park, dubbed Southyork for its *Dallas*-like ostentation, was finished in the summer of 1990, she was not prepared to live as a naval wife in married quarters or even in a rented house near Andrew's base, and when he was at home she found his preferred way of relaxation boring. Andrew liked to watch videos and play golf and, when the couple entertained, Sarah found his behaviour embarrassingly boorish. At dinner parties he was served first and gobbled down his food regardless of the other guests, and he had a fondness for telling loud and unfunny naval jokes. To the Queen's household it appeared that he had no control over his wife's behaviour, while to Sarah it seemed that he was not prepared to stand up for her when she was lectured by his mother's courtiers. Andrew, sadly, still loved his wife but, as Sarah's father had told his mistress, she had been in love with the Royal Family rather than her husband. Now both 'love affairs' were cooling from Sarah's point of view.

The man with whom Sarah had fallen in love was the handsome Texan Steve Wyatt, whom she had met in Houston at the home of his mother, the glamorous Saks heiress, Lynn Sakowitz Wyatt. Wyatt's stepfather, Oscar, one of the richest and toughest men in Texas, could offer Sarah all the luxury that a huge ranch and a fleet of private planes could provide. Sarah had flown to New York in the Wyatts' plane and stayed at their expense at the Plaza Athénée. Her affair with Wyatt continued when he was transferred to London; she was photographed with him and her daughters at the Wyatts' villa on Cap Ferrat (formerly the home of Somerset Maugham) and again, according to Sarah, at a weekend house party in Gloucestershire. Later that summer the extent to which Sarah had become involved with Wyatt was blatantly revealed. Declining an invitation to dinner with Lord McAlpine and his wife, she instead, at Wyatt's instigation, gave a dinner in her second-floor Buckingham Palace apartment to Ramzi Sultan, an Iraqi oil dealer, whose country was about to invade Kuwait and who was therefore very much *persona non grata* to the British government. Blithely unaware of the faux pas she had committed, Sarah took both Ramzi and Wyatt, uninvited, to join the

McAlpines later that night, making no secret of her attraction to Wyatt. With a complete lack of propriety, she obtained an invitation for Wyatt to the Christmas ball held that year by the Queen to celebrate the ninetieth, sixtieth and thirtieth birthdays respectively of the Queen Mother, Princess Margaret and Prince Andrew. Just over a year later Wyatt, warned off by his socially astute mother, returned to the United States, leaving behind on the top of a wardrobe in his former flat holiday snaps of himself with Fergie and her children to be found by a window cleaner and passed to the newspapers. (Sarah herself claimed that the flat had been searched and found to be 'clean', implying that the photographs had been placed there at the instigation of the *Daily Mail*.) By then Fergie had linked up with another Texan, John Bryan, in a liaison which was to prove her downfall.

Yet Diana, lacking in self-confidence and always aware that her affair with James Hewitt, even though temporarily in abeyance, could destroy her reputation, still kept up her competition with Fergie for public esteem. 'No matter what misfortunes publicly befell her sister-in-law,' Jephson wrote, 'the Princess would still torture herself with the thought that she might yet become a real rival rather than just a useful counterpart to her own good fortune.'[5] Sometimes she appeared to be in direct competition with her sister-in-law, as when she reacted to a newspaper report of 'caring Fergie'; she would complain to Jephson, 'Patrick! We seem to be reading rather a lot about the red-haired lady . . .'[6], whereupon a charitable counterstrike would be arranged. But if some of these charity duties were thus cynically motivated, Diana's actual performances were undertaken in a genuine spirit. Often her charitable forays took place when she was bored, cooped up in Balmoral, longing for an outlet and not totally unaware of the good publicity to be earned by being seen to visit a hospice while her in-laws were known to be slaughtering game. The less the Royal Family seemed to appreciate her, the more Diana felt the need to be wanted by the public, to receive from their response the unconditional love and understanding which she so badly needed. Yet Diana's responses, according to Jephson, who accompanied her on numberless public occasions and charitable duties, were not feigned. 'The impression I had formed on that first outing . . . – that she genuinely cared – was not untrue. It was the instinctive reaction of any sensitive adult, heightened by a strong maternal instinct and a personal acquaintance with pain . . . Not even the best actress could sustain such a convincing show of compassion for so long; nor would those on the receiving end be so easily fooled.'[7]

The Queen's courtiers, although wary of the future, still, unlike the principals themselves, hoped that somehow the Waleses' marriage would survive in some form. Sir William Heseltine, the Queen's private secretary, who retired that year, was relieved by Diana's assurance: 'Don't worry, I'll stick it out.'[8] Two tours that year, to the Far East and to Hungary, sent the spurious message to the world that all was well. Jephson described them as 'the last grand gestures of togetherness' which produced some misleadingly optimistic comments about how well they seemed to be getting on. Photo opportunities featured the couple gazing romantically across the River Danube, and enjoying themselves on the upper deck of a river boat, looking for all the world as if they were on holiday together. You had to be very close to the action, said Jephson, who accompanied them, to perceive the guerrilla warfare being waged below the surface. Point scoring against Charles was a game which Diana played with consummate skill: she was photographed holding hands with the Hungarian President's wife during the arrival ceremony (it was the story with all the papers at home, she later told Morton) and posing with romantic Magyar horsemen. Patrick Jephson, who was to leave her five years later in a mood of some disillusionment, described the delicate balance between sincerity and ulterior motive in her actions. There was no doubt, he wrote, that her underlying intention was 'to attract attention, to signal an independence from her marriage, and to exert by guile and gamesmanship the strength she felt unable to express openly. Foreign tours, no less than home engagements, were vehicles for a subliminal message: I am not a dumb clothes-horse, a junior player in a marriage that frustrates me: I am a figure in my own right, and none too scrupulous.'⁹

In private, Diana was playing a dangerous game. Hewitt returned from Germany before Christmas before being ordered to the Gulf War in January and they resumed their passionate affair. Prince Charles was aware of it, as he was also of the relationship with James Gilbey, probably through Superintendent Colin Trimming, head of the Waleses' protection squad, who reported everything back to his boss. Sometime around the end of the year Diana – possibly from Gilbey, who had been confronted with the tape by the *Sun* – learned that that newspaper had a copy of the recording. The owner, Rupert Murdoch, and Andrew Knight, chairman of News International, proprietors of the *Sun* and the *News of the World*, decided that the material was too controversial to publish and the tape was put into a safe where it would remain for two and a half years. The *News of the World* also had a story alleging Diana's affair with James Hewitt from Hewitt's valet, Lance Corporal Malcolm Leete, which they proposed to publish. Knight also sat on this story; the fact that he didn't believe it showed how skilful – or lucky – Diana had been in covering up the affair.

Diana was still in love with Hewitt after he flew out to serve with his regiment in the Gulf, where war had been going on since the previous August. She was obsessed with war news and wrote Hewitt a series of passionate letters, often as frequently as four times a day, expressing her longing and loneliness, putting her every thought down on paper. She said that she was 'finally trying to understand herself'. She told him that she could not stand the deception in her marriage any longer and that she had given Charles an ultimatum that 'something had to be done' about it. Moreover – an indication of the direction her thoughts were tending towards – she wrote that she felt frantic that 'the truth about Charles and Camilla . . . had not become public knowledge'.¹⁰ Some people, like Max Hastings, did know, but out of loyalty to the monarch and perhaps for fear of finding themselves in court (like Penny Junor, who was sued by Andrew and Camilla

Parker Bowles for misidentifying Camilla) kept their knowledge
to themselves. Diana determined to find a way to get the story
into the public domain, just as she was determined that Hewitt
should remain in the shadows.

But on that front, things were becoming difficult. The *Daily
Mail* now not only had a copy of the Squidgygate tapes, but their
chief royal reporter, Richard Kay, had made friends with the naïve
Hewitt in the Gulf, even to the extent of lending him his satellite
telephone to make calls – which he did, to his mother and to
Diana, their numbers registering on the telephone.[11] The previous
year Diana had made friends with the paper's editor, David English,
who was later to become her chief media mentor. Yet it was Nigel
Dempster who in February 1991 first publicly named Hewitt as a
friend of Diana's. 'Nigel Dempster outed him,' said a fellow
reporter. 'And I believe that Andrew Parker Bowles was the source,
and it was designed, I think, to take the heat off the Parker Bowleses
at that time.' Then, in the following month, Hewitt was exposed
in the *News of the World* by his estranged girlfriend, Emma Stew-
ardson, who revealed that Diana had been sending letters and
expensive presents to the Gulf (where Richard Kay had noted the
quality of the hampers of food which Hewitt enjoyed). No one,
however, went so far as actually to claim they were lovers. For
Diana, however, the hints were enough; as so often in her relationships, she became suspicious that he was using her, that he was
becoming 'too serious', that he was more in love with her position
than he was with her. This was unfair: James Hewitt was genuinely
in love with her and the relationship was almost as dangerous for
him and his career as it was for her. She had given him hope for
the future in her letters, talking of her belief that in July 'her life
would change'. 'Her determination to be free was so strong,'
Hewitt later recalled, 'that I had formed a real hope that some time
in the future we could be together.'[12] In fact the *News of the World*
revelations had sealed his fate. After a couple of meetings on his
return from the Gulf, Diana told him on the telephone that it
would be better if they 'cooled it'. The cut-off came in the usual
manner: when he telephoned the Palace, his call was not put

through. He was sent to Germany: when he returned to England, despite his being conveniently stationed at Knightsbridge Barracks, less than a mile from Kensington Palace, his dream was over. According to Ken Wharfe, with whom Diana discussed her relations with Hewitt, she had explained to him that she had to resolve the many problems in her life and could not do so while conducting an adulterous affair. Typically, when Hewitt accepted his dismissal with good grace, she was slightly irritated, having expected at the very least protestations of undying love.

With Hewitt out of the way, Diana concentrated on her war with Charles. Yet another joint trip, this time to Brazil that spring when, once again, the couple put up a good show in public, inspired optimism in the press. The *Sunday Mirror* described them as presenting 'a united front to the world . . . their closeness sent a shiver of excitement around the massed ranks of media men and women'. Yet only the previous December, Diana had told James Hewitt that there were times when she could not bear to be in the same room as Charles. And on the trip to Brazil, despite attempts to put on a show, Charles's jealousy of Diana manifested itself in dismissive comments, not just in private but in front of the British Ambassador to Brazil and the recently appointed Brazilian Ambassador in London, Paulo Tarso Flecha de Lima and his wife Lucia, soon to become one of Diana's greatest and most trusted friends. Onlookers observed that there was great tension: 'They were on speaking terms, but it was very tense. It was not a normal conversation between husband and wife. He would talk to her, she would answer. But he was already very dismissive of her. On the plane she was reading some papers, remarking to the Ambassadress, "This is my homework about Brazil." Charles chipped in, "Oh, she doesn't know a thing about Brazil." '[13] Public put-downs by the heir to the throne in front of high-ranking officials fuelled Diana's desire to escape from the sham her marriage had become.

According to Hewitt, Diana had planned an 'escape' in July, as her thirtieth birthday and the tenth anniversary of her marriage came up, determined that this period would be a watershed in her life. What kind of watershed it was to be he did not specify, but it seems probable that Diana envisaged a dramatic breakaway (with the inevitable exposure of Camilla), not divorce, but a separate court and acknowledgement of her position as mother of the future King. Again according to Hewitt, the timing she had worked out had been thwarted by the fact that the Yorks' marriage was also on the rocks. Sarah had been on the telephone to Diana wondering what to do. Lesley Player, Ronald Ferguson's mistress (whom at one time he had shared with Steve Wyatt), said that Sarah and Diana had a pact to leave their husbands at the same time. If such a pact existed, Diana was too canny to go ahead with it. Hewitt implied that pressure had been put on her by Buckingham Palace: 'There was no way the Palace was going to let both royal couples announce they were splitting up at the same time,' he wrote. 'Diana had been informed in no uncertain terms that the effect on the Royal Family would be disastrous.'[14]

Nevertheless, Diana forged ahead with her pledge made to Gilbey in the Squidgygate tapes when she had boasted: 'I'm going to go out and conquer the world, I'm going to leave him [Charles] behind . . .' 'Diana was obsessed with Charles,' a close friend said. 'And I think all the wrong steps she took in life were because of him . . . either to hurt him or to show off to him.' 'She was a very, very special person. She had a wonderful side to her – bright, courageous and unique. But she also had a very dark side to her personality, a very destructive side.'[15] This friend saw Diana's collaboration in Andrew Morton's *Diana: Her True Story* as 'the first move in her self-destruction'. Diana herself explained her decision as being a psychological necessity: 'It's because my life being as complicated as it is the only way for me to survive is to let people know what I have been going through.'[16] Her confidante thought there might be an element of vengeance on Charles and Camilla in her motivation. Morton himself was puzzled by her willingness to open her heart to a virtual stranger. 'If it was a way of getting at her husband, it's a remarkably reckless and foolhardy exercise,' he said. 'If it's a way of changing her life then the simplest way would be to speak to the Queen and Prince Charles.'[17] There was, he said, no deliberate decision to do a book with him; it just happened gradually. Diana knew Morton as a prominent member of the royal media pack. He was tall, good-looking, genial and university educated. They had met and chatted together on occasion, and he was also in contact with Dr James Colthurst, an old friend of Diana's who was to act as go-between for Morton and Diana. Morton, through Colthurst, had done Diana some favours, including advising her on the safest way to dispense with her hairdresser, Richard Dalton, without his going to the newspapers to sell his story. Morton advised her to write him an honest letter, buy him a good present and send him on his way. The strategy worked. Morton also kept her happy by writing sympathetic pieces about her in the papers.

'I think she wanted people to know what life was really like for her. I used the phrase "the prisoner in the Palace" and all that kind of thing. She felt constrained by the environment in which she worked. She felt there was no out, she felt disempowered both as a woman and as a human being. She felt trapped, not just in her marriage but by the system. And she felt, essentially, that when somebody comes along and is able to do something for her and make her look good – I mean I was writing pretty pro pieces and there was the Dalton episode, little things like that meant a lot because when you don't have any control over your life, then to have control through another agent – i.e. myself – was tremendously liberating.'[18]

Colthurst arrived at Kensington Palace armed with a tape recorder and a list of prompt questions one morning in May 1991. Neither he nor Morton was prepared for the deluge of words, which Diana delivered – thirty thousand in that one session. 'The first tape was just like – I can't emphasise it strongly enough – just like the desperate confessional, wanting to get everything out, it was ten years of her betrayal and unhappiness, depression and ridicule ... And it just came flowing out in a huge torrent ...' 'Did she really think it through? The answer is No. Because I and Mike [Michael O'Mara, Morton's publisher] and James had to do a lot of thinking it through for her. So, for example, the idea of bringing friends in, keeping her in the background, wasn't her idea, it was our idea.'[19] Added to that was a strain of aristocratic recklessness inherited from her Spencer forebears and, perhaps even more, from her mother, Frances, 'the bolter', which impelled her to go ahead regardless of the consequences. Morton also thought there might be an element of getting her retaliation in first, of putting Charles's adultery with Camilla in the public domain before her affair with James Hewitt was exposed. Diana wanted to expose the sham of her marriage and her role in the Royal Family, to expose the behaviour of Charles and Camilla and her own helplessness in the face of their betrayal.

Another reason for the involvement of Diana's friends was the dawning realization that Diana's version of events was not always strictly the truth. In *Diana: Her True Story*, Diana was recounting the reality of her life as she saw it in 1991–2 (towards the end of her life, Diana would frequently say that what she thought in 1991 was not how she saw things in 1996), a reality dominated by Charles and Camilla, her illness, the predictions of her astrologers and the constriction of the royal circle. Perhaps the most poignant testimony of all was that of Carolyn Bartholomew, who had known Diana since her school days and watched anxiously from the side-lines the deterioration in her health and happiness. 'She's not happy now, but once she was . . .' Carolyn told Morton. Diana's friends felt duty bound to help her by exposing the living lie she was enduring.

But if Diana felt threatened and constricted by 'the system', royal officials, even before the bombshell of the Morton book burst in June 1992, were wary of Diana as an unknown quantity. Buckingham Palace tended to regard the chaotic office of the Prince of Wales at St James's Palace as something of a joke. 'One of the reasons Buckingham Palace runs on smooth lines by and large is that people decades ago learned what the Queen wanted and how to do it and a way to get on with it,' one of Diana's aides said. 'I think from Buckingham Palace, St James's seemed a bit of a madhouse, and the maddest component was this strange, very tall, very blonde, very articulate, very charming, very powerful, very regal person' – Diana.[20] Until 1990 the charming Sir John Riddell had been private secretary and treasurer to the Prince and Princess of Wales. Aristocratic, with the required background of Eton, the Rifle Brigade and the City, Riddell's presence had ensured that relations with Buckingham Palace, where Diana's brother-in-law, Robert Fellowes, had now become principal private secretary, with the Marlborough-educated, Foreign Office-trained Robin Janvrin as his deputy, ran on an even keel. Even he, however, would treat the Princess's representatives, Anne Beckwith Smith and Patrick Jephson, as very much the junior branch of the operation, summing up a meeting with kindly condescension: 'And meantime Her Royal Highness will continue to do very little, but do it very well . . .' 'The Prince had had an organization before Diana came along and it was never really expected that she would make much of an impression on it, and when, rather irritatingly, she became more and more of a figure in her own right, the machinery didn't really exist to accommodate her in anything other than a purely decorative role. And as she became more productive in carrying out royal engagements, this was viewed with amused tolerance,' an aide to the Princess recalled.[21]

Riddell withdrew gladly from the Waleses' fray to the City, replaced briefly by Sir Christopher Airey and then, in what amounted to a palace coup, by Airey's deputy, Commander Richard Aylard, the grammar school-educated former naval officer who had read zoology at Reading University and acted as Diana's equerry from 1985 to 1988. Diana had regarded him as a turncoat when he left her to become assistant private secretary and comptroller to the Waleses' joint office. Later, she began to regard him as an enemy when in 1991 he became private secretary and treasurer to the Prince. In the background, the Prince's party at court regarded Diana as 'a mystery and a threat and somebody to be demeaned, mocked or briefed against, or constrained and restrained in some way. They used to talk very patronizingly about "putting her in a box where she couldn't do too much harm" . . .'[22] While the Queen's principal aides, Robert Fellowes and Robin

Janvrin, 'tried very hard to remain even-handed, to keep the Queen above the fray . . . people in the Prince's camp – and they were outside St James's as much as inside . . . liked to think they could invoke the authority of the Crown against Diana, which I thought was the height of arrogance and double standards, especially since the Crown herself chose to remain pretty much aloof.'[23]

The British Establishment, from courtiers down to aristocrats and their hangers-on in the country, can be a formidable and isolating force; small wonder, therefore, that Diana felt trapped and alone in what she felt to be her fight for survival. Beyond that she could not rely on her family: she had argued too much with her mother and grandmother. Frances, far away in the west of Scotland, had made her own life there where she ran a newsagent's and gift shop and was popular with the villagers as a crusader for local good causes. In the evenings, however, she could be incoherent. 'I can't speak to my mother after 5.30,' Diana complained, as she sought advice and comfort from mother figures Lady Annabel Goldsmith and Ambassadress Flecha de Lima. Frances Shand Kydd was still a remarkably attractive woman and loved by her grandchildren, who nicknamed her 'Supergran', but, as far as Diana was concerned, the relationship was volatile rather than supportive. 'I would say that, like the rest of her [Diana's] family, when the chips were really down, I'm afraid they weren't able, or perhaps willing, to give Diana the support she needed. She and her mother fought too much, there was far too much water under the bridge going way back . . .'[24] According to Andrew Morton, Diana felt 'constantly disappointed by her father'. 'She would say, "He arrives at six'o'clock", pointing to the entry in the visitors' book, "departs at 6.08." She adored him, loved him desperately . . . I remember he once rang from Japan saying, "I'm going to buy you a really lavish present." And she said to him, "I don't want that, I just want for you to be here with me." '[25] He was by now infirm and totally dependent on the devotion of Raine; moreover in September 1991 another Spencer family row broke out over the extent of Johnnie and Raine's sales of Althorp's contents. Nor was there support from her brother and sisters.

Charles, whom she adored, was involved in his own life and had problems in his marriage: Jane, mindful of her husband's career at Buckingham Palace, was in a very difficult position, while Sarah, in the words of a mutual friend, 'found it better to keep a safe distance between herself and Diana'.

So Diana was obliged to rely on the support of her friends and of her allies in the media. It was there that the war against Charles was publicly fought out. Sadly, the theme emphasized by Diana and the press was of Charles's failings as a father compared with her maternal devotion. A trip with the children to Thorpe Park brought headlines critical of Charles from her favourite *Daily Mail.* Under the headline 'CHARLES THE ABSENT ROYAL FATHER' the newspaper asked, 'Why do we not see from him the demonstrations of warmth, affection or closeness Diana frequently displays towards her sons in public?' Later Diana took William and Harry on a skiing holiday to Lech in Austria. Once again, Charles did not accompany them; once again his absence was noted by the press. In June media outrage stormed round Charles when William was hit on the head by a golf ball at his private preparatory boarding school, Ludgrove, sustaining a depressed fracture of his forehead. Both Charles and Diana accompanied William from Ludgrove to the Great Ormond Street Hospital for Sick Children in London for surgery. It was in no way to be a risky operation: Charles therefore decided to carry out a long-standing engagement to entertain British and European officials to a performance of *Tosca* and to travel to Yorkshire overnight to fulfil another official engagement. Diana spent the night in a bedside vigil at the hospital. Over the following days the press was in full cry, contrasting Charles's lack of caring with Diana's maternal devotion. 'WHAT KIND OF DAD ARE YOU?' the *Sun* shouted, while the *Daily Express* branded the Prince 'A PHANTOM FATHER', and another newspaper featured 'THE EXHAUSTED FACE OF A LOVING MOTHER'. Charles very much resented the mileage Diana extracted from the incident, accusing her of exaggerating the seriousness of William's injury for her own ends. Yet Diana did indeed feel bitter at the lack of support from Charles, expressing her feelings privately to friends.

The truth was that neither could bear the presence of the other and it must be asked whether it was not really better for the children for their parents to be apart. They were naturally aware of the fierce rows that took place: William used to listen at the door, taking in every word. Later, in her *Panorama* interview, Diana recalled her elder son pushing Kleenex tissues under the bathroom door as she sat sobbing on the other side. On one occasion Harry attacked his father, beating on his legs with his fists and shouting, 'I hate you, I hate you, you make Mummy cry . . .'

Diana continued her campaign in the press. The large-circulation popular press headed by the *Daily Mail*, the middle/upper-class tabloid, was on her side, thanks principally to its editor, David English, and royal reporter Richard Kay, deputed by English to be their contact with the Princess. Other well-known journalists were sympathetic: Anthony Holden, distinguished journalist and biographer; Andrew Morton, then a freelance who, while working with Diana on her life story, published favourable articles in the influential *Sunday Times*. In the tabloid press, James Whitaker and Harry Arnold tended to take the Princess's side, while Nigel Dempster of the *Mail* and Ross Benson of the *Express*, both of whom had contacts within Charles's circle, often stood out for the Prince.

Diana's thirtieth birthday on 1 July 1991 and her tenth wedding anniversary on the 29th, the two occasions which she had originally intended to use to make some sort of statement about her marriage, represented the next round. Now that she was engaged on the Morton book, Diana had shelved any plans for dramatic statements, but she did not intend to let the occasion pass without a demonstration. On 28 June a story, probably inspired by David English, was headlined in the *Mail* to the effect that Diana planned to spend her birthday apart from her husband.[26] She would be in London, lunching at the Savoy and hosting a party for her close friends, while Charles remained at Highgrove. 'That was PR straight from Diana,' Nigel Dempster told Sally Bedell Smith. Two days later he received a telephone call from one of Charles's friends, 'a well-bred lady's voice' putting the case for Charles: 'Charles has offered her anything for her birthday – lunch, dinner, a ball, but she has refused because she wants to be a martyr.' Dempster produced a front-page story for the *Mail*: under the headline 'CHARLES AND DIANA: CAUSE FOR CONCERN' he revealed that Diana had thwarted Charles's plans for her birthday and that there was 'a growing coolness in the marriage'.[27] After this furore, the couple spent their tenth wedding anniversary dining quietly at Highgrove; an article in the *Sunday Times* apparently celebrating this rapprochement, written by Morton, was headed 'Truce'. Far from representing any real reconciliation, however, the article, Morton admitted, was written specifically to prevent any momentum building up in the press over the unhappy marriage, to maintain his own reputation for inside knowledge of the royal scene but not so much as to allow his colleagues to 'cotton on so much that they would then start to follow the trail'. 'I wrote it quite deliberately to put them off the scent,' he said; 'the pieces I was writing were designed for her. You've got to bear in mind that for her, that the whole object for me was to get that book out unscathed . . . The game plan was that kind of balancing act, to show sophisticated observers . . . that I knew what I was talking about but at the same time not to let them get in on it.'[28] Morton, anxious for verification of the main story, indicated to Diana that he needed evidence of the Charles/Camilla relationship: in August she found notes from Camilla to Charles (how she did so has not been disclosed), which she found deeply upsetting, and showed them to Morton.

Meanwhile, according to Sarah Ferguson's account, 1991 was the year that she and Diana first put words to the unspeakable idea that they had been discussing for some time: that one or both of them might leave the Royal Family. They burned the phone wires into the night trading secrets and jokes that no one else would understand. Sarah even sent Diana a tape of the film *The Great Escape*. Sarah had been marked down as out of control for some time by the Queen's courtiers and her officials, dubbed by Sarah and Diana 'the grey men', principally 'Mr Z' (by whom she almost certainly meant Robert Fellowes, who also happened to be a cousin). The Ramzi Sultan affair had alerted them to Sarah's relationship with Steve Wyatt. These 'new American friends', she was told, 'were not the right sort of people' she should be mixing with. Sarah was in debt, her extravagance funded by unlimited credit at 'the Queen's bank', Coutts & Co. The miles she travelled on freebie holidays far exceeded those expended on official duties. In 1990 she had dropped to last in the royal engagements list, with ten fewer than the ninety-year-old Queen Mother. Sarah Ferguson was likeable, jolly and amusing but, in the famous words of one of the Queen's senior courtiers, she 'was never cut out to be a royal princess'.[29] 'Diana wasn't as bad,' said a royal official. 'But [for] Fergie who already had a life, it's like catching a wild animal and caging them up – they want to get out.'[30]

At Balmoral late that summer both girls behaved like rebellious teenagers. One night after dinner, Sarah and Diana slipped out of the back door, commandeered a quad bike and drove it at speed down the golf course, damaging the greens. And to compound their bad behaviour they were foolish enough to stop at the lodge occupied by Robert Fellowes and his family and ring the bell, although it was almost midnight. They then 'liberated' the Queen Mother's stately Daimler limousine and, with Diana at the wheel wearing the chauffeur's cap and Sarah in the back imitating the Queen Mother's royal wave, did wheel spins on the gravel drive surrounding the castle. Diana, Princess of Wales, was thirty years old, Sarah, Duchess of York, thirty-two – two spoiled princesses who had absorbed the adulation and cosseting to their every whim which membership of the Royal Family involved, but failed to understand the true implications of their position. 'The thing that was hard on Diana – and Sarah Ferguson,' one of the Queen Mother's ladies said, 'was that they were both totally uneducated. They had no idea of what the constitutional monarchy was, either of them. They thought it was a mixture of Hollywood and William Hickey, they really did, they thought it was endless freebies and romantic princes riding about and everybody cheering. I don't think they had a clue.'[31]

Typical of the 'me' generation, they were neither prepared to compromise on what they saw as personal fulfilment nor to consider fully the implications of what they were about to do. Between them they would be responsible for the greatest crisis of the British monarchy since Edward VIII had abdicated to marry 'the woman I love'.

13. The Volcano Erupts

'. . . *you got this flavour of intense unhappiness, real movement, almost as if the people at the Palace could see this volcano about to explode and just being petrified what to do about it. And in fact Diana wrote to someone before the book came out, "I can feel this volcano is going to explode but I can cope . . ."* ' (Andrew Morton[1])

While the royal household struggled to keep the lid on the swirling currents surrounding the Wales and York marriages, no one dared warn the Queen of what might happen. The year 1992 would mark the fortieth anniversary of her accession to the throne: the Queen in her Christmas broadcast message to her people, unaware that her family was crumbling around her, chose to emphasize the family theme as she affirmed her determination to serve as their monarch in the years to come: 'With your prayers and your help, and the love and support of my family, I shall try and help you in the years to come . . .'

The first shock to the family came in the first month of the year. On 15 January the *Mail* published the photographs of Steve Wyatt and Sarah on holiday with the children which a window cleaner and odd-job man had found on top of the wardrobe in Wyatt's vacant flat. This time the naïve, long-suffering Prince Andrew, in his father-in-law's words, 'hit the roof'. 'They were only holiday snaps,' Ronald Ferguson told Lesley Player, 'but they show that Texan fellow in a basket chair with his arm around her [Sarah] – and the one that really annoyed Andrew was little Beatrice with no clothes on being cuddled by him . . .'[2] Six days after the publication, Andrew and Sarah agreed to separate and travelled down to Sandringham to tell the Queen of their decision. According to Sarah, the Queen asked them to reconsider and no announcement was made for the time being. According to Sarah's autobiography she was determined to divorce Andrew in order to escape 'the Firm' in which 'grey man Z' (Robert Fellowes) had been joined by a new press secretary, 'grey man X' (Charles Anson). Without mentioning the developments in her private life which had led her to the decision, she blamed the grey men and their bully-boy tactics. They were determined to oust her and to protect Diana, she said. She did not mention Wyatt, who had left for the United States that month, apparently vowing eternal love, nor did she mention his replacement, another Texan, John Bryan.

Sarah was apparently expecting Diana to follow suit in bolting from the family but it soon became evident that she had no intention of doing so – yet. Perhaps in order to distance herself from the rumours surrounding Sarah, she appears to have been behind the lead in the *Daily Mail* on 18 March when a front-page 'exclusive' by Richard Kay and Andrew Morton declared that 'the Palace is preparing to announce the separation of the Duke and Duchess of York'. The story precipitated the Palace into action: the following day they did indeed issue a statement that lawyers acting for the Duchess of York had initiated discussions about a formal separation, accompanied by the pious hope that the media would spare the Duke and Duchess and their children 'any intrusion'. Their hope that the story could be kept quiet until after the General Election campaign then in progress had vanished. Sarah immediately suspected Diana since both Richard Kay and Andrew Morton were close to her and therefore the story must have been prompted by her, possibly to deflect any speculation about her own situation in the run-up to the publication in June of Andrew Morton's book. A representative of a public relations firm was summoned to Sunninghill Park. He arrived to find only Andrew there: Sarah was upstairs with John Bryan who had now taken over her affairs. They later appeared downstairs together in a state of high excitement. Sarah attacked the man for the bad publicity she had had to endure and indicated that John Bryan would be a more effective adviser. Tempers flared and the Yorks, with another guest, left the room (although it later transpired that they had been listening at the door). There was a scene during which champagne flutes were smashed. Witnesses commented that Andrew seemed to be frightened of Sarah and now hated Diana, his former friend, on his brother's account.

Diana was intent on her own survival and had no intention of becoming embroiled in her sister-in-law's self-induced troubles. She distanced herself from Sarah and carried on her own public relations campaign. In February she travelled with Charles on a visit to India which was to feature the famous 'Princess alone' photograph of a pensive Diana seated in front of the Taj Mahal, romantic monument to the enduring love of the Mogul Emperor Shah Jehan for his dead wife, Mumtaz Mahal. The impact of the picture showed Diana's phenomenal public relations skills. In itself, the location of the shot was absolutely normal; it was taken from the only spot to which the authorities would allow media access. Charles himself had sat on the same bench on his visit twelve years before, when he had given a hostage to fortune by saying, 'One day I would like to bring my wife here.' At the time, Charles himself was at a meeting for business leaders in Bangalore – the separation of itineraries was normal practice on intercontinental visits such as this. 'The trouble with these visits,' said Dickie Arbiter, the couple's press secretary who accompanied them, '[is that] they only last for four days, five at the most, and everybody wants a piece of the action. They are only two people and they can only do so much so they have to split and do what was required of them.'[3] The media, aware of Charles's previous pledge, put their own interpretation on the picture, following the precise line Diana intended. Famously, she followed it up with the cruel 'kiss that never was' at a polo match when, as Charles bent towards her to kiss her for a much awaited photo opportunity, she swiftly averted her head at the last moment, so that he was pictured pecking ineptly at her neck. 'Oh, Come On You Can Do Better Than That, Charles!' the *Mirror* admonished.

Such well-publicized images of a marriage in trouble caused consternation at the Palace, where the top officials had already picked up rumours of the Morton book and were desperate to shore up the marriage of the heir to the throne. It was only to get worse. On 29 March, Johnnie Spencer died suddenly of a heart attack in the Humana Hospital Wellington in north London where he had been recovering from mild pneumonia. His death was quite unexpected: Diana, who had visited him with William on 25 March, had left the following day for a family skiing holiday with Charles in Lech. None of the family was with Johnnie when he died, not even Raine who had felt able to go down to Althorp to supervise funding events. Diana, distraught in Lech, prepared to fly home without Charles. On this occasion of her private grief she could not bear the thought of yet another 'happy families' act for the media. Charles, his private secretary Richard Aylard and Dickie Arbiter tried to persuade her to go with her husband for the sake of the public image of the Prince and of their marriage. It took a telephone call from the Queen to persuade her to make a joint journey back to England. Even then the couple's private estrangement was such that, on arrival at Kensington Palace, Charles departed immediately for Highgrove, leaving Diana alone to grieve for her adored father. On 1 April she drove down to Althorp for the funeral at the family church of St Mary the Virgin, Great Brington. Charles flew over by helicopter to join her in the car for the church, maintaining the fiction of a supportive husband. Immediately after lunch, he flew back to London. Following her father's coffin out of the church with Raine, Diana's instinctive sympathy caused her to take the first step towards ending the feud with her stepmother. 'She did a very moving thing at Johnnie's funeral, Diana,' a relation who attended said. 'Raine was on that side and Diana was on this side, and when they left their seats she went over to Raine and held her hand and walked down the church with her. I was very impressed with that because I thought it showed a desire to reconcile everything, and in front of the whole congregation doing that . . . so that it was evident to every-body what she had done. And I thought that was very tender . . . bringing Raine in and not isolating her.'[4] Frances Shand Kydd did not attend, although she was present – making herself as inconspicuous as possible – at the London memorial service on 19 May.

By then Diana was standing on the edge of the abyss – the pre-publication serialization of the Morton book which would precipitate her isolation from the Royal Family. For some time she had hugged the secret triumphantly as she looked forward to putting her case to her public, exposing Charles and Camilla and revealing the sham of her 'fairy-tale' marriage. But, with less than a month to go, she began to be apprehensive of the consequences of what she had done. 'I was with them going to Expo '92 in Seville,' said one of her close aides. 'She said, "You don't know what I've done." She was scared, really scared.[5] I think she was just beginning to realize . . .' To David Puttnam, former film producer and future Labour peer, she confided, 'I've done something which I may really live to regret . . .' Sitting next to Puttnam at a dinner meeting of powerful media executives called the Thirty Club at Claridge's in March, she confessed that she was terrified of the consequences. Puttnam was then governor of the National AIDS Trust of which she became President. 'Before, she was talking about wanting to do something unusual, big,' Puttnam recalled, 'so I arranged for her to address all the media owners, Rupert Murdoch, Conrad Black . . . at the Thirty Club . . . she was absolutely terrified, so I coached her through it, we worked out what she would do, we even set it up so that there were some interviews by very, very young interviewers. And she was brilliant, and she knew she was brilliant. The speech about the incidence of AIDS in women was a really "grown up" thing to do.' It may be that seeing the media power ranked in front of her brought home to her for the first time what she was getting herself into. At dinner, to Puttnam's surprise, she 'suddenly started confiding in me how unhappy things were in her marriage. She said "Neither of us has been perfect, but I've done a really stupid thing. I have allowed a book to be written. I felt it was a good idea, a way of clearing the air, but now I think it was a very stupid thing that will cause all kinds of terrible trouble", adding, "I would like to reel the movie back. It is the daftest thing I have ever done.'⁶ On the day the serialization of the Morton book came out, she rang the Waleses' press secretary Dickie Arbiter in a panic: 'What do I do?' 'You don't do anything,' Arbiter replied. 'Why didn't you tell me when I first asked you four months ago what help you had given the Morton book? You swore you hadn't given any.' And on that day, Diana still repeated, 'I haven't given any help.'⁷

By now thoroughly apprehensive, Diana was given an opportunity to demonstrate both her courage in the face of private anxiety and her value as an ambassador of the Royal Family and the British nation with an official visit to Egypt on 10 May. Ironically, as her private secretary Patrick Jephson noted, while the Princess flew out on her official tour in an aircraft paid for by the British taxpayer, the plane was diverted to land the Prince (on his eighth holiday of the year) and a party of friends in Turkey. In yet another example of the Prince's poor PR, when Diana flew back to London the same plane was forced to double back to Turkey again since the Prince's plans had not dovetailed with the Princess's official schedule. Despite a sobbing fit on the plane, possibly induced by apprehension over the Morton book but also perhaps because of the presence of the Prince and his friends off on their holiday, underlining the separateness of their ways, she heroically pulled herself together before the arrival at Cairo. 'No matter how close she came to the edge of bottling out,' Jephson wrote, 'she always produced the last-minute effort of will that could turn imminent disaster into serene triumph.' Immaculately groomed, she played her part in the arrival ceremony with 'consummate professionalism, poise and devotion to duty'. 'I wondered,' Jephson added, 'if her opponents really understood the bloody-minded determination of the woman they were seeking to banish into the backwaters of royal life.'⁸ Not only was Diana a huge success with her hosts, President Hosni Mubarak and his wife, but she won the admiration of the travelling press pack, alert for any sign of weakness. A report in the *Sunday Times* congratulated Diana on her courage. 'It is a mark of her confidence that even after the recent publicity about her marriage she is prepared to walk into a room of tabloid hacks. The transformation in Diana is quite incredible. Diana will never be a great intellectual but she is a very shrewd sharp woman with amazing strength of character.'[9]

Yet even she had underestimated the bombshell effect of the public revelations of the reality of a marriage – which the majority had firmly believed, or wished to believe, was still the fairy tale of that July day in 1981 – when they were published in the *Sunday Times* beginning on 7 June 1992. The book told of Diana's psychological problems, the bulimia, self-mutilation and depression – including the Sandringham suicide attempt that never was. Charles's infidelity with Camilla and his unkindness to Diana were similarly revealed. The nation as a whole was shocked and angry. There was disillusionment with the Royal Family, and hence the monarchy, which had been building over the antics of Sarah and Diana; with *It's a Royal Knockout*; with the Yorks selling pictures of themselves with their babies to *Hello!*; with Princess Anne's divorce from Mark Phillips in 1992, accompanied by the rumours of her affair with one of her policemen. Middle England, brought up to regard the Royal Family as role models, 'ourselves behaving better', was shaken to the core. The heir to the throne came out worst of all: a cynical adulterer who mistreated his virgin bride and selfishly ignored his children. This last was a recent theme of Diana's which she had been putting across in the press: James Gilbey quoted her as saying. 'She thinks he is a bad father, a selfish father; the children have to tie in with whatever he's doing.'

The representation of Diana as a victim struggling to free herself from the crushing weight of an ultra-traditional family and an adulterous, uncaring husband won her widespread sympathy from the public at large, as she had intended. The trouble about the book from the Royal Family's point of view was that its essential presentation of Diana as a virgin sacrifice offered up on the altar of the dynasty was near enough to the truth to be believable. At first, however, it was dismissed as a journalistic fabrication. Diana's repeated denials of collaboration to her brother-in-law, Robert Fellowes, who assured the chairman of the Press Complaints Commission, Lord McGregor, that she had not been involved, led to his statement condemning the press for 'dabbling their fingers in the stuff of other people's souls'. Her friends who had collaborated in the Morton book were accused of betraying Diana by revealing her secrets. A photo opportunity was arranged at the request of Carolyn's husband, William Bartholomew, who was determined that Diana should be seen publicly supporting his wife.[10] A cousin of the Queen remembered being told by a photographer that Diana herself had telephoned him telling him to be at the Bartholomews' Fulham house at a precise time.[11] Diana's evident approval of what Carolyn had done and the use of photographs from the Spencer family album gave Morton's revelations authenticity. One of the contributors, Angela Serota, a friend of Andrew Knight, executive director of News International, told Knight that Diana had indeed authorized her friends to cooperate with Morton.[12] When the Bartholomew photographs appeared, McGregor, who had received Robert Fellowes' assurances, rang him in Paris, where he was with the Queen, to berate him for deceiving him. Fellowes, who had asked Diana several times if she had been involved and received direct denials from her, had believed her. He was fond of his sister-in-law, whom he had known since childhood, and, being an upright man of Christian principles, had thought it inconceivable that she could have lied to him. He apologized to Lord McGregor and the Press Complaints Commission for misleading them and offered his resignation to the Queen who refused it. The affair greatly damaged Diana's future relations with her sister and brother-in-law, whom she had lied to and betrayed, making him look ridiculous to his own official circle. She continued to deny that she herself had been responsible for the book or that she had spoken to the author. No one believed her on the first count, although her undoubted responsibility for the second was not to be publicly revealed until Morton published extracts from the tapes after her death.

While Diana had succeeded in her aim of revealing the sham of her marriage and gaining the sympathy of the wider public, the British Establishment and the upper echelons of British society were outraged at what they saw as a betrayal of the Queen and the monarchy on her part. It was the first self-destructive step towards the final parting of the ways. Diana never wanted a divorce; in her heart she still loved Charles to the point of obsession and saw him as her husband. She still hoped that she could have it all: remaining in the Royal Family, keeping her children and her title as Princess of Wales, while keeping a separate court. 'Diana would never have got out,' Dickie Arbiter affirmed. But, although at a private meeting with Charles the day after the serialization began they agreed to separate on the grounds of incompatibility, Diana continued to feel a passionate resentment over her treatment, refusing to play an accommodating Queen Alexandra to Charles and Camilla's Edward VII and Mrs Keppel. Like Sarah Ferguson, she was a child of a modern generation which was not prepared to accept the upper-class conventional marriage in which fidelity and romance did not play a part. But, unlike Sarah Ferguson, who for selfish reasons turned her back on a husband who loved and supported her through all her infidelities and antics, Diana had every reason to complain as the loving, inexperienced bride who had been used and abused by an uncaring, selfish husband incapable of giving her the love she craved, nor even the normal married life she had dreamed of. Moreover, as she saw it – and who is to say she was wrong? – he was backed up by a powerful social set and ultimately by the Palace, who had tried to silence and sideline her.

Jonathan Dimbleby wrote of the aftermath of the serialization:

After the publication of the first instalment of the Morton book, a handful of the Prince's closest friends, including the Romseys and van Cutsems, felt compelled to tell both the Queen and Prince Philip how stoical they thought the Prince had been through the long trauma of the marriage. Perhaps nudged by this intervention but certainly shocked by the media blitzkrieg surrounding the publication of the book, both the Queen and the Duke, who had been at pains not to take sides, rallied to the Prince; in particular, the Duke wrote a long and sympathetic letter to him in which he praised what he saw as his son's saint-like fortitude. It was in this atmosphere that the Queen and Prince discussed for the first time whether he should seek a separation from the Princess.[13]

The Prince went on to consult Lord Goodman, lawyer and adviser to the powerful, as to his position, but took no further steps.

As Charles's authorized biographer, Dimbleby is well informed and reliable on the Prince's side of the story, although no official biographer can be entirely impartial. What he did not say, however, is that despite their initial shock at the effect of the book in battering down the wall of confidentiality traditionally surrounding the family, and at Diana's deviousness in first encouraging it and then concealing its progress, the Queen and Prince Philip were not at heart totally unsympathetic to Diana. The Prince's first reaction was anger at his daughter-in-law for bringing the situation and its accompanying scandal into the open. With the Morton book, she had 'destroyed everything', he wrote to her. Yet the Queen and Prince Philip disapproved of Charles's adultery with Camilla which, far more than any unreasonable behaviour of Diana's, had brought scandal on the monarchy. Indeed, at Easter the following year, a courtier was amazed when Charles, who was sitting beside her, exploded in fury at his father: 'You should have seen the letter he wrote me . . . !'[14] 'What Charles has done is very wrong,' Prince Philip wrote in a compassionate letter to his daughter-in-law. Both the Queen and Prince Philip were – and are – strong in their religious feelings and convictions; divorce was abhorrent to them and they hoped above all that it need not come to that, both for the sake of the young princes and the monarchy – 'the image of a family on the throne', as Walter Bagehot had put it. It was the Prince's party at the Palace and in society who undermined Diana by implying or saying publicly, as one certainly did, that Diana was mad – 'that bad Fermoy blood'. The general Palace view – but not in the Queen's office – was detestation of Diana for her revelation of family secrets and sympathy for 'the poor Prince'. The fact that the basis of her story was the truth counted for nothing in the face of her breach of the rules.

Yet, despite everything, the royal show rumbled on: the traditional celebration of the Queen's official birthday, Trooping the Colour, went ahead with Diana as part of the family party standing on Buckingham Palace balcony for the RAF fly-past as if nothing had happened. Fergie, however, was nowhere to be seen. As the second instalment of the Morton serialization hit the news-stands on 14 June, the family were at Windsor for the racing at Ascot. The following day the Queen and Prince Philip had a meeting with Charles and Diana, during which the subject of divorce was mentioned but rejected. The Queen was led to believe that Diana would stand by Charles and suggested a six-month cooling-off period. Once again Diana was asked if she had collaborated on the book and once again she denied it, in tears. Prince Philip, by her later account, was 'angry, raging and unpleasant'[15] and later cold-shouldered her in the royal box.[16] On the opening day, as the Queen and the rest of her family drove in open carriages down the course, the disgraced Sarah took her two daughters to wave at their grandmother from the rails. The Queen waved back but inwardly she no doubt despaired at yet another manifestation of what the press now liked to call her 'dysfunctional' family. Guests at lunch at the Castle noted that the Queen seemed to be 'in a pretty bad temper' and when she did talk to her guests she was less than her usual gracious self. In the royal box after lunch, again, no one dared speak to her.

At the end of June Diana gave yet another demonstration of the crowd-pleasing qualities which made her such a valuable royal asset. On a visit to Belfast (security had been breached by the leaking of her visit the night before), she paid a spectacularly successful visit to the Republican heartland, the Falls Road, the dominion of the IRA. An estimated twenty thousand people came to 'shout for Diana'. The Morton revelations had evidently made their impact and there was no doubting where the popular sympathies lay. As the *Daily Mirror* front page put it under a banner headline 'WE WANT DI!', frontline Belfast had 'a message for the Royals'. Even the normally anti-monarchist Dublin press reported sympathetically on the Princess. It was a timely reminder of her popular appeal, and her enemies responded accordingly. On the same day as the papers published ecstatic reports of her success in Northern Ireland, others carried stories that could only have been planted by her enemies, clearly suggesting that the Princess suffered from mental instability.[17]

At the end of July both Charles and Diana attended a dinner to celebrate the Queen's fortieth anniversary on the throne and in August, after a brief, unsatisfactory 'family holiday' on millionaire John Latsis's yacht, they flew up to Balmoral for the annual family holiday. They were all there when, on 20 August, the *Daily Mirror* published the notorious 'toe-sucking' pictures featuring Sarah and her 'financial adviser' John Bryan on holiday in the South of France with the two little princesses. Nothing was said when Andrew, forewarned by Sarah, went down to face the younger members of the family at the breakfast table littered with newspapers blaring headlines and explicit photographs. Sarah herself went to face a furious Queen at 9.30. One can only imagine the conversation. While the scandal raged in the press, at Balmoral it was as if nothing had happened. Sarah remained for a further three days, sitting in her usual place beside Andrew. A young member of the family said to a relation, 'You won't believe it – nobody said a word. There was Fergie sitting next to Andrew and the topless pictures all over the papers . . .'[18]

Four days after the publication of the 'toe-sucking' pictures of Sarah and John Bryan, it was Diana's turn for embarrassment. The *Sun* published the Squidgygate tapes of the conversations between Diana and James Gilbey on New Year's Eve 1989 under the heading 'MY LIFE IS TORTURE', which not only underlined the deep rift between herself and Charles but her difficulties with the Royal Family in general and, more damagingly, her close relationship with Gilbey. The terms in which she had spoken of the family's ingratitude and lack of appreciation of her dutiful public efforts – 'after all I've done for this f . . . family' – were difficult for the Palace to come to terms with. The *Sun* then alleged that Diana and Hewitt had had a 'physical relationship' with no evidence beyond analysis of their 'body language' in photographs of them together. Diana suspected a conspiracy to destroy her but there was none beyond the destructive effect of the relentless

tabloid circulation war. In these circumstances and after the publication of the Morton book which, however much she may have
regretted it, still represented her 'manifesto', her protest against the
sham of her marriage, it was hardly surprising that she dug in her
heels over the projected joint tour of South Korea.

'As the Prince's staff contemplated the nightmarish task of
explaining to the Korean authorities that the Princess would not
after all be accompanying her husband on the first royal visit to
their country,' Dimbleby's official account ran,

Peter Westmacott, the deputy private secretary to the royal couple, was
obliged to do the Korean 'recce' as if he were organising a joint visit –
which, from his conversation with the Princess, he was convinced would
not in fact take place. At Balmoral, the Prince tried to persuade the
Princess to change her mind. Even the Queen intervened to advise her
daughter-in-law that she ought to go. Finally the Prince told her bluntly
that she would have to come up with an explanation of her own for
staying behind. At this, the Princess finally relented, saying meekly that
as the Queen had asked her to go she would after all accompany him.[19]

The resulting tour, as Diana knew it would be, was a public
relations disaster. The glum faces of the couple only served to
indicate the depths to which the marriage had sunk. There could
no longer be any pretence that the situation was salvageable. On
the aeroplane returning from Korea, the Prince wrote one of his
gloomy, self-pitying letters, recounting his despair that Diana could
not be 'a friend' to him and how he had been battling the tempta-
tion to cancel his engagements: 'I feel so unsuited to the ghastly
business of human intrigue and general nastiness . . . I don't know
what will happen from *now* on but I *dread* it.'[20]

In contrast, Diana's subsequent solo visit to Paris on
13 November represented in Jephson's eyes her 'apogee'. Greeted
with the welcoming message 'COURAGE PRINCESSE!', Diana went
through the perfectly orchestrated schedule at the peak of her
beauty and professionalism, charming President Mitterrand, the
French public and the press alike. For Jephson that moment rep-

resented Diana at her best. Strengthened by her stand over the Morton book, she had not yet encountered the pitfalls which awaited her bid for independence. 'To my eyes,' Morton wrote, 'knowing what she had already endured and what lay ahead in the immediate future, there was something heroic in her.'

For Diana the endgame of the first phase was near. The final confrontation of the year came in a quarrel over one of Charles's annual November shooting weekends at Sandringham, planned for the 20th and timed to coincide with an exeat from Ludgrove so that William and Harry could join them. In a last act of defiance, Diana decided not to go and, moreover, to inform Charles that she would be taking the children to see their grandmother, the Queen, at Windsor, or, if she could not stay there, to Highgrove. The Prince metaphorically stamped his foot and threatened her with his authority – he could not be defied in the eyes of his friends. Diana held her ground. His intemperate attitude gave her the excuse she needed to write a defiant letter which, paraphrased, said, more or less: 'Given the way things are between us I'm not sure I want to subject myself to the company of your friends and I certainly don't want to subject the boys to the company of your friends given that we both know who might be there . . .'[21]

According to Dimbleby, it had 'become the custom for the royal couple to invite some sixteen friends to stay for three days of relaxation, shooting, and walking'.[22] In practice, the 'friends' were all Charles's, not Diana's, and by now they had almost no friends in common. Charles's friends, Diana well knew, would include the inner circle who provided safe houses for his rendezvous with Camilla. As Diana complained to Jephson, 'They're all *his* friends. I'm going to be completely outnumbered.'[23] And as a friend said, 'She'd been put through this Sandringham ordeal over and over again . . . it was a real little love-in for the Prince's buddies and his whole household was mobilized to make it an extraordinary expression of his regal position. It was a [Michael] Fawcett production in overdrive, playing King in the Queen's house . . .'[24] Diana's position, while absolutely understandable as regards her own presence in the house, was less tenable when it came to preventing the boys from seeing their father. Unfortunately, they were her principal weapon and in her rage and distress she was not above using them as pawns in the war with her husband.

Charles's patience finally snapped. He would not be defied like this in front of his friends, or, as Dimbleby judiciously put it: 'Unable to see any future in a relationship conducted on these terms, he decided he had no choice but to ask his wife for a legal separation.'[25] On 25 November he and Diana met privately at Kensington Palace and agreed to put the matter in the hands of their lawyers. Discussions continued for some weeks over the matters to be agreed, principally arrangements over the children, secondly a financial settlement for her upkeep, and lastly and most controversially, Diana's future role as a working member of the Royal Family, described, according to Jephson who took part in the negotiations as 'a semi-detached member of the Royal Family'.

'It was at about this time,' Jephson commented with distaste, 'that the phrase "loose cannon" became popular.'[26] The Queen herself, he said, was taking great trouble to remain neutral, but the Prince's advisers (he did not name them but hinted that they were not his legal ones) seemed determined to thwart Diana's ambitions to become an independent royal operator, attempting to restrict her use of the Queen's Flight and the royal train, and downgrading the protocol accorded to her when on official visits. In the end, since the Queen declined to come down on the Prince's side, Diana got almost everything she wanted in the final negotiations except for the financial settlement which was not agreed until the divorce was finalized in 1996. The only stipulation made by the Queen was that Diana should not represent her abroad. Significantly, in an attempt to promote fairness and bipartisanship between the households and staff of all the Palaces, the Lord Chamberlain circulated a letter impressing on everybody the necessity of understanding for both sides. Whether it actually made any difference to the attitudes in the opposing camps is doubtful but it was useful in emphasizing the neutrality of the Crown (that is, the Queen) in the disputes between the Waleses.

On 9 December in the House of Commons, the Prime Minister, John Major, read out the prepared statement issued by Buckingham Palace:

It is announced from Buckingham Palace that, with regret, the Prince and Princess of Wales have decided to separate. Their Royal Highnesses have no plans to divorce and their constitutional positions are unaffected. This decision has been reached amicably and they will both continue to participate fully in the upbringing of their children.

Their Royal Highnesses will continue to carry out full and separate programmes of public engagements and will, from time to time, attend family occasions and national events together.

While the first statement was received by Members of Parliament in respectful silence, the Prime Minister's following words to the effect that 'there was no reason why the Princess of Wales should not be crowned Queen Consort in due course . . .' produced a collective gasp. The idea that the Princess of Wales, living apart from her husband and at daggers drawn with him, could still be crowned Queen Consort struck most people as absurd. The idea that the Prince of Wales's succession was assured as Head of the Church of England, even if constitutionally correct, also required some swallowing. The Archbishop of Canterbury, when officially consulted before the statement, said that for the separation to be widely accepted two important provisos should be met: 'both parents would have to be seen to maintain close bonds with their children; and extra-marital love affairs that might be brought to public attention would need to be avoided'.[27] It would soon become obvious that the Archbishop's second proviso was very far from being met.

Symbolically, on Friday 20 November, the start of the fateful Sandringham weekend, Windsor Castle caught fire. The images of flames shooting from the great castle on the hill, home of the British monarchy for almost a thousand years, seized the

Lech, Austria, 30 March 1992: Diana and Charles leave their skiing holiday after news of Earl Spencer's death. Diana could not bear the thought of yet another 'happy families' act for the media and it took a telephone call from the Queen to persuade her to make a joint journey back to England.

Public sympathy causes Diana to break down on a visit to Ashworth Hospice, Liverpool, in 1992, just as Andrew Morton's book, *Diana: Her True Story*, is serialized.

Oliver Hoare, 1994, pictured as the news breaks that Diana has been making anonymous telephone calls to his house.

Diana and her sisters, Sarah (left) and Jane (right), after a night out.

South Korea, November 1992. 'The Glums': Charles and Diana on their
last official trip together, attending a presidential banquet in Seoul. Their
separation would be announced one month later.

and Diplomatic Protection Department; a message was conveyed from the Palace to Kensington Palace, intimating that a prosecution under nuisance call laws might be considered. The calls stopped but Diana's relationship with Oliver Hoare had continued.

Andrew Morton, who was preparing a follow-up book on Diana post-separation (*Diana: Her New Life*) for publication in 1994, asserted that the influence of Diana's astrologers could not be ruled out in the motivation of her decision and its timing. Diana believed that she would never be Queen but, equally, that Charles would never be King, his exit being either voluntary, abdication in favour of William, or involuntary, by accidental death. Recently, apparently, one of them had predicted that, owing to his unpopularity, Charles would have to resign as heir to the throne, leaving that position to William.[9] Another version of this continuing theme was that he would retreat to Italy with Camilla and fulfil himself by painting. Diana saw her eventual role in relation to the monarchy as Queen Mother, guiding the destinies of William, the future King.

'My boys' – or, as Gilbey had put it in the Squidgygate conversation of 1989, the 'lovebugs' – remained the unchanging focus of her life. Both were now boarding at their preparatory school, Ludgrove. When they were away, Diana was lonely at home by herself at Kensington Palace. She deeply missed her greatest friend, Lucia Flecha de Lima, and her family with whom she had been used to spend the weekends, when they left for a new post in Washington in November 1993. When the boys were at home for the prescribed weekends or part holidays, her life revolved around them. Diana has been pictured as an empty-headed woman with no idea beyond her personal benefit, but, perhaps because of her own experience of a hereditary position, and the importance of 'the heir', she understood very well the meaning of the hereditary monarchy and William's place in the scheme of things. Despite her own difficulties with her husband and his family, she was not about to reflect those problems on to her children. She was determined that they should be brought up in as 'normal' (one of her favourite words) a way as possible both at home and in the world outside. This went beyond expeditions to Thorpe Park and Disneyland, or shopping expeditions when they, unlike other members of the Royal Family, paid with their own money; she took them to share her own experiences of people much less fortunate than themselves. While some of the Royal Family – including the boys' father – disapproved of the ultra-democratic way in which they were brought up, Diana believed it was essential for them to see life beyond the royal enclave in a way which it had not been thought important for their father to experience.

William in particular learned to be at ease with the homeless; later, when Harry was old enough, she involved him too. Diana had already visited The Passage on her own in June 1989. On two subsequent occasions, inspired by her friend the Catholic Archbishop of Westminster, Cardinal Basil Hume, she took first William and then both boys to The Passage Day Centre and Night Centre attached to Westminster Cathedral. Diana and William arrived on 20 December 1993 unannounced; there were no press with her, nor did the people in The Passage know that she was coming. Sister Bridie Dowd, director of The Passage at the time, recalled how, when they walked into The Passage, a long area with people sitting at tables along the wall, the atmosphere was electric: 'They just moved to their feet right away. They were so taken with the fact that she was there.' Diana, shadowed by Sister Bridie, had difficulty moving among the people and talking to them because 'they wanted to hold on to her, because she had that great ability to listen to people and really to make you feel that she heard every word that you were saying and even what you weren't saying . . . She made you feel that she was listening with her eyes as well as her ears. Her eye contact was very very special . . .'[10]

Diana told Sister Bridie that she 'wanted William to be aware of the other side of life. She didn't want him to grow up cosseted. And she had talked to him about it and he had seen photographs and said he would like to visit. So that was his first visit to any centre for homeless people. It was before he went to Centrepoint. And that was a huge thing for him to do because going into The

Passage was very intimidating. There could be a hundred people in The Passage at any one time. People from all walks of life who for one reason or another had experienced difficulties, who had dropped out of society for whatever reason. Some who had been to university . . . two university lecturers, ex-priests, a very broad mix of people . . . Many of them were street homeless, others were homeless living in hostels . . . people who were insecurely housed, people who were lonely or people who had drink problems . . .'[11] 'There were people who have been in the army and when they left just weren't able to cope, two nurses who were not well enough in themselves to keep a job, people whose marriages haven't worked out, people who have been made redundant.' They would be made welcome, given a cup of tea, breakfast, lunch; there were washing facilities, showers and clothing stores, education classes and counselling. And William? 'He was very shy initially and stayed close to Mum for a while,' Sister Bridie said. 'But the people were very good and very sensitive to his needs and talked to him about football. Once he got talking to them he was absolutely fine. He was reserved. He was a child, but you could see the potential there.'[12] Later both William and Harry accompanied their mother to the Night Centre and played chess with the people there. Diana's vision of a popular monarchy was a potent one which was to survive her death, even in an attenuated form.

Diana was concerned for William who was sensitive and to some extent, like his father, a worrier. It was, after all, William on whom she leaned in her unhappy periods, who had listened at doors and heard things it would have been better for him not to have heard. Despite that, theirs was a very normal, not a neurotic relationship. Anybody who has listened to the Settelen tapes broadcast on NBC will have heard the boys jeering their mother good-humouredly when they thought she had gone too far – 'Isn't she *awful*!!' She was less concerned about Harry, a cheeky, cheerful boy who had inherited her optimistic temperament but none of her problems. Sensitive to the fact that the boys' future positions would be so very unequal, she was intent on involving them both

in their future role. William would be King but it was important
to them both that Harry should be there to support him.

In the background over the two years since the separation
were the long drawn-out divorce negotiations, pressed by Charles,
fended off at a meeting in October 1993 by Diana, who repeatedly
told friends that she did not want to divorce. Both sides man-
oeuvred to win over public opinion. Since the summer of 1992,
Charles's camp had planned a riposte to Andrew Morton's book
that would win back the high ground for the Prince. 'Prince
Charles wanted it as a justification after the Morton book,' one of
his close circle recalled.[13] This was to be a biography by the
broadcaster Jonathan Dimbleby, already seen by the Prince as a
sympathetic figure for his green views and the fact that he had
once worked at Windsor Home Farm. It was to be an authorized
book based on interviews with the Prince's friends and staff and
use of the Prince's correspondence and diaries. Officially, it was to
mark the twenty-fifth anniversary of Charles's investiture as Prince
of Wales. It had initially been intended as a television documentary:
'Well, the original concept when I was involved was a celebratory
documentary to mark his twenty-fifth anniversary,' recalled Dickie
Arbiter. 'Harmless sort of thing, jolly fine fellow, the organizations,
bland but big plug for the organizations rather than for the man,
because the organizations are the key . . . so we use that vehicle.
Then Aylard moved the goalposts. "The Prince has decided that
[it should include personal matters]" and I said, "I'm sure the
Prince hasn't decided that, I'm sure you've decided, but you do
realize it's going to be warts and all?" He said, "Oh, we'll do that."
And I said, "Richard, I really do mean WARTS AND ALL."
And he said, "Yes, go ahead." So I said, "Well, I'll do your bidding
because that's my job to lay on the facilities for the crew, but I
don't agree with it." '

The project was given a cautious welcome by the Palace who
may have hoped to monitor it – 'fact-checking' – but refused
cooperation by Diana's staff who, rightly as it turned out, foresaw
that a panegyric to the Prince could hardly fail to be unfavourable
to the Princess. The Prince and his camp cannot be blamed for

aiming to raise his public profile and to emphasize the good work he did, which was still often derided or ignored. The effect of the Morton book on his reputation had been devastating, and the efforts of his friends through the media had been largely unsuccessful. A tabloid editor said, 'Charles's friends, Romseys, van Cutsems, etc, were at it all the time, ringing me up, giving me stuff . . .'[14] Charles, it seems, could not win. Diana worked her magic even on Jonathan Dimbleby. Although she had refused an interview, exposure to her personality over lunch had its intended effect.

'The Princess,' Jephson wrote, 'put on a great performance in which regality and informality were mixed in proportions that would frustrate the most determined critic. She ate her lunch with obvious enthusiasm and laughingly sympathised with Dimbleby's Herculean task on the Prince's behalf. After she had departed in a cloud of fond farewells, I caught on Jonathan's face the dazed look familiar to me from so many others who had just received her dazzling best . . .'

Asked how the impression he had received compared with what he had been told, he seemed 'momentarily uncomfortable', replying: 'if I can't believe what I've been told about her . . . then I can't believe any of it'.[15]

The programme went out on 29 June 1994. Given the personal content, it seems unlikely that the Palace would have had any input beyond providing facilities. There was apprehension among the Queen's circle, and rightly so, as it turned out. 'He's on a hiding to nothing' was the general opinion, hoping that it might not be even worse. They were as yet unaware of just how personal the programme would turn out to be; those who were begged the Prince not to do it. One of his aides resigned. The main thrust of the programme, the public man, his charities and his views of the causes he believed in, came across as a sympathetic portrait of a good man with serious intentions. The programme was aimed at the young, the future King's constituency, showing the Prince, normally an indifferent television performer, at his best as an environmental crusader, speaking articulately, passionately and without notes. With pop star Phil Collins at a holiday camp organized by his successful inner-city youth help foundation, the Prince's Trust, he appeared at ease and in his element.

Unfortunately, the 'hook' of the programme for which it would always be remembered was his answer to Jonathan Dimbleby's direct question as to whether he had been faithful in his marriage. Charles replied that he had – until his marriage 'had irretrievably broken down'. He went further to describe Camilla Parker Bowles as a 'very dear friend' whom he would continue to see. Nothing could have been calculated to infuriate Diana more. It invited a response and, in due course, one would be forthcoming.

While the general public applauded the Prince for his honesty, people close to the Royal Family, and indeed the Waleses and Camilla, were unanimous in their condemnation. Charles had complained of the media's insensitivity to the feelings of his sons with their 'Charles v Di' stories but here he was on television watched by millions, first pictured relaxing with his sons and then confessing that he had been unfaithful to their mother. The royal establishment from top to bottom was shocked. Chief among Diana's crimes had been 'speaking to the media' but here was the heir to the throne publicly proclaiming his adultery and, not only that, his devotion to his mistress and his intention to carry on exactly as he had been doing in the past. The most charitable view was that he and Diana 'had been driven mad by the media'. 'That's what brought the house down . . . the advice had been "Look, don't talk about your marriage at all, let Jonathan ask you as many questions as he likes but you just say 'Look, my marriage, just like anybody else's, is entirely private'." [He should have said] "It's not your business and it's not the audience's business" and the whole of England would have stood up and said, "Good on you. Absolutely right." So what mileage was there in talking about it? It was a red rag to a bull . . .'[16] At Balmoral Charles asked a close friend, the Duchess of Westminster, what she thought about the interview. 'She was very outspoken and she said, "Well, actually, Sir, I didn't think it was very good" and he got into a frightful rage, didn't speak to her the whole weekend – he's very petty, Charles. He went straight to the private secretary [Aylard], blamed him, just flew at him, he screamed and shouted and yelled at him. I mean Charles is terribly spoiled . . .'[17]

Whatever the public approval rating may have been, in the words of the Palace aide the interview 'brought the house down' as far as the loyal household staff was concerned. It was indeed 'a red rag to a bull'. Several bulls, to be precise. Talking to the media had been the ultimate sin, inconceivable for a member of the Royal Family to do, and yet here was the heir to the throne admitting his adultery on television and pledging his loyalty to his mistress. Loyal servants were outraged. Charles's valet, Ken Stronach, 'the most loyal and discreet of all' according to colleagues, beside himself, went to a newspaper with damaging stories about Charles and Camilla. He repented and tried to withdraw; the newspaper went ahead anyway. The experience destroyed him. 'The general feeling was,' said his colleague, 'that having been made to sign things and lying down the line for their master, this has been [for them] the ultimate betrayal.'[18] Loyal staff, trained to absolute discretion following the example of the Queen and the Duke of Edinburgh, were dismayed, fearing that the monarchy was disintegrating. The reaction of a royal aide who went with a colleague to view the interview was: 'God Save the Queen, long may she reign over us.'

The other consequence of the programme, which in the end was to be more far-reaching in its effect, was Andrew Parker Bowles's decision to divorce Camilla. While he had been perfectly willing to countenance his wife's relationship with Prince Charles as long as it remained discreet – or, at least, not public knowledge – Charles's admission, coming as it did only just a year after the Camillagate tapes, had put their relationship beyond question, placing Parker Bowles in an impossible position. The day after the programme was broadcast, the Prince's private secretary, Richard Aylard, admitted in a press conference that the woman in question was Camilla. In January 1995 Andrew and Camilla Parker Bowles divorced.

Diana feigned indifference. On the evening the programme was shown, she fulfilled a long-standing engagement at the Serpentine

Gallery, photographed wearing a sexy, clinging black dress which showed off her tanned, toned legs. Her whole manner radiated confidence. 'She bounded out of the car in that wonderfully athletic way she had,' Peter Palumbo, who, as chairman of the gallery, was on hand to greet her, recalled.[19] The underlying message was, 'Look at me . . . look what you've thrown away and see how much I care.' The photograph appeared on all the front pages. The *Sun*'s take on it was: 'The Thrilla he left to woo Camilla', accompanied by an unflattering photograph of Camilla. While Diana was angry under the surface, she had a certain admiration for Charles's courage and honesty in revealing what he did, as, it appeared, did the general public. Her own riposte would have to wait until the notorious *Panorama* interview eighteen months later.

Beneath the radiance, Diana was concerned that her media image was slipping: the press knew that Diana manipulated her own publicity, tipping off favoured newspapers as to her whereabouts when she wanted them to be known. She had been hoist with her own petard in early June 1994 when she was photographed having a clandestine rendezvous with Richard Kay of the *Daily Mail* in his parked car. At the instance of his editor, David English, Kay had been assigned to Diana 'as a sympathetic ear' and had been working closely with her since 1993. Tall, lean, good-looking and transparently trustworthy, Kay had become genuinely friendly both with Diana and the Spencer family and had been acting as her media mouthpiece for some time. Jealous rival newspapers now had photographic evidence of her closeness to Kay, and a hypocritical howl of rage went up.

More trouble lay ahead. In March James Hewitt, at Diana's instigation, gave an interview to Anna Pasternak which was published in the *Daily Express*, giving an anodyne account of the relationship. Diana had asked him to talk to Andrew Morton but he had refused, finding in Pasternak what he thought to be a more sympathetic ear. As far as Diana was concerned, Hewitt said, 'It was a pre-emptive strike, but the rumours grew stronger than they were before.' Diana's strategy failed: where she had intended the public to swallow the story of an innocent friendship, Hewitt was roundly condemned for cashing in on their relationship. 'Diana was happy for it to go out,' Hewitt told Bedell Smith. 'But once it backfired, the support I got from her was non-existent . . .' Hewitt had already been ostracized in high-level quarters when knowledge of the affair became widespread. As an officer and a gentleman, it was thought, he should not have contemplated a physical affair with the wife of the heir to the throne. In March he had had to leave the army and his future seemed uncertain. Now Diana had cut him off for doing her bidding. He felt bitter and abandoned; the result would be Pasternak's Mills and Boon-ish version of the affair to be published in October 1994 as *Princess in Love*.

In mid-August 1994 Diana was holidaying with the Flecha de Limas on the fashionable island of Martha's Vineyard off the Massachusetts coast. Sally Bedell Smith, invited to join the party for lunch on the beach, noticed that Diana 'seemed strikingly subdued . . . preoccupied', moving her chair apart from the group to talk intently with her confidante and mentor, Lucia. Later she cut short her holiday and returned home. The reason was that she had learned that the Pasternak book about her affair with James Hewitt, based on the passionate letters she had written him in the Gulf, was to be published in the autumn. She was deeply upset at what she saw as this betrayal, although, had she been shrewd enough not to cut Hewitt, it might have been avoided.

August was not to be a good month in the media for Diana. Quite apart from the Hewitt rumours, the newspapers had picked up on the nuisance calls story with regard to Oliver Hoare: the public were amazed to read of Diana as a 'phone pest' which suggested that she was psychologically unstable. Diana asked Hoare to make a public statement; understandably, in consideration of his family, he refused. Women were understanding, considering that Diana, lonely and in need of reassurance, had wanted to hear Hoare's voice. Yet the fact that Hoare was married with children did show her in an unfavourable light. The scandal subsided but the negative publicity she had attracted and the revelation of her two affairs, which it implied, unnerved her.

Anna Pasternak's account of the Hewitt affair, which confirmed their physical relationship, was published on 3 October. However, Diana escaped lightly: after all, she had been abandoned by Charles for his lover and Hewitt was unmarried, so there was no 'marriage wrecker' shadow hanging over it. The ceiling fell in on Hewitt, who from then on became a tabloid hate figure. 'Love Rat and Cad' declared the *Sun* and it is by these epithets that he is apparently to be forever known. It was, after all, Diana who dumped Hewitt when it no longer suited her and she had found a new interest in Oliver Hoare. Hewitt had fallen genuinely in love with her and, if her later television confession is to be believed, she with him. He had given her confidence through some of her darkest days and she had emerged stronger with her confidence revived. Hewitt was naïve, gullible, the reverse of streetwise. He should have kept his mouth shut and never have allowed himself to be lured into cooperation with Pasternak but he did and paid for it. After that he was dead in the water while Diana sailed radiantly on.

At the time, however, she felt the betrayal deeply. In a letter dated 11 October 1994 to Chryssie Fitzgerald, the reflexologist who also carried out her colonic irrigation treatment, she described what had happened as 'THE toughest week yet I have had to face'; when she had come for her appointment she had been 'in a total state of shock and very distressed about Hewitt's so-called revelations'. She had been equally hurt, she wrote, on hearing what Sarah, Duchess of York, had said about her. The two women shared most of their therapists and psychics – Sarah to an almost excessive degree. Despite their rapprochement over the past two years, when they had made common ground over their troubles with the Royal Family, there was no real depth to their relationship and a considerable tinge of jealousy. Sarah, not infrequently and always unwisely, made her feelings about Diana known, sometimes to whoever answered the telephone at Kensington Palace. In this case she had obviously unburdened herself to Chryssie Fitzgerald. 'I never expected to hear on top of all that [the Hewitt revelations] about someone else's hatred for me & what accompanies those feelings,' Diana wrote. 'It hurt so [double underlined] much to hear from you, Chryssie, that Sarah found me a problem . . .' Chryssie and Diana appear to have parted company around that time, a frequent occurrence where Diana was concerned.

The great publishing event of the autumn was to be Jonathan Dimbleby's biography of the Prince, something to which Diana, with reason, had been looking forward with some apprehension. Dimbleby had done his estimable best to be fair; his remark to Jephson after his lunch with Diana was indicative of the kind of information he had been receiving about her from Charles's circle. It was, of course, the case for Charles, as opposed to Morton's case for Diana. Since Diana herself had first brought her depression, lack of self-confidence, bulimia and attempts at self-harm into the public domain with the Morton book, she could hardly complain about finding them reported in Dimbleby's biography. A quick glance at the index to the book would be enough to reinforce her fears: 'weight loss', volatile behaviour', 'jealousy of Camilla Parker Bowles', 'attempts to control the Prince's life', 'resentment of the Prince's interests', 'self-absorption', 'marriage breaks down irretrievably' . . .[20] This last, Dimbleby, forced to give a date by the Prince's television confession, attributed to 1986, illustrating this particularly with the Prince's failure to sympathize with Diana when she fainted in Canada on their official visit for Expo '86. 'The truth was that he had started to withdraw the support which for so long had drained his reserves of sympathy and compassion.' The truth was, rather, that Charles's failure to respond to her need for affection and his lack of understanding for her predicament (unlike his sympathetic reaction to her sister Sarah's anorexia) had been evident far earlier than the summer of 1986. Basically, the cause of Diana's affliction was not only post-natal depression after the birth of William but her early realization that Charles did not truly love her and that this marriage in which she had invested so much hope could never approximate to her romantic dreams. Charles's true love for Camilla Parker Bowles and his powerful sexual attraction to her above all other women had made those dreams impossible. Charles had abandoned Diana, not she him.

From the point of view of the monarchy, something which Dimbleby glossed over, the failure of the Waleses' marriage was a tragedy of missed opportunities.

16. Towards a New World

'A friend . . . once asked her if she gambled. "Not with cards but with life . . ." '[1]

Increasingly, as problems at home mounted, Diana had begun to see a new life for herself in the United States prompted, perhaps, by the refuge which the Flecha de Limas' embassy in Washington represented for her, as a home from home, just as the Mount Street embassy had been for her before they left. Jacqueline Kennedy Onassis's death from non-Hodgkin's lymphoma at the early age of sixty-four on 19 May 1994 had made worldwide news, her iconic status as American royalty confirmed by the solemn public manner of her passing. Mourning spectators and television cameras focused on her Fifth Avenue apartment, retailing pictures round the world. After JFK's assassination in 1963, Jackie, then as pressured by publicity and semi-royal status as Diana now was, had made her escape into the protection of Aristotle Onassis, whose vast wealth, private island and ocean-going yacht could provide her with the privacy she craved. When Jackie had returned to America permanently after Onassis's death, her friends had formed a praetorian guard around her and her quasi-royal status had won her respect and consideration from the paparazzi (with the notable exception of Ron Galella). If Jackie could do it, why couldn't she? Diana thought. Jackie still had her beauty, trailing clouds of glamour when she left America to marry Onassis in 1968 aged thirty-nine; when she returned for good in 1975 she was still beautiful but in her late forties and, to her fans, distant and mysterious. Diana was in her thirties, at the height of her radiant beauty and glamour. It was a delusion to think that she would ever have been left alone.

And there was even an Onassis figure on the horizon: billionaire

Teddy Forstmann, partner of Forstmann Little and chairman of Gulfstream Aerospace, whom she had met through one of her particular mentors, Jacob Rothschild. Lord Rothschild, who was on the advisory board of Forstmann's company, had introduced her to Forstmann at an Independence Day dinner which he had given at Spencer House. Forstmann was charming with dark good looks and they had quickly become firm friends: later that summer they had met again and played tennis together when she was on holiday with Lucia Flecha de Lima and her family on Martha's Vineyard. 'He came over two or three times to see her,' a friend said. 'Friendly visits, I don't think they even held hands.' 'They didn't have an affair,' she went on, '[although] he was besotted by her . . . when she flicked those eyes [at him] . . . in a way Teddy would have been the ideal man for her, [but] Teddy is a very selfish man.' But, although Diana's thoughts were definitely tending in that direction, Forstmann's were not. He was level-headed enough not to want the disruption marriage to Diana would have caused in his life. 'She thought that way [i.e. marriage],' the friend said, 'but he didn't. There was a moment when she thought it would be a good idea for her because he had a private plane; she could come and go across the Atlantic to see her children. It was a problem for her to see her children but not to live in England. [But] I think in a way she knew that the only way out would be a non-Englishman with money.'² Patrick Jephson, who was with Diana on her second tour, was impressed with Forstmann: 'I think it was his common sense, delivered straight and with the confidence that only experience and pots of self-made money can bring, that was his greatest service to the Princess,' he wrote; '. . . what's more, he was kind to her.'³

In October she made a five-day visit to the United States which was an unqualified success. As opposed to the implacable hostility of the British Establishment and the hot and cold treatment given her by the British media, she was met with enthusiastic and uncritical appreciation. In New York the artist Nelson Shanks, who had painted what was generally considered to be the best portrait of Diana, gave a dinner for her at the National Arts Club in New

York where she was welcomed with a bear hug by one of her greatest admirers, Luciano Pavarotti. She stayed at the Carlyle Hotel (from then on her favourite hotel), where the manager, James Sherwin, made it a home from home for her, before flying by private jet, a Gulfstream IV provided by Forstmann, to Washington the next day to stay with the Flecha de Limas. Forstmann was her escort at a dinner given in her honour by the most influential woman in Washington, Katharine 'Kay' Graham, owner of the *Washington Post*.

Kay Graham had first met Diana when the Flecha de Limas brought her over to Graham's private beach on Martha's Vineyard. Later, Kay Graham recalled being immediately struck by Diana's 'natural, low-key charm'. 'We seemed to enjoy each other,' she wrote. 'From that point on we were able to have easy and candid conversations during long walks on the beach.' Diana came over to play tennis at Kay Graham's house. On the drive back to the Flecha de Limas, Diana talked 'lovingly' to Kay about her sons: 'I want them to grow up knowing there are poor people as well as palaces,' she said. 'If you spent time with her,' Kay Graham wrote, 'you felt Diana's extraordinary strength, as well as vulnerability and her somewhat mocking and ever-present sense of humour.' 'I asked her if she had ever thought of going to college now that she was alone,' she recalled. 'She found my question hard to believe, and commented with irony, "I've already had an education".' A friend of Graham's who met Diana on 'the Vineyard' once asked her if she gambled. 'Not with cards,' she answered, 'but with life.'[4]

On the Vineyard in August, Diana, just after she arrived, had heard that Elizabeth Glaser, with whom she had corresponded and who was a well-known AIDS patient, was on the island. Diana dropped everything to pay her a long private visit. In Washington that October, Diana was still searching for the right way to focus her energies. She had, she said, heaps of requests but she had to decide in which area she could do most good. 'Make sure it matters to you,' a fellow guest told her. 'Because if it doesn't you can't make it matter to others.'[5] Later she told Kay Graham that if she had to talk about a cause she would make sure that she went to see the problem and learned about it first, saying that she was only going to work in areas where she thought her presence could make a difference.[6]

At a lunch given the next day in her honour by the British Ambassador, Sir Robin Renwick, and his wife, Diana sat at a table which included two major figures in American public life, the President's wife, Hillary Clinton, and the hero of the Gulf War, General Colin Powell, only recently retired as Chairman of the Joint Chiefs of Staff. Diana and Colin Powell hit it off immediately: then, after lunch, she retired for a private talk with Hillary Clinton whom she had first met at the D-Day celebrations in June. The two women had much in common: 'We talked of the challenges of public life and the struggle to protect our children from the scrutiny of the world,' Hillary recalled. 'She told me of her new hopes and plans for using her position to focus attention on the needs of suffering people. Although she seemed vulnerable and unsure about the direction her life was taking, I sensed in her a reservoir of resilience and determination that would help her take charge of her own life and help others, despite great obstacles.' Later in their relationship, Diana spoke with heartfelt feeling of the 'disease' of not being loved.[7]

On her return to London Diana, still exhilarated by her experiences, wrote a note to Patrick Jephson, thanking him for his 'strength and support' and saying how 'thrilled' she was 'by the new path we are treading'.[8] Jephson called it a delusion to think that anything positive could come out of what had been not much more than a happy social trip but at least, he added, it was a positive delusion. After a year of more or less minor activity which had included backing out of a suggested presence on the International Committee of the Red Cross, Diana took up her charity work again with enthusiasm. She visited two special hospitals for mental patients, Carstairs in central Scotland and Broadmoor in southern England, visiting Carstairs in the company of Jayne Zito, whose fiancé had been killed by a schizophrenic mistakenly released into the community. At Broadmoor, Diana attended – alone – a meeting of the patients' council which consisted of the patients themselves. 'I watched her take her seat in what was to be a private session of the council, surrounded by men who were thought to be a serious threat to the public,' Jephson wrote. 'As the door closed, I heard her voice and whatever she said raised an immediate warm laugh of greeting.'⁹ She ended the year visiting Paris in her role as President of Barnardo's, touring the community projects in the poorer parts of the city but ending on a regal note with a banquet in the Hall of Mirrors at the Palace of Versailles given in her honour where she charmed President Mitterrand. As she 'made a majestic exit', she was applauded by nine hundred guests: it was Diana 'going out to conquer the world'.

Meanwhile, Jonathan Dimbleby had published his biography of the Prince, serialized in the *Sunday Times* that autumn: Diana returned to find her husband and not herself the focus of publicity, very little of it favourable. Well written and authoritative though the book was, it was also, unsurprisingly, one-sided. Everything that had gone wrong in Charles's life was somebody else's fault, particularly inadequate parenting by a remote mother and a bullying father who had been 'unable or unwilling to proffer . . . the affection and appreciation' Charles had craved. Diana's neuroses were to blame for the failure of the marriage. Only Camilla emerged with any credit from the Prince's self-pitying account. As one reviewer put it, she was portrayed as a kind of virginal Mills and Boon heroine: 'Her warmth, her lack of ambition or guile, her good humour and her gentleness endeared her to the household . . .' Dimbleby wrote.

In mid-September, pre-publication, there had been 'a terrific explosion from the Queen' when it was discovered that the Prince had handed over to Dimbleby a drawerful of papers which included not just his childhood diaries but also State Papers, without bothering to check what was there. He was forced to take them back and go through them. Recently he had been staying with his grandmother at Birkhall. 'He'll only be coming here for one day,' the Queen said grimly. 'And he chose the day of the Ghillies' Ball when there wouldn't be time to talk,' a courtier recalled.¹⁰ The general opinion among the Royal Family and the household was

that 'it was a great error to do this book at all. In fact washing your
dirty linen in public for somebody in that position is a very stupid
thing to do,' said a courtier. 'There's no doubt that their policy of
never talking or giving interviews in the past has been a very good
one.' 'Things have been rather difficult here,' a courtier told a
member of the family from Buckingham Palace, 'but they've
calmed down a bit, thank God.'[11] 'I remember having long conversations with him [Charles] about his children and how he mustn't
do anything to hurt them. So what does he do? He does this book,
the most hurting thing in the world.'[12] Whatever else he may have
been trying to achieve by the book, publicly blaming his father
and mother for his own shortcomings was unkind and hurtful, to
say the least. Princess Anne and her brothers telephoned Charles
objecting to his depiction of his parents: 'they rang and told him
off and he sulked against them for weeks,' an aide recalled.[13]
Publicly everyone blamed Richard Aylard, who was to be the
scapegoat for the affair.

Monarchists who had condemned Diana over the Morton
book were outraged by the Prince and the Dimbleby book. Even
Charles Moore, a prominent media figure and stalwart monarchist, was prompted to say: 'When the Royal couple separated I
wrote a column in this space [the *Spectator*] which criticised the
Princess for indulging her "craving for private happiness" and
ended "how do you know some will object that the Prince does
not suffer from this same debilitating craving? I do not know but
since he is the next King I do not think we should discuss the
matter." Now he is forcing us all to discuss it, wrenching the
conversation back, just when we hoped it might stop, to him and
his woes.'[14]

Tensions were aroused by the Dimbleby episode between Buckingham Palace and St James's Palace. The Waleses' media war was
irksome and embarrassing for Buckingham Palace. That Charles
should let Diana take command of the press and in fact provoke
her to it and then lose the moral high ground was a source of
discomfort. 'I think that sense of frustration and anger and disappointment which undoubtedly radiated from the centre of the

royal establishment is directed on the Prince,' said one of Charles's aides, 'and it's hard to argue against it sometimes.'[15] There was a distinct feeling that, as far as St James's Palace was concerned, things were out of control.

And it was true that Diana commanded the media heights. Margaret Thatcher's public relations guru, Gordon Reece, had introduced Diana to David English, editor of the *Daily Mail*. The parent company, Associated Press, then took what English described, apologetically, to representatives of the Prince as 'a commercial decision' to support Diana, who sold newspapers, as opposed to the Prince, who did not. The powerful Murdoch press, proprietors of *The Times*, *Sunday Times*, *Sun* and *News of the World*, was, for much the same reasons, inclined to favour Diana. 'Diana was quite friendly with Murdoch himself,' said an expert in the media field. 'They had a correspondence. They would see each other occasionally and they would write to each other. She wrote to him . . .'[16] Relations between Charles and Murdoch, who was not naturally a monarchist and hated inherited privilege, were non-existent. A meeting between them in the late eighties organized by ex-King Constantine of Greece had had the opposite effect to that intended. '. . . Murdoch went away thinking that the Prince was this sort of pinko commie leftie sort of weirdo – and I think those kind of words were used – and the Prince went away thinking he [Murdoch] was a kind of crypto-fascist megalomaniac, so that didn't work. So I think that News Corporation generally had an agenda and Diana was very, for them, commercially she was very powerful . . .'[17] The Telegraph Group, the most conservative and naturally pro-monarchist media organization, was then owned by the Canadian-born tycoon Conrad Black. 'Conrad Black and the Prince of Wales didn't get on,' said the aide. 'Max Hastings, when he was editor [of the *Daily Telegraph*] couldn't stand the Prince of Wales – it's all in his book – thought the Prince was unfit to be King, should stand aside for William . . . Express Newspapers were the only real group which were friendly with him [the Prince of Wales]. She [Diana] commanded the media, there's no doubt about it. Because a picture of Diana sold papers . . .'[18] And, while the Prince dealt with the press through his aides, Diana had deliberately set out personally to charm the editors, from the broadsheets to the tabloids, influential columnists like Auberon Waugh and Paul Johnson, and media celebrities like Clive James.

Diana's seduction of one of the more ruthless tabloid editors, brash thirty-year-old Piers Morgan of the *Daily Mirror*, which he recorded after her death in his memoirs, provides an interesting illustration of her methods. Meeting at a reception for the charity Childline at the Savoy in January 1996, Diana asked Morgan jokingly how all these editors claimed to know everything about her when they hadn't even met her. '"Now's your chance to enlighten me, your royal highness," I replied. She eyed me up. "Hmm . . . I don't have the time, I'm afraid . . ." Then she giggled. "Or the inclination, come to that!"' She moved on, leaving Morgan agape. 'It was fascinating just watching her work the room,' he wrote. 'Everyone, and I include myself in this, just melted in her presence. She is radiant, sexy, and very direct – so you get the feeling you're the only one she cares about for the few seconds she's talking to you. It's a class act.'[19] On 8 May she invited him to lunch at Kensington Palace. Morgan was as excited as a schoolboy. 'Diana's the biggest star in the world and I am getting a private audience . . . *Wow!*'[20] Morgan was even more excited when William joined them for lunch. It was a frank conversation and Morgan was allowed to ask Diana anything he liked, despite, surprisingly, the presence of William, who, he noted in his memoirs, 'is clearly in the loop on most of her bizarre world, and in particular, the men who come into it from time to time'.[21] But Morgan, despite the temporary intimacy, knew that Diana was calling the shots. 'She knows she's got me over a barrel,' he wrote later. 'If I want any more from her, I am going to have to play the game by her rules.'[22]

At the opposite end of the press spectrum was Peter Stothard, then editor of *The Times*. Their meeting had come in May 1994 when Diana had concerns about leaks on the subject of her expenditure, put at more than £3,000 a week, via her husband and his friends. 'My husband said it at a dinner party last week,' she told him, 'where it got to Ross Benson and to Nigel Dempster . . .'[23] Diana's approach to the intellectual Stothard was not quite the same as her dealings with Piers Morgan. He found her extremely sophisticated 'about the media, her use of it and its use of her'. The interview was conducted on her terms, within strict but surprising lines. Flatteringly, inside those lines were 'the very aspects of her life which most people keep outside in discussion with media editors – her husband, his mistress, her in-laws, her own fragile sense of herself. Within minutes I felt I was talking to someone I knew. By the time she had toyed herself through her foie gras and lamb, I knew things about her that I did not know about my closest friends . . . The speed with which she ran through her list of subjects would not have disgraced a bank chairman anxious to catch the Ascot train.'[24] Lacking Diana's sophistication, it seems, Stothard quite failed to catch the story Diana had meant him to take in – how she had saved a tramp from drowning in the Serpentine. Although she dragged him to University College Hospital where she was to visit the rescued tramp, Stothard still failed to see the light until the story appeared in all the newspapers the next day, including his own – but without a briefing from him. Diana the Good Samaritan had been designed to counter Diana the Spendthrift.

As an estranged member of the Royal Family, Diana was in limbo. She relied ever more on her close friends, particularly Lucia Flecha de Lima, even though she was in Washington. Lucia was, according to Diana's butler, Paul Burrell, best friend, mother figure and counsellor rolled into one. Even now that the time difference between England and America made communication more difficult, their relationship continued to grow, becoming stronger as the years went by. In Washington, Lucia would set her alarm clock for 3 a.m. so that she could speak to Diana at the start of her day. 'If the princess needed advice or consolation, she rang Lucia,' Burrell wrote,[25] and Lucia was ready to answer whenever Diana needed her. 'I faxed an endless stream of messages across the Atlantic to her,' Burrell continued. Diana repeatedly told him how 'marvellous' Lucia was, that she could not cope without her, and that Lucia was 'like a mother to her'.[26] According to Burrell, who was best placed to know, Diana's 'surrogate family' now included first of all Lucia, then Lady Annabel Goldsmith, Rosa Monckton, Susie Kassem and Diana's doctor, Dr Mary Loveday. Richard Kay had by now transcended the role of media mouthpiece: he was a confidant – at least for what she needed him to hear – and helped her with her speech writing and correspondence. Sarah Ferguson was also close to Diana at that time. She was living apart from Andrew, although not yet divorced, with her daughters Beatrice and Eugenie at Romenda Lodge, Virginia Water. Diana frequently went down there to lunch, particularly at weekends, taking William and Harry, if they were at home, to see their cousins. Diana adored the York children and kept their childish paintings on her walls. At this time, the two women were constantly on the telephone to each other, gossiping, complaining about the treatment they were receiving from royal circles and the press, or discussing the latest words of wisdom from one of their gurus.

Outside this inner circle, Diana had a wider network of advisers – such as Clive James – who would lunch with her at Kensington Palace to offer her their expert wisdom when she asked for it. As with all her friendships, she compartmentalized these relationships. They came to Kensington Palace or lunched with her in restaurants *à deux*; only Diana knew what she had told each of them, and Diana was absolutely in control of the friendship. Apart from Raine de Chambrun, these counsellors were all men, intelligent, successful, who were nonetheless besotted with the Princess and protective towards her. Clive James, indeed, was an admirer of Charles yet he could not resist the lure of Diana. 'Even before I met her I had guessed she was a handful . . . Clearly on a hair trigger, she was unstable at best, and when the squeeze was on she was a fruitcake on the rampage,' he recalled. 'But even while reaching this conclusion I was already smitten, and from then on everything I found out about her at first hand, even – especially, her failings and her follies, only made me love her more . . .'[27] James forgave her even when she lied to him, as when she denied having anything to do with the Morton book: '"I really had nothing to do with that Andrew Morton book," she said. "But after my friends talked to him, I had to stand by them." She looked me straight in the eye when she said this, so I could see how plausible she was when she was telling a whopper.'[28]

Another confidant and friend was David Puttnam. It was he who had arranged the Thirty Club dinner for her in 1994 to address and impress the media magnates, he who had – with Patrick Jephson – urged her to form a Princess of Wales Trust to fund her charitable giving. (She later rejected the idea – apparently on the advice of Colin Powell – since it would be seen as setting herself up in opposition to Charles's cherished Prince's Trust.) 'She drew you into her life in quite a definite way,' said one of her friends, 'the drawing-in involved deep confidences which she knew the person in question would never betray, as if it were a secret compact.'[29] She would talk about her personal life in what one friend described as 'sometimes . . . excruciating detail'. Diana was fascinated by the cinema, identifying with some of the stars, particularly Marilyn Monroe. 'She loved Marilyn Monroe, she really did,' said a friend. 'And I got hold of a fantastic biography, a documentary from America, and I don't know what made me do it, but before sending it to her I thought I'd have a look at it. And I looked at it and never sent it. And I never sent it because I thought this is not good stuff for Diana to be looking at. So the point here is that I was dealing with a sufficiently vulnerable person, that this ostensibly fascinating piece of material about someone she admired could actually have a different context . . . I think without doubt she [Diana] had suicidal tendencies. But people with whom I've had that conversation have said that in a sense she was too selfish for that, that's not the way she would have done anything – and then there were the children . . .'[30]

Extraordinarily, Diana would be the same age as Monroe when she died. (Charles, who of all people would have been aware of her recklessness and her bravery, is alleged to have said that she would either get herself killed or end up in a wheelchair.) Perhaps with hindsight (these conversations took place some eight years after Diana died) the theme of death ran through several such conversations. Clive James wrote: 'I was even convinced . . . that she would get herself killed . . .'[31]

17. Fall from Grace

'Events of the last few weeks . . . have enforced the perception of the Princess as a predatory figure preying on other women's men'[1]

Early in 1995, Diana drew up what her secretary called 'her own, very private manifesto'. She wanted her 'true worth to be recognised', the chance to use her 'healing interests and abilities', to 'address increasing world problems', 'to make a contribution on a world platform . . . and to deal with many countries'.[2] In essence she saw her priority as being 'survival against the forces who had so nearly suffocated her'. That year she was to make no fewer than ten overseas trips. Sadly, as Jephson revealed, these brilliantly successful trips, which did more good for the British image abroad than months of trade visits and business initiatives, were regarded with suspicion at Buckingham Palace and the Foreign Office. 'I think they're all scared of the Princess of Wales,' a member of the Royal Family said at the time.[3] Diana had cultivated a relationship with the Foreign Secretary, Douglas Hurd, who had regarded her with 'a kind of paternally concerned interest' but he left office that year to be replaced by Malcolm Rifkind. If not to the bureaucrats, 'the grey men' whom Diana so resented, Diana's beauty, charisma and fame made her welcome wherever she went in the world. 'While I fenced tensely with officials in Buckingham Palace and the Foreign Office about the precise definition of the Queen's stricture that the Princess should not represent her abroad,' Jephson wrote, 'Presidents, Kings and even − in the case of Japan − an Emperor let it be known that they expected the Princess of Wales to come to tea when she was in town.'[4]

Typically of Diana, she had called in the best advice before the Japanese tour − her friend Clive James, the Australian writer, wit,

poet and broadcaster who had been among her legion of platonic
admirers for the past few years. James presented a television show
which featured Japanese wannabes doing the most outrageous
stunts. He was also a serious student of the Japanese language and
Japanese literature. Diana asked him what would be the best thing
she could do there, apart from her hospital visits. James advised
her to learn some Japanese phrases and sent her his Japanese teacher.
Diana, in his words, 'flew to Japan, addressed a hundred and
twenty-five million people in their own language, and made the
most stunning impact'.[5] The published purpose of the visit was to
enable Diana to acquaint herself with the work of various charitable
centres for the old, the young and the disabled, and to formalize
the link between Great Ormond Street Hospital for Sick Children,
of which she was president, and Tokyo's National Children's
Hospital. As Jephson put it, 'such innocent objectives nevertheless
attracted scrutiny from those now convinced that the Princess of
Wales was a dangerous guided missile, ready at a moment's notice
to explode with devastating effects for British diplomacy and the
prestige abroad of the British royal family'.[6] Diana was invited to
tea at the Imperial Palace, the ultimate accolade for a visitor to
Japan. She mischievously made the most of it. Already towering
over the diminutive imperial couple, she chose the highest heels
she could find. 'It's very important to wear really high heels,' she
joked with Jephson. 'I'm already taller than the Emperor, but it
won't do any harm to look just that bit taller!' Next day the
eye-catching photographs of the meeting featured Diana,
curtseying respectfully low, the main feature of the picture being
the consequent exposure of 'a generous expanse of athletic royal
thigh'.[7]

    Diana followed this up with a highly successful fund-raising trip
to Hong Kong under the auspices of entrepreneur David Tang
and with the blessing of the Governor, Chris Patten. In one
evening she raised a quarter of a million pounds for medical and
youth charities in Hong Kong and China, notably for the work of
the Leprosy Mission, a cause to which she was especially attached.
She made fund-raising charity trips to Venice, Paris and New York

and two more official visits – to Russia and Argentina. She carried out 127 public engagements as compared with only ten in 1994 following her 'time and space speech'. On one such trip, Diana's companions witnessed one of the odder manifestations of her compassionate impulses. While they were eating their dinner in first class, Diana was sitting apart listening to her Walkman. Suddenly she snatched off the Walkman, leapt to her feet and dashed into the compartment behind, to return with a yelling baby in her arms. Despite all her efforts to calm it, the baby continued to scream and there soon appeared its anxious and somewhat alarmed mother to whom Diana had no alternative but to relinquish the child.

But at the same time as her public exploits were winning her praise, the old, reckless, self-destructive Diana was at work. In February Oliver Hoare's chauffeur went to the *News of the World* with damning details of their affair. By now even Diana recognized there was no future in their relationship and, after the *News of the World* revelations, that it was positively dangerous for her to continue. She dumped Hoare, who wrote her a characteristically charming letter thanking her for all the happiness she had given him and returning her present of a pair of her father's cufflinks. Despite her resolutions as to her public career, in private she could not find happiness. The year 1995 was to be a particularly difficult and unstable year for her. She was lonely at Kensington Palace with both the boys away at boarding school. During one of her visits to the Chelsea Harbour gym in Fulham, she met England rugby hero Will Carling, whose dark, rugged good looks and sporting celebrity appealed to her. They met at the Harbour Club and at Kensington Palace; Carling confessed that his marriage was in trouble, Diana sympathized.

Diana led him on, while at the same time mocking him to the staff at Kensington Palace as 'my puppy dog'[8] (he always visited accompanied by his black Labrador). The same 'puppy' simile was used by Carling's former personal assistant, Hilary Ryan, in a *News of the World* report in August that Diana had been having 'secret trysts' with Carling at Kensington Palace. She told of furtive meetings, long, secretive phone calls, and the pet names they used for each other. No evidence was produced of any physical relationship, although it was rumoured that Carling had made some indiscreet – indeed ungentlemanly – remarks about Diana to fellow rugby players. Will Carling gave a newspaper interview confessing that his meetings with Diana had been a mistake, and that he regretted the distress he had caused his wife Julia. Julia Carling herself was no shrinking violet and experienced at dealing with the media. She told the same newspaper that she did not want her husband seeing Diana again, saying, 'She picked the wrong couple this time.' (Ever supportive, Prince William told Diana in front of Piers Morgan that at school he used a photograph of Julia Carling as a dart board.) The effect of Julia Carling's stand on Diana's public reputation was to tarnish her in a way that had not happened before. Following on the Hoare affair, and now this, the tabloids described her as a home wrecker. She became the butt of snide jokes. On the BBC's sports quiz *They Think It's All Over*, the England cricketer David Gower and the footballer Gary Lineker laughed heartily at jokes about Diana and men made by comedienne Jo Brand. It was no secret that Diana had asked Lineker to lunch and that his wife had absolutely forbidden it. Asked by presenter Nick Hancock if he had lunched with her, Lineker replied ungallantly, 'That woman's too much trouble.'[9] But Carling, it seems, could not keep away from Diana. The stories were repeated at the end of September when the Carlings split. In Diana's circle it was alleged that Diana had turned her back on her old friends Kate Menzies and Catherine Soames when they had criticized her over the Carling affair.[10]

On 20 August 1995, a vicious attack on Diana appeared in the *Mail on Sunday* under Nigel Dempster's byline: 'Is Diana the Mistress of Manipulation?' the headline asked. The subhead was even more damaging: 'Mental anguish behind fall of Diana the "saint"'. 'Events of the last few weeks, concerning Diana's so-called relationship with Will Carling, the recently married captain of the England rugby football team, have enforced the perception of the Princess as a predatory figure preying on other women's men,' the article announced. She was known as 'Zuleika' (after the *femme fatale* of Max Beerbohm's novel *Zuleika Dobson*) 'among those who wish to see her marginalized from mainstream British life'. She was like her mother, who was a bolter, and had failed to sustain a marriage, the newspaper asserted, adding a comment by 'an observer': 'The apple does not fall far from the tree.' Worst of all, the article asserted that Diana was suffering from a mental illness.

Rumours of mental instability had been circulated by Diana's enemies within St James's Palace. It was alleged at the time the Dimbleby book was being written that Diana had a psychological profile which was found to fit a well-recognized if controversial condition called Borderline Personality Disorder, or BPD for short. Eight symptoms characterizing BPD had been put forward at the time, most of which neatly fitted Diana's behaviour, all of which were quoted in the *Mail on Sunday* piece. This theory was allegedly considered unsuitable for inclusion in the Dimbleby biography; it was, to put it mildly, diagnosis from a distance and extremely damaging. Put otherwise, it was another manifestation of the continuing argument between partisans of the Prince and those of the Princess: was Diana disturbed before she married or did his behaviour with Camilla and the circumstances surrounding the couple drive her to bulimia and irrational behaviour? Diana was not unaware of the whispers in Charles's circle and from his defenders in Buckingham Palace that she was 'mentally unstable' as a result of 'bad blood' (a favourite in aristocratic circles, in which bloodlines were so important) deriving from the Fermoys – dating particularly from the suicide of her uncle Edmund in August 1984. In 1994, however, the BPD allegation had been considered too scandalous to make public. But for Diana's enemies it was too good to waste, hence its publication in Dempster's column. The allegations were repeated later that year on a television programme, but their first formal manifestation did not come out until the publication of the book by pro-Charles author Penny Junor, entitled *Charles: Victim or Villain?*, published in 1998, after Diana's death. According to Junor, it was several years before the Prince realized that Diana had a problem.

In fact, the theme of Junor's book went further: Diana had always been mad, bad and dangerous to know and this had been the case long before she knew the Prince. The father of one of Diana's Norfolk schoolfriends had gone so far as to make specific inquiries about where Diana would next be going to school. He was concerned about the effect his daughter's friendship with Diana would have on her. Junor's book also included what is rumoured to have been Ruth Fermoy's deathbed statement to Dimbleby, that she could have kicked herself for not having the courage to warn the Prince about Diana before they married, a statement that hardly fitted the facts as they were in 1980. The argument that the unfortunate Prince was dealing with what amounted to a madwoman was too basic to the case of Charles v Diana and it was never going to go unsubstantiated for long.

At the time the *Mail* article was published, Diana was suffering feelings of continuing insecurity and increasing paranoia. Alone in the claustrophobic atmosphere of Kensington Palace, she would imagine all sorts of things; among them was her conviction that she was being bugged: 'She had a wild and vivid imagination,' a former aide said. 'You know, talk of bugs – I have to say this was absolute nonsense because besides the private lines, the other lines there came through Buckingham Palace switchboard and if they wanted to listen in they could listen in without putting bugs on and she knew as well as anybody else that the majority of her calls went through Buckingham Palace because it was a safety valve. Because all sorts of peculiar people would telephone. So to avoid that, she would give the switchboard number and they would filter. They wouldn't put anybody through without talking to the principal first, saying I have so and so on the line . . .'[11] A senior ex-police officer also dismissed the idea that Diana was being bugged: 'Some people are very ready to believe that there is this undue interest, that their house is being bugged or their letters being opened or their phone is being tapped . . . but the reality is that it's terribly difficult to get permission to do any of those . . .

There are not the facilities to do instant tap at the drop of a hat. The permissions one has to get, the difficulty in getting it, the difficulty in actually technically doing it is quite considerable. That doesn't stop people believing that they are being tapped or followed or whatever. And it's usually the sign of someone who's quite paranoid . . .'[12]

But beyond actual bugging, Diana did have grounds for her suspicions in another way. 'It must have been very difficult for her,' a close friend said. 'She was spied on, I've no doubt about it. I think that after she withdrew her police bodyguards, I think the police continued to maintain an interest in her, they say because they needed to be sure she was safe but one wonders . . . there's a lot of prurient stuff went on, a lot of people took a great deal of pleasure in finding out who she was seeing and making sure it was leaked to the papers . . .'[13]

One day the well-informed *Daily Mail* told Jephson that the Princess did not trust the loyalty of even those close to her. 'I knew my employer well enough to recognise a career prospects review when I saw it,' Jephson wrote. That year others who had served Diana long and loyally were made redundant, namely head butler Harold Brown and the head chef, Mervyn Wycherley, surplus to requirements now that Diana's divorce was approaching. Brown's loyalty and discretion were recognized by Princess Margaret who hired him herself, ensuring he kept his apartment.

The beneficiary of all these redundancies was Paul Burrell, the former Palace footman, who had not wanted to leave his comfortable family cottage at Highgrove when the division of the Waleses' staff had taken place in 1992. 'He was on to a good thing down there,' said a former aide of Diana's. 'He liked the country, was used to the country, and it wasn't a case that Diana had asked for him, it was a case that the Prince didn't want him because he had shown whose camp he was in. And so you could hardly fire someone because they happened to be in someone else's camp; you find him another job and that's what he did.'

By 1995, however, Burrell had become to some extent Diana's

confidant, or at least confidential servant. Despite having a wife and two children, Burrell was besotted with his employer, even to the extent of adopting her mannerisms; nothing was too much in order to please her. He spent long hours at Kensington Palace with her, to the annoyance of his wife, who might have said, as Diana was subsequently to say, that there were 'three of us' in the marriage. It was an emotional attachment: Diana became the centre of his world. 'She got rid of all her dressers and staff and people like that,' said David Griffin, Princess Margaret's chauffeur, who had frequent conversations with Diana while waiting outside the Palace for his employer. 'And then he [Burrell] started to take on a role, like we used to call him Mrs Danvers [the sinister housekeeper in Daphne du Maurier's *Rebecca*] and everywhere she used to go he'd appear, and that sort of thing. Stupid things, like she used to ask me "Can you give my car a going-over", which I did. He came out one morning and said, "I'll do this from now on . . . he thought it was a great honour for me to do it . . ."[14] Diana was as popular with the Kensington Palace staff as her butler was not: no doubt jealousy may have played a part but, used as they were to serving the Royal Family, the relationship between the Princess and her butler was a source of comment: 'We used to call them "the Odd Couple" sometimes,' Griffin said. 'It wasn't done in a detrimental way, but it seemed sort of strange . . .'[15] Even Burrell was not exempt from Diana's suspicion and, in some cases, understandably. On one occasion Griffin was passing her front door when Diana came out. 'She slammed the door with such ferocity that I thought "Oh!!" and I said, "Good morning, we're not in a very happy mood today, are we?" "No, we're not," she said. "Oh," I said, "what's happened?" And she said, "He'll have to go." And I said, "Who's got to go?" She said, "He [Burrell] will", and I said, "Who?" "I caught him going through my letters," she says.' Later, Diana seriously intended to sack him when she discovered that he was running up huge telephone bills on her account.

One piece of evidence illustrating Diana's state of mind in the autumn of 1995, the famous 'letter' stating that her husband planned to have her killed, was published by Paul Burrell and dated, he said, October 1996. The letter ran:

> I am sitting here at my desk today in October, longing for someone to hug me and encourage me to keep strong and hold my head high. This particular phase in my life is the most dangerous. My husband [not in the book but published later] is planning 'an accident' in my car, brake failure and serious head injury in order to make the path clear for Charles to marry.
>
> I have been battered, bruised and abused mentally by a system for 15 years now, but I feel no resentment, I carry no hatred. I am weary of the battles, but I will never surrender. I am strong inside and maybe that is a problem for my enemies.
>
> Thank you Charles, for putting me through such hell and for giving me the opportunity to learn from the cruel things you have done to me. I have gone forward fast and have cried more than anyone will ever know. The anguish nearly killed me, but my inner strength has never let me down, and my guides have taken such good care of me up there. Aren't I fortunate to have their wings to protect me . . .[16]

Friends of Diana say that the mood in which this statement was written was more indicative of her state of mind in the autumn of 1995 than 1996. It could also be pointed out that in October 1996, after their divorce had come through, there would have been no necessity – even if he had had the inclination – for Charles to have her killed so that he could remarry which, by October 1996, he was legally free to do. Colin Tebbutt, ex-Royalty and Diplomatic Protection Department, now running his own security firm, was asked by Diana in 1995 to drive for her and provide protection with a two-man back-up when she needed him. Tebbutt had concerns about the letter: '. . . because being in charge of transport and still being a great friend of the private secretary, Michael Gibbins . . . why wasn't it pointed out to me? Why didn't somebody say to the team who were driving the car . . . and I knew the man who supplied it and the car was always under lock and key and always in a garage with an electrical lock. Could nobody say to me, "Colin, the brakes are dodgy" or "Somebody's going to make an attempt on her life"? Why didn't Burrell tell the private secretary to tell the chauffeur or the security team?'[17]

Other people who worked closely with the Princess did not believe that, although the text was undoubtedly in Diana's hand, it was addressed to Burrell in particular. 'Now, if she'd written that to Paul, it would have been "Dearest Paul" and in that case it would have been very much in his [Burrell's] interest to show that letter, but the very fact we didn't see it [the superscription] and the very fact that it wasn't even on the letter with not even a signing off [signature]. I know for a fact that it was a memo to herself and she would not bullet point it, she would just get it down.'[18] Another aide confirmed, 'this alleged letter to Burrell, yes she wrote it, the paper was genuine, the writing was genuine, but she did write notes to herself'. Often the theme of these memoranda would be the result of a conversation she had had recently and wanted to jot down as a memo to herself. They might, equally, be the result of some consultation with one of her therapists or clairvoyants. The point is that the memo was an expression of Diana's state of mind at the time and an illustration of the forces driving her towards what would turn out to be the greatest mistake of her life, the notorious *Panorama* interview. A year later, the idea of writing a memo such as this would never have crossed her mind. Yet, such had been the impact when Burrell's book was serialized, and so seriously was it taken when Burrell reproduced the text in his book, that Lord Stevens, the retired head of the Metropolitan Police, went so far as to interview Prince Charles about it for the purposes of his inquiry in 2005 into the death of Diana.

The idea of giving a spectacular television interview had been taking shape in Diana's mind throughout 1995, sparked by her meetings with two media giants of American television, Oprah Winfrey and Barbara Walters, both of whom she had invited to lunch with her at Kensington Palace, while her friends Clive James and David Frost had tried to lure her on to their shows as the ultimate celebrity guest.[19] In the end it was a rank outsider, Martin Bashir, who persuaded her to give what was to become perhaps the most notorious television interview of all time. Bashir, then a junior journalist on the BBC's *Panorama*, succeeded where the other luminaries failed and he did so by preying on Diana's fears for her security and safety. His original idea had been to do an investigative programme on the current fears about the activities of the Security Services in monitoring the lives of celebrities and the Royal Family which had been prevalent since the publication of the Squidgygate and Camillagate tapes in 1992 and 1993 respectively.[20] Andrew Morton, in his last book on Diana, published in 2004, was convinced that there would have been no interview had Bashir not tapped in to Diana's secret fears. According to Morton, Bashir first met Diana's brother, Charles, at Althorp in the summer of 1995 in order to discuss his suspicions of being bugged. Charles was suing the *Daily Express* for a series of articles alleging that he had helped to launder the proceeds of a multimillion-pound fraud carried out in New York by his close friend and best man at his first wedding, Darius Guppy. Spencer won £50,000 damages and an apology. At the same time he had taken out an injunction against his former head of security, James Waller, forbidding him from disclosing information about his private life and that of members of the Royal Family; this had followed the publication in March 1994 of a letter Charles had written to Diana in December 1993 warning her that her public appearances were damaging her popularity.

Allegedly through Spencer, Bashir secretly met Diana, whose insecurities he fed by convincing her that her apartment was being bugged. In order to advance his cause with Charles Spencer and Diana, according to Morton and, later, the *Mail on Sunday* (April 1996), Bashir had a set of forged bank statements made up by a graphic designer showing payments made to James Waller and a former business partner of Waller's, Robert Harper, from *Today*, the newspaper which had published Spencer's letter to Diana, and a Jersey-based company for unspecified services. Whatever the truth of the matter, something happened to persuade Diana to give the interview. The prime motive, according to this reading of the affair and the sentence of her October memo, written at the time of the negotiations with Bashir about the interview, about Prince Charles arranging her 'accidental death' and her references to 'my enemies', was fear for her own safety and a determination to make herself so popular as to be invulnerable. The interview was to be a pre-emptive strike. Diana's biographer, Sally Bedell Smith, attributes this paranoia to Bashir's warnings and it was at about the time of their meetings that Diana had insisted on having her apartment and her car swept for bugs. Bashir also apparently warned her not to trust Catherine Soames and Kate Menzies, although she had in fact already parted company with them, and, significantly, Julia Samuel, one of the most intelligent of her friends, whom she then dropped.[21]

Diana had previously consulted three of her media mentors, David Puttnam, Clive James and David Attenborough, about doing the Bashir interview. 'Because we had told her not to do it,' said one, 'in all three cases she gave us the impression that she'd listened to us and had decided not to do it and all three of us got quite a shock when she did.'[22] 'I mean, my argument was very simple, rather cynical in a way . . . whenever she used to bang on about the possibility of doing something like these interviews, was – you'd be mad to do it because once you've done it the weapon that it is ceases to exist, so you're handing over the one serious weapon that you have, and in a sense you're then just a victim of events, you have no control over events; whilst you haven't done it you are actually in control of events. So that was my position . . . and when I said that she always said, "You're absolutely right, of course you're right, I absolutely understand that." '[23] Clive James wrote in his remembrance of Diana after her death: 'I counselled her against it. I said if that happened the two camps thing would go nuclear, and continue until there was nothing left. She would be on the run forever and there would be nowhere to go . . . She seemed convinced, but of course she was pretending. She had already decided.'[24]

Several things moved Diana to take the fatal step of the *Panorama* interview: her longing to put her case to the people over the heads of her 'enemies' in the Establishment; her love of publicity on her own terms; her intrinsic belief in the rightness of her own instinct even over all the wise opinions she had been given by people who had only her interests at heart; her determination to counter allegations of Borderline Personality Disorder; and lastly, and, least attractively if understandably, the desire for vengeance. This was evident in her instructions to the BBC over when to release the news of the broadcast. On Diana's specific instruction[25] the BBC released their press announcement on 14 November, an unwelcome forty-seventh birthday surprise for Charles, on an official visit to Tokyo. Photographs taken at the time show him cutting a celebratory cake, his face expressing total dismay.[26] That morning Diana called the Palace to inform them of the interview which was to take place in six days' time. The Royal Family were, with justification as it turned out, appalled at what they regarded as the second betrayal after the Morton book. It was by now too late to do anything but wait and see.

The fifty-five-minute programme went out on 20 November. Dressed in black, wearing little jewellery, her eyes heavily ringed with kohl, Diana was in victim mode but nonetheless defiant, and seemingly oblivious to the significance of what she said in the context of the monarchy. Her words echoed the October 1995 letter as she spoke of her sufferings, her betrayal by her husband, the efforts of people to destroy her by painting her as mad, her bulimia; she admitted to her love affair with Hewitt, but with no one else. ('Yes, I adored him, yes, I was in love with him. But I was very let down.') Above all, the attack was directed at her husband, his mistress and their friends. They – 'her enemies' – had said she was 'unstable, sick and should be in a home of some sort in order to get better', and, when asked if Charles agreed with them, she said, quoting (without attribution) from a book by the former hostage Brian Keenan, 'there's no better way to dismantle a personality than to isolate it'. Asked what part Camilla Parker Bowles had played in the break-up of her marriage, she replied in the most memorable phrase of the evening, 'Well, there were three of us in this marriage, so it was a bit crowded.' She admitted to helping with the Morton book because she had wanted the true story of her unhappy marriage to be made public: 'I was at the end of my tether. I was desperate. I think I was so fed up with being seen as someone who was a basket-case, because I am a very strong person and I know that causes complications in the system that I live in.' The word 'strong' came in no fewer than four times. Some people 'in the Establishment that I married into, have decided that I'm a non-starter. Because I do things differently, because I don't go by a rule book, because I lead from the heart, not the head.' She, however, wanted to reign not officially but as a Queen of Hearts (a phrase borrowed from the works of her step-grandmother, Barbara Cartland) and to be an ambassador for Britain, giving affection and helping 'other people in distress'.

The key moment of the programme – the point at which Diana cut herself off from the monarchy and the Royal Family – came when she cast doubt on Charles's fitness to rule, and raised a further doubt as to whether he would succeed to the throne. 'It's a very demanding role, being Prince of Wales', she said, 'but it's an equally more demanding role being King. And because I know the character, I would think that the top job, as I call it, would bring enormous limitations to him, and I don't know whether he could adapt to that.' 'My wish,' she added with a sly dig, 'is that my husband finds peace of mind.' Speaking of herself in the third person, always a bad sign, she declared with an undertone of menace as well as defiance: 'She won't go quietly.'

It was a stunning – and to some a shocking – performance, watched by fifteen million people in Britain and millions more round the world. Diana's friends were horrified: 'Diana at her worst,' Rosa Monckton wrote. 'A brilliant suicide note,' said another. Camilla, watching with her family, apparently laughed at the theatricality of the 'Mad Cow', as she sometimes referred to Diana (possibly in reference to BSE) but its effect on her standing with the public would be even more drastic than the Morton book had been. Nicholas Soames loyally rushed on to the BBC's serious news programme *Newsnight* to declare that the interview showed 'the advanced stages of paranoia'.

The week before the broadcast, when it was too late for him to derail her plans, Diana finally told Patrick Jephson she had done the interview. He immediately rang the Queen's press secretary. Over the car phone Charles Anson was his usual laid-back self but there is no doubt that the news of what Diana intended to do caused consternation to the Queen and her staff. Diana refused to reveal the content of what she intended to say to anyone and the fact that it was to go out on *Panorama*, the BBC's flagship current affairs programme, only served to increase nervous suspicion. As it happened, even the chairman of the BBC, Sir Marmaduke Hussey, had been kept in the dark for the simple reason that he was married to one of the Queen's and Charles's favourite Women of the Bedchamber, Lady Susan Hussey. Had he been told of the project he would undoubtedly have moved heaven and earth to stop it. The director-general, John Birt, Hussey's chief executive, was in on the plan but did not inform his chairman, nor did he make any effort to stop it or even to tone down the content. The result was a serious rift between the Palace and the BBC. Nothing the Palace, Jephson or even Diana's lawyer, Lord Mishcon, could put forward succeeded in getting Diana either to reconsider or to reveal what she was going to say. After watching *Panorama*, the Palace, Jephson and the Princess's press secretary, Geoff Crawford, were in a state of shock. Crawford resigned immediately, although he accompanied the Princess on her tour of Argentina two days later. Jephson, his plans for Diana's rehabilitation and reintegration into the royal circle in ruins, determined to resign as soon as he decently could.

Diana remained resolutely convinced she had done the right thing. The night before, she had telephoned one of her mother figures: 'She rang me and said to me, "I've done the most wonderful interview, I've put everything right." I was slightly worried about it. She said, "You will watch it, won't you, and tell me in the morning?" I watched it, and it was so frightful I – literally – was thinking I'm never going to be able to stand up for her again

because it's so frightful, the *Panorama* thing. She rang me. The
telephone rang at eight o'clock in the morning – she was an early
riser, like me – and I couldn't . . . I had to pretend to be on the
other line because what was I going to say to her? Well, it was so
frightful that I did, I told her that I wasn't mad about it and she
was furious . . . I said it was a frightful mistake, and she didn't like
that at all, she hated being criticized. But it was appalling, it was a
total error of judgement.'[27] Diana's friend, who knew both Charles
and Camilla well and was much liked in court circles, encapsulated
the reaction of everyone who wished her well. In terms of a
royal future, she had thrown herself off the edge of the cliff. The
interview finished her friendship with Princess Margaret who was
outraged by Diana's remarks about Charles and the succession and
wrote her a stinging letter to tell her so, and Margaret's children,
previously so friendly, avoided her. The interview was devastating
for her sons; in her lack of consideration for their feelings and her
public admission of adultery she had behaved no better than
Charles. It was rumoured that William would not speak to her for
several days.

In public relations terms, however, the interview was a popular
success. Diana had appealed to her own followers, the converted:
favourable results of newspaper polls helped convince her that she
had done the right thing. Two days after the interview, buoyed
up with confidence, she left for a pre-arranged charities trip to the
Argentine, Britain's erstwhile enemy in the Falklands War. The
democratic President, Carlos Menem, took Diana's visit as a signal
that 'Argentina has gradually regained a position in the world
which it had lost'. Faced with her return to London and normality
– at least her form of it – realization of the possible consequences
of what she had done had begun to dawn on Diana. Patrick
Jephson commented sharply, 'she had taken the biggest possible
injection of her favourite drug, and now she felt even worse'.[28]

While St James's Palace may have been happy to see Diana
publicly imploding, Buckingham Palace was not. Jephson was still
trying to put together the broken pieces of Diana's relationship
with the Palace, presenting a blueprint for their future dealings.

He suggested that Diana's secretarial staff should move to offices in Buckingham Palace, and that the Queen's press office should deal with her public relations. He proposed removing her from dependence on Charles for her financial support, and that Buckingham Palace should provide domestic back-up for her apartment at Kensington Palace. Finally, her areas of work both abroad and at home, charitable and public, should be clearly defined and agreed. Both he and Diana attended a meeting at the Palace, when it became obvious that, while Jephson might have hoped to lure his thoroughbred into the safety of the Palace stable, the Queen's staff were not entirely willing to receive her, having been bruised once too often by Diana's initiatives, of which the *Panorama* interview had been just one too many. On 29 November, Jephson and Diana attended a meeting with the Queen's principal officials at the Palace, headed by her brother-in-law, Robert (Sir Robert since 1991) Fellowes. Given the guarded response his proposals received, Jephson soon realized they were doomed. 'Whatever goodwill there might have been at Buckingham Palace towards her as a person,' he recalled, '– and I had no doubt there was plenty, not least from Robert himself – the offence she had caused was too great. It was a classic case of "love the sinner hate the sin".'[29] Furthermore, the Prince's team were not willing to see the Princess transferred to the shelter of Buckingham Palace, as Jephson proposed. 'A move under the wing of the senior household, and hence to the centre of royal power, was hardly going to have the marginalising [of Diana] effect they undoubtedly hoped for,' Jephson commented.

Still unaware that events were moving on without her, Diana flew with Jephson by Concorde to New York to receive a humanitarian award from her old admirer Henry Kissinger on 12 December. It was an American occasion of the kind which always stimulated and empowered her in distinct contrast to the difficult atmosphere reigning at home. 'There were motorcades, Secret Service agents, adoring crowds and rooms full of rich, powerful and beautiful people to be charmed,' Jephson wrote of his last foreign trip with his employer. As a gesture of appreciation,

Diana appointed her old friend and supporter Liz Tilberis, formerly editor of *Vogue* in London, now New York editor of *Harper's* and suffering from what was to be terminal cancer, as her honorary lady-in-waiting. She returned to the Harlem Children's Hospital, scene of her moving visit six years earlier. As always, the welcome she received in America had its effect on her: Diana in New York, Jephson recalled, was a different person from his temperamental London employer.

She returned to the gloomy confines of Kensington Palace full of confidence to take on 'her enemies', the first of whom was to be Alexandra 'Tiggy' Legge-Bourke, employed by Charles to be his Girl Friday and to look after William and Harry. Diana had been jealous of Tiggy's closeness to her sons since her appointment, when a photograph of Charles kissing her on a skiing holiday had convinced her, quite groundlessly, that Charles and Tiggy were having an affair. Tiggy's visits to her private gynaecologist that year prompted Diana, disastrously, to conclude that she had had a termination and that the baby had been fathered by Charles. At the Christmas staff lunch on 14 December, she confronted the unfortunate young woman. '*So sorry* to hear about the baby,' she smiled. Tiggy was horror-struck, almost fainted, and had to be helped from the room by Charles's valet Michael Fawcett. Diana was triumphant but at St James's and Buckingham Palace, where Tiggy was universally liked, there was consternation and disgust. Tiggy instructed her lawyers; Sir Robert Fellowes telephoned Diana to find out precisely what her allegation implied when Diana gleefully repeated the allegation to him. Sir Robert investigated and found the whole affair groundless, as he informed Diana in a stern official letter rebutting what she had said. Her allegations were completely without foundation, he told her; Tiggy's relationship with the Prince had never been anything other than a professional one: 'on the date of the supposed abortion, she was at Highgrove with William and Harry. It is in your own best interests that you withdraw these allegations . . .' Attached was a private note to Diana: 'This letter is sent from one who really believes that you've got this whole thing dreadfully wrong, and that you *must* realise it – please.'[30] Later that month, lunching with friends at a favourite Italian restaurant in Chelsea, La Famiglia, before going down to Eton to meet Charles for the Christmas carol service, she was 'very pensive' and 'very nervous': 'she was very brittle and her mouth was much tighter, she was doing that whole lowering the head thing,' an observer said.[31] Diana, the goddess of New York, had metamorphosed into Diana, the Naughty Little Girl, about to meet the Grown-ups.

The blow fell a week before she was due to take William and Harry to Sandringham for Christmas. A letter arrived from the Queen, addressed in her handwriting to 'Dearest Diana' and ending 'With love from Mama'. Its content, however, was stark: having consulted both the Prime Minister and the Archbishop of Canterbury, the Queen had come to the conclusion that it would be in the best interests of the country to end the uncertainty and for Charles and Diana to take steps to divorce. Diana, according to her butler Burrell, to whom, he said, she showed the Queen's letter, sat down to reply, saying to her mother-in-law that she needed time to reflect. Time, however, was exactly what she was not going to be given; a letter from Charles arrived. Their marriage was beyond repair, he wrote, representing a 'national and personal tragedy'; since divorce was inevitable, it should be done quickly in order to resolve the 'sad and complicated situation'.[32] The 'fairy tale' was definitively over.

As a gesture of goodwill, the Queen still extended her invitation to Diana to spend Christmas at Sandringham. A royal invitation amounts to a royal command but Diana had gone too far to care. Discussing the Queen's letter with her butler, she had shown no interest in the constitutional issues of divorce. Enraged that the government and the Church had been consulted over her marriage, she had 'yelled', 'This is my marriage and it is no one else's business.' As for the Queen's reference to 'the interests of the country', her reaction was 'In the country's interests, is it? What about the interests of me? What about the interests of my boys?'

celebrities, she had a worldwide public not only for her beauty and charm, but for her compassion for the poor and sick which communicated itself to anyone who saw her. And, as she frequently said, she was determined to use this power to help people.

She had already taken a step which symbolized the sloughing off of her old life, deciding to auction her old wardrobe for charity. The idea had been William's. He had said, 'Mummy, you're running out of cupboard space and you're not going to wear any of those again, and I really think something should be done with them, and what will you do with them, send them to a charity shop?' Diana said, 'No, I can't do that. They're too well known, they're too well photographed, why don't we make some money for charity out of it?' When Meredith Etherington-Smith asked William if it had been his idea, 'He said, "Yes, it was my idea – we don't want Mummy wearing any of those again" – and he said it rather firmly.'[5] Some of the clothes were more than ten years old, dating from her earlier, frillier period, before Victor Edelstein had given her a more sophisticated look.

The vehicle was to be a Christie's sale of the clothes for the benefit of the National AIDS Trust, which included two of her friends, Marguerite Littman and Christopher Balfour, chairman of Christie's, with whom she had first discussed the project at lunch in July 1996. Meredith Etherington-Smith, then marketing director of Christie's Worldwide, was to be their representative for the sale, handling all aspects of it, including the cataloguing of each item.

'Christopher Balfour summoned me one morning and said, "Interesting project for you. The Princess of Wales wants to sell her clothes." I said, "Don't be stupid, what are you talking about?" And he said, "She wants to sell her clothes because she's not going to be wearing kind of big ball dresses any more, she's got a new life, she wants to sell them in aid of Marguerite's AIDS Crisis Trust and the Royal Marsden . . . You leg it down to Kensington Palace and meet her . . ."'[6] Wearing her good luck black jacket with starfish buttons, Meredith arrived at the Palace to be met by Burrell, 'smiling but looking slightly nervy'. He took her coat, asking her to wait. 'He nips upstairs and I subsequently learned from her that he'd actually gone to say, "She looks all right . . ." because she was actually rather nervous, she was as nervous as I was about meeting me for some reason. Apparently I passed muster – I was filtered through by the butler and went up this very grand staircase which was obviously part of the original baroque KP, to see this amazing human being dressed in a white T-shirt and sneakers and a navy blue cardigan, also looking rather nervous . . .'

'It's very curious,' Meredith recalled. 'I've met a lot of very famous people but no one as famous as Diana, visually famous anyway. But there's a difference between visual fame and people who are famous for who they really are. In the months after September 1996 when we first met, I formed a very different opinion of her from the one I had read about. What I'd thought she was like was totally unlike the side of her she presented to me.'[7]

Meredith surmised that Diana was very comfortable in the company of older women. 'I think possibly, without being too psycho-therapeutic about it, because of the lack of a mother . . . most of her confidantes apart from Rosa Monckton, were actually older women – Annabel Goldsmith, Elsa, Marguerite – and I think she felt very comfortable, they weren't competition, they were fun and she could become slightly girly with them without the baggage of "I'm the most beautiful person in the world" . . .' It was decided that Diana should be involved all the time. ' "It's going to be partners",' Meredith said. ' "I'll never do anything and make any decision without referring to you." ' 'There wasn't one decision that wasn't discussed with her, faxed to her, okayed by her . . . And as a result of that, I worked with her for nine months, pretty much, and we didn't have one what I call eyelash moment.' Asked what she meant, Meredith explained: 'That sort of look, when she kind of retreated into herself and that hair came over the forehead and the head went down and she looked up [through her lashes] . . . it was a very nice and fun working partnership.'[8]

Meredith bought a green leather book which Diana filled with the catalogue entries in her big loopy writing. 'That writing reminds me so much of so many people who were at West Heath . . . She was not a stupid Sloane, she was much more perceptive about herself than you would ever think from just looking at the image or reading the press or seeing her on television. I think she was one of the smartest people I've ever met. Because West Heath was basically knitting for Sloanes when she was there. In my generation we used to laugh at them, we used to say they did O levels in Hamster Husbandry, and I think it was a shame because she had great natural common sense . . .'[9]

Meredith realized that it would be wise to keep a certain distance between them. 'She was a tremendous charmer in the fact that she wanted to draw people into her web and then, having drawn them into the web, when they were totally enslaved by her, then she got bored . . . I felt my job was to always be slightly removed . . . At the second or third meeting, she said, "You must call me Diana." I said, "Actually no, I'd be happier with Ma'am, because as far as I'm concerned that's what you have been and you are . . ." Which went down really well. She said, "Come on, call me Diana", and I said "No", and a slight distance was maintained. Because she talked about other people, "so and so is getting kind of boring, she's ringing up the whole time", I said to her, "Your problem is you are too damn charming and they get completely enthralled by you and have to have the fix", and she laughed and said, "I suppose you're right." And I said, "It's a weapon isn't it, charm? You can convert people." And she said, "You're quite right, but I haven't had that many weapons in my life. What you've got you use."'[10]

Among other things, they discussed Diana's campaign against the use of landmines. Diana told Meredith that she had written to the Foreign Office asking them if she could become a roving ambassador – 'Of course they turned me down . . . I've decided to do it on my own and I'm going to do it for a cause and the cause is going to be landmines. It's appalling the damage they do, and no one cares and they just spray them all over the place like ghastly bulbs. At least I can do something good with this kind of presence, you know, the opportunities I have, well, they're not opportunities, they're huge open gateways . . .'[11]

'Discouraged from becoming a roving unofficial ambassador,' William Deedes, who accompanied her to both Angola and Bosnia on landmine research trips, wrote,

she sought to address herself to various issues in the world which were being neglected. There were millions of them [landmines] scattered round the world. They lurked wherever there had been conflict. A few charitable organisations were engaged in locating and lifting them, but it was discouraging as well as dangerous work because more mines were being constantly laid in the wars bedevilling Africa. The manufacturers of these mines represented a huge vested interest, which reduced the chances . . . of an international ban . . . defence forces in Britain, America and much of Europe saw the mines, properly laid and charted, as legitimate means of defence . . .[12]

Diana had been in discussion with Mike Whitlam, head of the British Red Cross, about renewing her work for the organization. The result was a visit in January 1997 to Angola, the scene of prolonged civil war, under the auspices of the Red Cross and with a BBC television crew in attendance to film a documentary to raise money for the British Red Cross Landmines Appeal. Lord Deedes, who had been an advocate of a landmines ban since 1992, travelled with her for the *Daily Telegraph*, accompanied by mostly unenthusiastic and cynical members of the press corps. Deedes, who had been briefing Diana about landmines on visits to Kensington Palace, paid tribute to the drawing power of Diana's presence: 'Nobody took a blind bit of interest in landmines until she came along,' he said. The journalists, accustomed to accompanying royal visits in daintier surroundings than Angola, were, Deedes said, 'dismayed' by the state of the capital, Luanda, with stinking rubbish piled high in the hot streets. *Sunday Times* reporter Christina Lamb, young but nonetheless a veteran war reporter, had certainly been cynical about Diana in Angola. She was impressed: despite the heat and the smells Diana had come to work and work she did. Angola, said Lamb, was one of the few remaining places in the world where most people had no idea who she was, and therefore it was all the more remarkable to see the effect she had on the amputees she went among. 'The Red Cross whisked us from one hospital to the next,' Lamb wrote,

each with ever more horrific scenes of skeletal figures with missing arms, missing legs, and blown off heads – victims of some of the 16m land-mines scattered round the country. Many of the injuries were so grue-some I could not bear to look, despite years of Third World reporting. But Diana never turned her head away. Instead, she had something I'd only ever seen before in Nelson Mandela – a kind of aura that made people want to be with her, and a completely natural, straight-from-the-heart sense of how to bring hope to those who seemed to us to have little to live for.[13]

Diana insisted on going to Huambo and Cuito where the war had left the countryside infested with mines. The television reporter Sandy Gall described Diana's action as extremely cour-ageous: he had encountered mines in Afghanistan and knew how dangerous it could be to walk through 'cleared' minefields. Just before it was reluctantly agreed to allow her to visit these 'hell-holes', as Deedes described them, in London two journalists from *The Times* and the *Daily Telegraph* had entertained a junior minister, Lord Howe, to lunch. Expressing the usual Establishment view of Diana, he had been critical of her visit and called it political interference – the usual cliché 'loose cannon' came up. The minis-ter's remark caused heightened interest in Diana's trip: as Deedes put it, 'if it was causing offence to the Tory Government, that doubled its news value'.[14] Diana's comment to Deedes when he approached her in private next morning was 'idiot minister': to the cameras she insisted more diplomatically that the purpose of her visit was humanitarian and in no way political.

By now, Christina Lamb admitted, the visit had 'wiped out' all her past cynicism about Diana. 'That Lady-with-the-Lamp performance wasn't just for the cameras,' she wrote.[15]

Once, at a hospital in Huambo when the photographers had all flown back to their air-conditioned hotels to wire their pictures, I watched Diana, unaware that any journalists were still present, sit and hold the hand of Helena Ussova, a seven-year-old who'd had her intestines blown to pieces by a mine. For what seemed an age the pair just sat, no words needed. When Diana finally left, the young girl struggled through her pain to ask me if the beautiful lady was an angel . . . At the end of the Angola trip Diana said that the lasting image she'd take away was of that terribly ill young girl.[16]

The Angola visit was not the end of Diana's involvement with landmines that year. In mid-June she spoke at a conference in London on landmines under the auspices of the Mines Advisory Group held at the Royal Geographical Society, chaired by Deedes, who helped her draft her speech. With Mike Whitlam's advice she had drawn up a chart of landmine sites across the world, marked with red pins, which she kept in a corner of her sitting room at Kensington Palace. She told Deedes they should make another landmines expedition that summer, and, with the cooperation of Norwegian People's Aid and Landmine Survivors Network (LSN) from Washington, a three-day visit to Bosnia was arranged from 8 to 10 August. The party, which included Bill Deedes and Paul Burrell, by now Diana's inseparable shadow, flew out on a private jet owned by multimillionaire philanthropist George Soros. On the drive to Sarajevo they were joined by two Americans, Jerry White and Ken Rutherford, who had formed LSN after being maimed by landmines. White had lost one leg, Rutherford both. As the two Americans climbed awkwardly into the back of the Landcruiser, Diana turned round from her front seat to say, 'You can take your legs off, boys!' That broke the ice, Burrell recorded; the men had felt that they should keep their artificial limbs on in the presence of royalty.[17] Burrell, the Boswell of the landmines visits, recorded one very significant remark. Landmine victims can recall exactly where and when their accident happened: as they were discussing this, Diana remarked, 'My accident was on 29 July 1981 . . .'[18]

Deedes recalled with amusement his memory of Burrell, the protector. 'We stayed in a brand new hotel in Bosnia, and our rooms were opposite – she was one side of the corridor and I was the other side and I came out of my room in the morning and met Burrell coming out having delivered her breakfast, so I said to him, "Are you going downstairs? Let's have breakfast together." He said, "Yes, sure." I went downstairs, had my breakfast, went up to my room and found Burrell with a chair against her door looking very determined. And I said, "Hi, I thought you were coming to breakfast?" And Burrell said in tones of outrage, "The manager of this hotel burst into her room to ask her whether she approved of it because it's new." I said, "That's very continental, in Paris managers do." Anyway, he was not pleased, he sat there and said, "I'm staying here until she's dressed and ready to go out." That was an indication of the relationship – he was her protector.'[19]

On the last day of the visit they toured the ruins of Sarajevo. 'It had suffered cruelly during the Bosnian war, with mortar bombs falling constantly on the city, and much of the open space had been given over to burial grounds. Diana saw a woman tending her son's grave in one of the huge cemeteries there, walked up to her and embraced her silently, the two touching each other's faces with complete empathy.'[20] The same scene had taken place previously with a young widow whose husband had been killed by a mine while fishing. 'There being no interpreter present there could be very little said. What passed between them is beyond reckoning. When we parted, the widow seemed restored to life.' Diana had the unique gift of silent empathy. Deedes saw the two sides of Diana – 'All this,' he said, 'in the middle of a fling with Dodi Fayed.'[21] The same Diana who stood quietly embracing the bereaved mother in the Sarajevo cemetery would, within hours, be on the jet giggling with Burrell at the tabloid frenzy over her new affair. Aboard the plane she discussed with Deedes the prospect of attending an Oslo conference on landmines with a view to calling for a ban. 'Be careful,' Deedes told her. 'It's political.' 'I was going to write the speech with her . . . saying exactly how to keep out of politics for her but to get the landmine ban.'[22] On

the plane, Diana made a toast: 'Here's to our next country . . .'
Cambodia and Vietnam were on the list for October. She never
got to Oslo or to Cambodia or Vietnam. It was 10 August 1997
and she had only twenty-one days of life to live. 'She was only
involved with landmines from January 1997 until her death in
August,' Bill Deedes said. 'And there's no doubt at all that while
she was on the job she woke the world up as nobody else has
done.' In December 1997, in the wake of a surge of opinion
after Diana's death in favour of a ban on landmines, the Ottawa
Landmine Accord banning landmines was drawn up, to be signed
by forty countries. Mike Whitlam said: 'They would not have
been talking at the Canadian meeting, where they ratified the
Convention later that year, had she not gone to Angola. I would
stake my life on that. They actually acknowledged what she'd done
– at that meeting.'[23]

The landmines campaign had given her a new purpose in life;
she publicly announced in a speech in May, about eating disorders,
that she had finally beaten bulimia. She looked radiantly healthy.
Even her physical appearance had changed 'from a puppy to a
gorgeous lady', as one of her designers, Jacques Azagury, put it.
Catherine Walker, who had dressed Diana for much of her adult
life, said, 'the demure phase was over and so was her marriage but
what I hadn't anticipated was how quickly she would change and
begin wearing my sexier evening wear . . . her looks had changed
dramatically since she had first come to see me as a pale, slightly
plump, fragile-looking girl. Now she was tanned, fitter, more
muscular. She had become a perfectionist, working hard on her
body because of the scrutiny it was under and to help keep her
sane through her marital upheaval . . .'[24] In keeping with this free,
independent image, her skirts became shorter, her heels higher,
the lines of her dresses simpler and sexier. Now outside the royal
circle she could wear black for the first time since the disastrous
outing in 'that dress' at the Guildhall.

'She was growing up in front of my eyes,' said Meredith Etherington-Smith, who saw her from September 1996 through to July
1997. 'It was the most amazing year seeing this person growing

up and making choices, really important kind of choices, about landmines, taking that on, being serious about it, being really serious about this [Christie's] sale. She was professional, she was serious, she was grown up.' Even Diana's posture had changed, from the shy upward glance and hunched shoulders, to sitting erect and standing up straight. She was even stopping chewing her nails. Her fingernails, Meredith observed, 'got better as we went on'. 'She was generally more confident, she became a different sort of person, less the Princess of Wales and more Diana.'[25]

One thing she did take seriously was her role first as mother to the boys and second, as Meredith put it, as the Queen Mother of the twenty-first century. 'Her relationship with the boys was patently a wonderful one . . . She was a very good mother.[26] I expected them to be more protective of her than they were, and they weren't, they weren't mewling and puking and clustering round her. They didn't have a neurotic relationship. It seemed to me to be perfectly healthy and normal and nice and a great tribute first of all to Diana and secondly to Charles.'[27] 'Constitutional plans – well, she felt her long-distance role was to be the Queen Mother of the twenty-first century, that the influence the Queen Mother had had on her grandchildren in a way, she felt that was the kind of role which in a curious way she had been chosen for and one did feel that there was a bit of divine right entering into this, a little bit of fate. And she felt that William should be a democratic King, that the boys needed to have friends, that they needed to know their generation, they needed to know politicians, not just Tory ones, that they needed to know the Blair children. They needed to be part of contemporary English life, not an English life that was really out of date by the end of the war – and I'm paraphrasing some quite long conversations about this. And her job was to make sure they were released from the glass cage, and that when he did come to the throne, a lot of people would know him, and he wouldn't be a mystery, wouldn't be a royal freak, that he would be a person.[28] I think that she very much thought she would be a power behind the throne . . .'[29] Diana emphasized her desire that William should be 'a very English King': she felt that her Spencer blood had a lot to contribute. 'She felt that because of the spider's web of marital alliances and blood they [the Royal Family] weren't English. "I come from an English family," she had said proudly, and "we [the Spencers] are a lot older than they are." She was very proud of the Duke of Marlborough, for instance.'[30]

Diana was very anxious that her boys should not become isolated as the previous royal generation had been, as indeed their father had been. That was why she had wanted the boys, and William in particular, to go to Eton because they would have proper friends there and not sycophants. 'Diana said, "There's no messing around at Eton about someone being the heir to the throne. If you're not popular, charming, intelligent, or good at games, you're not going to rate, are you?" And so William knows a lot of people. And the interesting thing about that she said, "I think they'll be protection, those friends too. They've grown up together and they'll be protective."[31] And they are. You don't see grab shots of William that often, and why? Because his friends don't utter. She'd thought all this through. That's what I mean by being smart.'[32] 'They had money which they carried and spent and they went shopping. In other words she was trying to provide as normal a life as possible – they could come out from behind the glass window, and that was her great legacy.'

Meredith helped her shape her new modern image, with photographs by Mario Testino. One day she had commented to Diana how much better she looked in real life – without make-up, in jeans and a T-shirt and natural hair. 'You know you look so much better like that rather than with all the lacquered hair and the make-up. You've got wonderful skin, you don't need to slap all that stuff on. It's not modern. Jewellery isn't modern except for one of those little Tiffany diamond crosses – those chokers – for God's sake!' A set of photographs in the grand manner had been taken by Snowdon for the sale. 'They were fine but I wanted much more the girl who walked through the minefields. I wanted the woman I saw who looked amazing and modern. Discussing who should do them, Diana asked Meredith to choose someone she hadn't worked with before: 'I want someone new and I want to look how I feel inside. I feel like I belong to the twentieth century now, I really do. I'm doing modern things and I'm trying to lead a modern life, and I'm a single woman and that's how I want to look.'[33]

At the shoot with Testino in a Battersea studio, Diana had enjoyed herself immensely. Afterwards, as they were packing up, with music booming in the background, she started playing around, arm in arm with Mario Testino, imitating Naomi Campbell doing catwalk and Kate Moss doing catwalk. 'Everyone was screaming with laughter, including her, and she went that amazing rose pink colour [Diana always had blushed easily] and she looked fantastic, so full of energy and life. It was so sweet and so sad when I took the work prints [of the photographs] back and she said, "It was one of the happiest days of my life – and I really mean it." Looking at them she said, musing, "But these are me. Really, really me." She also said, "God, I think I look like Marilyn Monroe in those pictures ..."' She was quite obsessed with Marilyn Monroe, Meredith said, and in one of the pictures she did look like the young Marilyn. She often talked about her, and how she had fought the studio system in Hollywood on her own and won, because they had dumped her and then had to take her back. 'I think perhaps she felt there was another woman against the world,' Meredith said. 'I remember having a conversation about it with her once and her saying that she [Monroe] wasn't just a blonde fluffy thing, she was smart, and I think she identified with that.'[34]

Diana still felt beleaguered by court circles. She told Meredith she had 'a lot of enemies'. 'That sounds a bit paranoid,' Meredith replied. 'No, you know how it works. It's justification – I'm the baddie.' 'Well, all you have to do is to be a goodie, and you are a goodie by the example you set. That's why landmines – patently you have an enormous sympathy with people less fortunate than you are.' 'You call me fortunate?' 'I do, actually. I call you fortunate because you have the rest of your life in front of you and you have amazing opportunities to do amazing things ...' 'Yes,' she said, repeating that she had enemies and felt very much on her own sometimes. 'But you have good friends.' She replied, 'Yes. But you try fighting them [the Establishment enemies].' She was right, of course. It took a great deal of courage to face down her powerful enemies who saw the Establishment threatened by her very existence. Despite her supportive friends in all walks of life, the hostile pressure was very much alive and relentless and ready to pounce when 'goodie' Diana fell back into the ways of 'baddie Diana'. Diana believed that there was an agenda among Camilla and her circle and certain jealous courtiers to paint her as mad and sideline her in public life. 'They would have preferred her to disappear,' a friend said; 'she was deeply inconvenient – and enjoyed being deeply inconvenient.'[35]

Unfortunately, Diana could not remain 'goodie' Diana for long, without tripping up on her needier, more foolish and self-indulgent instincts. She quarrelled with her staff, helpers and 'star' friends. She quarrelled with her personal assistant Victoria Mendham, presenting her with her bill at the K Club which represented an astronomical sum for the woman to pay (Prince Charles later settled it). She quarrelled with Martin Bashir, backing out of a book she had contemplated doing with him. Under the terms of her divorce agreement, with its confidentiality clause which did not allow her to discuss her life in royal circles, the huge sums quoted by her potential publisher did not seem realistic. Moreover, it was alleged that Paul Burrell had repeated to her some disobliging comments Bashir had made to him about her. She quarrelled with Gianni Versace and Elton John when she backed out of contributing a foreword she had written to a book of photographs to raise money for John's AIDS Foundation, because, just after her divorce came through, she became nervous of what the Queen would think when she saw the book's suggestive images next to pictures of the Royal Family. (She was reconciled with Elton John at Versace's funeral in Milan on 22 July after the designer's murder in Miami.)

She did not abandon hopes of Hasnat Khan, nor of her dream of marrying him. In May she flew to Pakistan again on the pretext of helping Imran Khan and his hospital. She intended to meet

Hasnat's parents, his mother in particular, and if possible to convince them that she would be a suitable wife for their son. She persuaded Jemima Khan to go with her and Jimmy Goldsmith to lend them his jet. This was Diana at her most selfish and inconsiderate; Jimmy Goldsmith, as all his close circle knew, was dying, in fact was soon to die, and the last thing a member of his family wanted to do was to leave him and fly to Pakistan. Jimmy apparently told Jemima to go but to have the jet in readiness to leave Pakistan at any moment if necessary. This time Cosima Somerset did not go with her; she had been the victim of one of Diana's cruelly abrupt breaks, the reason apparently relating to something within the Goldsmith circle.

Diana had done everything she could to get close to Hasnat Khan's family, visiting his uncle Omar and his English wife Jane at their home in Stratford, and inviting Jane to stay at Kensington Palace. Through them she had made friends with Hasnat's grandmother, Nanny Appa, and she hoped to follow Jane's example and win acceptance into the aristocratic Pathan clan. Above all she needed to win acceptance from Hasnat's mother, the formidable, university-educated Naheed, who had bitter memories of the British when, after Partition, her family had been uprooted from their home in India. In Muslim society the mother is given great respect in the close extended family where arranged marriages are the rule, and each member of the family supports the other, often sharing the same house. Naheed did not approve of Western cultural images and her son, for all his Western ways, at heart shared her cultural beliefs. Although Diana hoped to follow the example of her friend Jemima, who in marrying Imran had converted to Islam and lived in the family complex in Lahore, that marriage was eventually to fail. It was a complicated situation both for Diana and for Hasnat's parents, anxious to see their son married (two arranged engagements had not led to marriage) but nervous of the consequences where Diana was concerned. Diana was staying with Imran and Jemima in Lahore when she was invited to visit Khan's family at their Model Town home in Jhelum, some one hundred miles to the north of Lahore, to meet not only

Hasnat's mother and father but also eleven members of his family. She dressed in a blue shalwar kameez which Jemima had had made for her in Lahore, and travelled incognito with two of Hasnat's sisters in an old black Toyota Corolla to avoid press attention. Nothing was said about marriage during Diana's visit and Diana appeared sombre as she left, but in the car with one of Hasnat's sisters she seemed confident that she could continue with her modern life and her campaigns at the same time as being married to Hasnat. On her return she confessed to Imran Khan how much she wanted to marry Hasnat.

The Hasnat Khan relationship continued on and off through the summer. Although he loved her, he continued to be undecided about the prospect of marriage and Diana's needy behaviour – constant telephone calls, sitting in a car in the street outside his house – following the pattern of her previous affair with Oliver Hoare, unnerved him. When Diana tried the old tactic of jealousy, being seen and photographed with Sikh businessman Gulu Lalvani, he was so angry that he broke off relations with her, not for the first or the last time.

With her private life in turmoil, Diana had her public life to distract her. In late May she had taken William to lunch with the newly elected Prime Minister Tony Blair and his family at his official country residence, Chequers, when they had discussed a possible future role for her. Blair, who displayed a unique ability to gauge popular feeling, saw the promotional potential of Diana as other more conventional politicians had not. June was a busy month: on 19 June she was in Washington for a meeting with Hillary Clinton; she then flew to New York to see her idol, Mother Teresa. (She had met her in Rome in February 1992 after visiting her hospice and orphanage in Calcutta on her India trip with Charles. This had greatly inspired her.) They walked hand in hand through the Bronx. Two days later, back in England, she drove herself up to Stratford to see the Omar Khans and eleven members of the family over from Pakistan, including her particular friend, Hasnat's grandmother, Nanny Appa. Two days after that, on 23 June, she was back in New York for the pre-sale party at

52

Diana enjoys the freedom of Nevis – her first holiday after her separation.

53

Diana is painted by Nelson Shanks as she sits for her first portrait as a
separated woman.

In 1994 Diana gave up police protection, which made her increasingly
vulnerable to the ever-merciless paparazzi.

Post-*Panorama*,
December 1995: Diana
accepts an award from
Henry Kissinger at the
'Humanitarian of the
Year' awards ceremony,
New York.

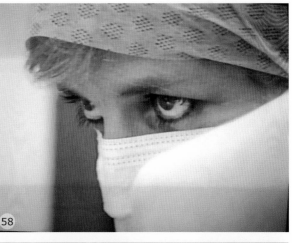

1996: Diana watching heart
surgery at Harefield Hospital,
Middlesex.

Diana with
Imran and
Jemima Khan
and Lady
Annabel
Goldsmith at
a fundraising
gala for Imran's
hospital charity
in Lahore.

28 August 1996: Diana on the day of her divorce from Charles, accompanied by Lucia Flecha de Lima.

61

Hasnat Khan.

New York, June 1997: Diana at a gala party to launch the Christie's auction of her dresses held in order to raise money for her charities. She is wearing a dress by Catherine Walker.

63

Diana visiting the Lord Gage Centre for old people, a Guinness Trust home in Newham, East London. Despite her global success, Diana was always dedicated to home-grown charities.

London, June 1997: Diana at the Christie's pre-auction party.

64

1997: Diana comforts a grieving mother during her final campaign to ban the use of landmines in Bosnia.

65

Angola, January 1997: Diana at Neves Bendinha, an orthopaedic workshop in Luanda.

66

August 1997: Diana and Dodi on the yacht *Jonikal* in St Tropez.

Diana and Dodi leave the Ritz moments before their fatal accident.

6 September 1997: the funeral of Diana, Princess of Wales. Her coffin is followed by her ex-husband, her ex-father-in-law, her brother and her two sons.

Tribute to the 'People's Princess': flowers and wreaths outside Kensington Palace after the death of Diana – an expression of the extraordinary popularity of a princess who touched the lives of many.

Christie's, flying back before the auction took place on 25 June to avoid the media circus. The sale was a great success: all the dresses sold, for a total of $3,258,750; the catalogue sales alone accounted for $2.5 million. The top price of $222,500 was paid for the 'White House dress' by Victor Edelstein which she had worn dancing with John Travolta.

While in New York before the sale on 23 June, Diana had continued her campaign to win over – and perhaps to learn from – powerful women. After seeing Katharine Graham and Hillary Clinton in Washington, she lunched at the fashionable Four Seasons in New York on 23 June with Anna Wintour, editor of American *Vogue*, and the British journalist Tina Brown, then editor of the *New Yorker*. The lunch had been arranged by Anna Wintour, with whom she had worked on a breast cancer fashion benefit the previous September. Despite her brave talk of her 'strength', the joy of giving help to people who needed it and her purpose in life – speaking of the landmines campaign, apparently, with an 'eerie' expression in her eyes – Tina Brown perceptively diagnosed 'the frantic Diana' lurking beneath the shining surface, so soon to be revealed in her summer antics with Dodi Fayed.

Beneath the glitter of her public life, her worldwide celebrity, the beauty which bewitched everyone she met, she was still insecure and a prey to the sense of rejection which never left her, encapsulated in the failure of her marriage. Out of the limelight, she was lonely, shut up in the gloom of Kensington Palace with the butler and addicted to soaps (*Brookside* was a favourite). The loneliness struck hardest at weekends when the boys were with their father: 'I stay in town. If I go out, I keep my eyes down or straight ahead. Wherever I go the press find ways to spy. Often I visit a hospice.'[36] Evenings, again, were hard; sometimes accompanied, first by Patrick Jephson, then driven by Burrell, she toured the seedier parts of London, spotting drug dealers or prostitutes to whom she often gave money in an effort to make them go home. The media siege served further to isolate her; to escape them she sometimes went out sitting on the floor of a taxi; from the time she dispensed with her protection in 1994 the hunt was on. Often the paparazzi waiting outside places like her therapist Susie Orbach's house would shout obscenities at her, 'spraying her down', hoping to catch shots of her distress and tears. Her fame and her royalty made it worse; 'that three-foot royal aura' around her, which Meredith Etherington-Smith had observed, made her almost unapproachable in an intimate way. At times on private social occasions, such as a dinner party at Taki Theodoracopulos's house, she seemed almost desperate to make friends, zeroing in on people, reaching out and drawing them in. Then, in order to seem 'one of the girls', she would rivet, and sometimes repel, people with her indiscreet talk, 'inappropriate', sexual conversation, venomous remarks about former friends, and raucous 'common' laugh. She was sadly aware that the baggage of her past would make it difficult to find the Barbara Cartland married life she still yearned for. 'Who would take me on?' she said. Yet at times she concluded that she would be better off single, the mother of the future King and the promoter of great causes.

Again, she was alone, even as far as her family was concerned. Sarah McCorquodale was the closest to her and sometimes acted as her lady-in-waiting, but she lived with her family on a large farm in Lincolnshire and therefore was physically distant. Relations with Jane, who lived close by, were awkward: despite Robert Fellowes' friendly attitude to Diana, he was still the Queen's principal private secretary and could not afford to take sides. For almost all the past four years, relations with her brother Charles had been tense, first in the misunderstanding over the house and then as a result of an unkind letter written by him in April 1996 referring to Diana's 'mental problems' quoted by a ferociously loyal Paul Burrell.[37] In private conversations Charles had made no secret of his opinion that his sister was dangerous to know. The terms of Spencer's letter were bitter: 'After years of neglect on both sides, our relationship is the weakest I have with any of my sisters . . . perhaps you have more time to notice that we seldom speak . . . I will always be there for you . . . as a loving brother: albeit one that has, through fifteen years' absence, rather lost touch – to the extent I have to read Richard Kay to learn that you are coming to Althorp

. . . I long ago accepted that I was a peripheral part of your life, and that no longer saddens me. Indeed, it's easier for me and my family to be in that position as I view the consternation and hurt your fickle friendship has caused so many.' Worst of all, from Diana's point of view, went on to refer to her 'illness' (presumably bulimia) and 'mental problems': 'I fear for you. I know how manipulation and deceit are parts of the illness . . . I pray that you are getting appropriate and sympathetic treatment for your mental problems.'[38] Recently, however, they had had a rapprochement when Diana had flown to South Africa in March, ostensibly to see her brother but actually in pursuance of her campaign for Hasnat Khan, and to check out the possibilities of South Africa as a place where they could eventually live.

Saddest of all, Diana had not been on speaking terms with her mother since Frances had given an interview to *Hello!* (for charity) in which she had claimed that the withdrawal of the HRH title did not matter and made other observations to which Diana objected. Diana had not been consulted over the article but in any case their relationship had been difficult after a series of telephone calls in which Frances had criticized Diana's behaviour with men. Frances had been convicted of drink-driving the previous year and was in a fragile emotional state. She was so anguished by the breakdown of relations with Diana that she even telephoned William Tallon, the Queen Mother's page, imploring him to get Diana to speak to her. Diana, as always when she felt she had been betrayed or let down, was implacable and sadly they never spoke again.

21. Fatal Summer

'Whom the gods love, die young' (Lord Byron, *Don Juan*, Canto IV, xii, from the Greek)

At the lunch in New York in June with Tina Brown and Anna Wintour, Diana had displayed 'unease' when asked how she was going to spend the summer holidays. The truth was that at that moment she had nowhere to go. July and August are difficult months for fashionable people without an invitation to a villa or a yacht for the sun, or a country house estate in Ireland or Scotland for the fresh air and the shooting. In any case, country house life was no longer an option for Diana who had cut herself off from that set long ago. Diana and 'the boys', with their concomitant detectives and paparazzi, were not normal guests. For Diana, it was the Jackie Kennedy Onassis dilemma: how to combine great celebrity with a need for privacy and family life. Later that month, she thought she had found the answer.

Mohamed Fayed, or, as he preferred to be called, 'Al' Fayed, had been born in 1929 in a village near Alexandria, Egypt, into a modest background which he preferred to forget.[1] Fayed had risen from his lowly beginnings through his connection with the Kashoggi family, Saudis of Turkish descent, who owed their position to their connection with the rulers of Saudi Arabia. In 1954 he had married Samira, the sixteen-year-old sister of Adnan Kashoggi, his contemporary, son of the head of the family Dr Mohamed Kashoggi. Their son, Emad, always known as 'Dodi', had been born in 1955; after Fayed's divorce from Samira shortly afterwards, Dodi had been brought up in straitened circumstances by his uncle, Salah, his father's younger brother, and his Italian wife, and strictly forbidden to associate with his mother. While his father travelled the world in search of a fortune through a series of dubious enterprises, the wretched Dodi had been left at home in Alexandria. Fayed's biographer wrote that Dodi was the casualty of his father's unsuccessful ambitions. 'Barely literate, speaking poor Arabic . . . Dodi endured an isolated and loveless childhood. Frequently he cried, and he even screamed during the night. Anguished by the suffering, the father would comfort his son in a shared bed, and, the following morning, would spend over-generously on toys. Torn between earning his fortune and caring for his son, Fayed . . . did little to alleviate the boy's misery.'[2]

By 1969, through his connections with Dubai, Fayed had amassed a fortune of £2 million, a considerable sum for those days. Within two years he had acquired a Rolls-Royce with chauffeur, a chalet in Gstaad, apartments at 60 Park Lane and the honorific 'Al' before his name. By 1972 he was the proud owner of a Scottish castle, Balnagown, a villa in St Tropez, and a yacht named *Dodi*. Dodi himself had been enrolled at Sandhurst, the British military training college, attended not only by British officer candidates but also by the sons of Arab princes like King Hussein of Jordan. After only four weeks, uneducated, materially spoiled, hopelessly indolent and unathletic, the boy had begged to be withdrawn. Mohamed Fayed, meanwhile, had added Barrow Green Court, Oxted, Surrey, to his property portfolio, qualifying him to be considered as the owner of a country estate. In 1975 he bought shares in Lonrho, the company set up by 'Tiny' Rowland, a capitalist adventurer whose wealth surpassed even Fayed's. Alarmed by the Department of Trade and Industry inspectors' adverse report into Lonrho's dealings, Fayed sold out, having made £8 million on the transaction. In 1979, still in search of the social position and prestige which eluded him, he bought the Paris Ritz.

Dodi, meanwhile, was pursuing a playboy life of girls and nightclubs: his aimlessness both irritated and alarmed his father. Dodi dreamed of a career in films and, as a reward for introducing his father to a Finnish beauty queen, Heini Wathen, whom he later married, Fayed set up a film production company for Dodi. Interested only in girls and drugs, Dodi had little to contribute to the enterprise. Financial success came when Fayed's company, Allied Stars, invested 25 per cent in the Oscar-winning film *Chariots of Fire*. Dodi was billed as executive producer – in fact he had done nothing but spend money on friends, girls and cocaine, even succeeding in getting himself thrown off the set of *Chariots*. Mohamed, furious at his son's decadent lifestyle, cut off his financial support. It was not for lack of love: 'Mohamed only wanted the best for him but the way in which he went about achieving the best for him, didn't help,' said a friend. 'But he loved him, worshipped him, adored him and if anybody tells you differently, they're wrong.'[3] In 1984, Mohamed Fayed had found a new source of wealth, becoming financial adviser to the Sultan of Brunei. In 1985, after a protracted war with his old partner, Tiny Rowland, Fayed bought the House of Fraser and became the owner of what was then a British national treasure, Harrods.

By then, Mohamed and Dodi had become reconciled; when Dodi's mother Samira died in March 1986, his father forbade him from attending her funeral, definitively cutting him off from his Kashoggi relations. He gave Dodi a £150,000 monthly allowance, free accommodation in Park Lane, Paris, St Tropez and his suite at the Pierre in New York and use of his fleet of cars, including a Mercedes, a Lagonda and two Aston Martins.[4] Meanwhile, a vengeful Rowland had asked that Fayed's purchase of Harrods should be referred to the Monopolies Commission, alleging dishonesty in its financing. Questions were asked by MPs friendly to Rowland in the House of Commons and another investigation, once again by the Department of Trade and Industry, loomed. Fayed gave donations to the ruling Conservative Party and, in tandem with a parliamentary lobbyist, Ian Greer, payments for questions to MPs. This, however, did not prevent the DTI from launching an investigation into the Harrods purchase. The investigation branded the Fayed brothers, Mohamed and Ali, 'liars' but the behaviour of Rowland in pursuing his vendetta led Lord Young at the DTI to decide neither to refer the case to the Monopolies Commission nor to release the inspectors' hostile report. The report was eventually released but Fayed's devious behaviour and that of Rowland had tarnished both of them. As a result of the DTI report, when the Fayed brothers applied for British passports in 1993 their application was rejected. Fayed had been deeply offended and, as a result, turned against what he liked to imagine was the corrupt British Establishment. Despite his wealth, he was a deeply controversial figure.

And the wealth was, to say the least, ostentatious. Fayed's Gulfstream jet was decorated in deep pink with Egyptian motifs and hieroglyphics woven into the fabrics covering the walls and floors. A penthouse in the style of a Roman villa adorned the new eighth floor of 60 Park Lane, with solid gold fittings on his double bath. In Harrods, the escalator was decorated with gilded Egyptian statues cast with Mohamed Fayed's features. He had nine houses to commute to with his Gulfstream, a Sikorski helicopter and a fleet of red armoured Mercedes limousines. Yet the British Establishment, shocked by his vendetta against the Conservative government which had refused him his passport, began to turn their backs on Fayed. By 1996 he needed Diana to add to Harrods, the Villa Windsor in Paris which he had acquired in 1986, Turnbull & Asser, the Prince's shirtmakers, and *Punch* magazine.

Fayed was determined to rise to the top in British society after his acquisition of Harrods. He relished his annual meeting with the Queen at the Royal Windsor Horse Show, contriving to be photographed with the monarch even if he had to retreat to the stands as a mere spectator afterwards. Cleverly, he had diagnosed that the route into the British Royal Family lay through polo: sponsorship of a Harrods polo match in July 1986 would, he knew, lead to an introduction to the Prince and Princess of Wales (a photograph shows Diana at the event with Dodi in the background). In September 1996 he had offered Diana a directorship of Harrods; when she refused it, he offered it to Raine, who accepted.

Diana was the ultimate prize and the honey trap was his wealth. Diana had persuaded him to sponsor *The Nutcracker* for the English National Ballet. 'It was at a gala,' Pamela Harlech remembered, 'and she just said to him, "Come on, you can afford it, come on, just give it!" It was something like £400,000 – and she said, "You can afford it. It'll be good for you." And of course it was, it was terrific for Harrods because it was Christmas.'⁵ At another ballet gala dinner in early June, Fayed was sitting between Pamela Harlech and Diana when he saw his chance. 'He said, "What are you doing this summer?" And she said, "I don't know, I haven't decided what to do with the boys." He said, "Why don't you come and stay with us?" Pamela and Derek Deane, who was sitting on her other side, winced. "Don't do it. Really bad idea." But she said something like, "Well, how lovely . . .".'⁶ Dismissing her friends' warning about Fayed's reputation, she later sent a message that she would be delighted to accept.

As always with Diana, there were several reasons for her decision to take her children to stay at St Tropez with Fayed. Much as she might talk about not worrying about Camilla any more, she could not restrain her natural reaction to her old rival. Camilla's success raised the old nightmare feelings of helplessness, jealousy and despair, always potent triggers for some of her most misguided actions. July 1997 was to be Camilla month in the Prince of Wales's household. ITV were to screen a documentary about her. 'When I got to know Diana,' Richard Kay said, 'Camilla as far as she was concerned was a fading influence on her life. She was obviously always going to be there and she would always blame her [for the failure of her marriage] but she developed almost a sense of pity towards her . . . She felt that Camilla was now having a pretty hellish life in the mid-1990s because she was now undergoing the same level of interest that she herself had had many years earlier, and yet she wasn't getting anything back from it. She was getting a very bad press which I'm sure Diana was delighted about. But there were certain things that did freak her out. She was very unhappy when Channel 5 decided to do the first television biography of Camilla which ran in July 1997 and that upset her a lot. She wanted to know why television would be interested in her.'⁷ Worse, on 18 July Charles was giving a fiftieth birthday ball for Camilla at Highgrove, staged, of course, by Michael Fawcett. Two days before, on 16 July, Diana with William and Harry took

Fayed's helicopter from Kensington Palace to lunch at Barrow Green Court, then went on to Stansted for the flight to Nice on Fayed's jet, and from there via his yacht, the *Jonikal*, to the Castel Sainte Hélène, a ten-acre estate on a cliff overlooking St Tropez.

Having secured his prize, Fayed had pulled out all the stops. He even invested something in the region of £15 million buying the *Jonikal*, a 195-foot yacht built in 1991 and requiring a crew of sixteen, from a Milanese textile tycoon, just to entertain Diana.[8] More, he now saw Dodi as the ideal companion for his prized princess. Despite failure in almost all the other areas of his life, notably the business positions his father had procured for him, Dodi had had success with women. He was charming, kind and generous, reputedly good in bed, and had the ability to focus his entire attention on a woman who interested him. He had had affairs with several beautiful and well-known women and indeed would find women for his father and uncle. His principal drawback was a well-known cocaine habit. Now aged forty-two, he had one failed marriage behind him and, as Fayed well knew, a fiancée, the American model Kelly Fisher; he was due to marry her three weeks later in Los Angeles where Fayed had just paid $7.3 million for Paradise Cove, a six-bedroom seaside house in Malibu, formerly the property of Julie Andrews and her husband Blake Edwards. Determined to bring Dodi to entertain Diana, Fayed telephoned him in Paris, ordering him to dump Kelly Fisher, and sent his Gulfstream to bring him to St Tropez on 14 July. In fact, Fisher was brought down by Dodi two days later and installed to alternate between his father's lesser yachts, moored near the *Jonikal*, the 'love boat' destined to woo Diana. In London society the rumour ran that Fayed had promised Dodi $30 million if he could land Diana – but not for himself, for his father.[9]

On the morning of 18 July, the day of the Highgrove party, the tabloids were full of pictures of Diana, as she had intended they should be. She had taken particular care to make herself known to the accompanying press party, moored offshore from the Fayed villa. Wearing a sexy leopard-print bathing suit, she posed beside the swimming pool, occasionally breaking off to execute a gracefully athletic dive, in the 'look-at-me' fashion of her childhood. She rode behind Harry on a jet ski, showing a handsome cleavage. The press, assembled in boats off Fayed's beach, had no idea what was going on. They had not yet picked up on Dodi who, when he was seen with Diana and the boys in St Tropez, they assumed to be a sailor off the Fayed yacht. 'Why the press was so excited about it all,' Richard Kay recalled, 'was because they just didn't know what the hell was happening. They never knew where the story was going. In fact James Whitaker admitted that he was on the verge of a nervous breakdown and if it had carried on he would probably have cracked up. He said he just couldn't cope with the sheer stress.' Diana was not about to enlighten them but to mystify them further. Commandeering one of Fayed's speedboats, she dashed up to the press boat to announce that they should wait for something great: 'I'm going to surprise the world . . .' Questioned later by Richard Kay, she more or less admitted that it had been a meaningless stunt and a tease. Asked what this 'great' thing was, she shrugged, 'Oh, it's nothing . . . I've just had enough of everything . . .'[10] That same day, photographs flashed round the world of Fayed on the deck of the *Jonikal* with his arm round Diana, she – several inches taller than her host – with her hand resting on his shoulder. Fayed then gave an interview with a journalist in which he claimed that Diana saw him as a father figure, that her attitude to all the criticism of her stay was that these people 'can go to hell if they don't like it'. He boasted of his superb security for her to keep the press away, that he was on good terms with the Royal Family, yet was unable to resist a dig at Camilla. Diana, he said, 'doesn't think or care about Camilla Parker Bowles. She is something out of a Dracula film . . .'[11]

What, indeed, was Diana doing accepting Fayed's hospitality for herself and even more for her son, the future King of England, and his brother? When advised by friends not to go, she had replied, 'Oh, he's very naughty . . .' Fayed's speech was normally littered with his version of the English expletive 'fuggin', and he was happy to retail lurid details of his sexual exploits even to other women who didn't want to hear them. But he was expansive, a cheerful figure on holiday surrounded by his wife, Heini, and their four children, with the kind of family atmosphere that appealed to Diana. Moreover, it was a Muslim family, even if not quite on the lines of her still beloved Khans. The fact that the Establishment might look askance at Fayed made no difference whatsoever to her. Diana had never thought along Establishment lines; indeed, their disapproval may indeed have enhanced his appeal. 'Fayed has always been very nice and courteous to her and she had nowhere to go and he offered his house and she accepted,' said an old friend.[12] 'But she had a very good sense of the ridiculous and she knew how ridiculous Al Fayed is with his plane and his house and his bad taste. He gave her a watch with pearls, the kind of watch that had a pearl bracelet. And she hated it.'[13]

Diana returned to London on 20 July to face what appeared to be the final showdown with Hasnat Khan. Despite their previous troubles she had by no means given up on him and had telephoned his London flat to tell him the date of her return. Sometime during the few days she spent in London in late July – she flew to Milan on 22 July for Gianni Versace's funeral – they parted, seemingly for ever, Hasnat having told her that their marriage was impossible. Diana had told close friends that she wanted to marry Hasnat. 'He was a wonderful person and he was in love with her, he was completely besotted with her but he did not want to marry her,' said one.[14] 'Hasnat Khan has only one interest in life,' Richard Kay said. 'He was very fond of Diana but he wanted to be a very good doctor and his ultimate aim is to take the skills he's learned here back to Pakistan. And the idea that he could become Mr Diana of Wales and still be a practising doctor was just absurd, it was never going to happen. And I think she knew that too. I mean, who do you marry if you've once been married to the future King? She went almost from the sublime to the ridiculous. The idea that she could marry an impoverished hospital doctor was a wonderful Mills and Boonish sort of story line.'[15] Diana persisted, despite having told two of her mother figures that, on her Pakistan mission to meet his parents, they had been horrified at the thought of the marriage and had told her it was impossible.[16]

But now, in late July, with London emptying as people went off on their summer holidays and the boys departed with their father, romance with Dodi offered an escape. On 26 July she flew to Paris for twenty-four hours to be met by Dodi and enveloped in the Fayeds' world – private helicopter to the centre of Paris, then on to the Ritz Hotel where she was given the Imperial Suite. After dinner at Lucas Carton, the couple returned briefly to Dodi's flat in his father's apartment block on rue Arsène Houssaye, its windows overlooking the Champs-Elysées, then took a romantic walk along the Seine, hand in hand, and for once alone (the trip had been kept secret). Diana spent the night by herself in the Ritz, breakfasted with Dodi and then flew back to London. Diana was exhilarated, touched by Dodi, the first man ever to cherish her with so much thought and attention.

On 31 July she was back on the *Jonikal* for a cruise alone with Dodi (if you except numerous crew and bodyguards, butler, chef and masseuses), cruising off the coasts of Corsica and Sardinia. Dodi Fayed was simple, gentle and considerate of her every need. On this, and subsequent trips, the two of them talked unceasingly of loveless childhoods, the cinema and gossip. Importantly for Diana, Dodi was intellectually unchallenging and never made her feel inferior; at the same time he looked after her in the way she had always dreamed of and never hitherto found. It was a stress-free experience where Diana could behave in a relaxed, almost childlike way. Significantly, numbers of furry stuffed animals figured prominently in both their bedrooms: in Dodi's Paris apartment three Harrods bears sat on a table in the bedroom, three more on chairs in the dining room. He also had a collection of model aeroplanes on display in his bedroom. They played the soundtrack from the film *The English Patient* over and over again, watched DVDs and television; sometimes Diana played the piano: 'All my family play,' she told the astonished butler, René Delorm. When Dodi was busy, Diana read. She was reading, Delorm noted, a book entitled *On Being Jewish*, a curious choice for Muslim company.

Unwittingly, however, she had become caught up in a Fayed-controlled environment from which she would not escape.

Mohamed Fayed monitored the romance from afar: Dodi was in high favour owing to his obvious success with the Princess. Father and son spoke daily on the telephone, sometimes more often. Fayed was determined to extract the maximum good publicity for his son's coup. He employed the publicist Max Clifford as his adviser to supplement the skilful efforts of his spokesman, former BBC royal reporter Michael Cole. The results of his campaign were to dog the remainder of Diana and Dodi's days. On 4 August, a noted photographer, Mario Brenna, arrived in Sardinia from Monaco following a tip-off. Fayed's biographer, Tom Bower, suspected a Fayed employee was responsible; another well-informed author, Kate Snell, however, claims that Brenna was acting on a tip-off from another notorious paparazzo, Jason Fraser, who had obtained the information from a different source. Brenna had spotted the *Jonikal* moored off the bay of Cala di Volpe on the Costa Smeralda, but subsequently lost her. Later, however, he spotted the yacht travelling between Corsica and Sardinia. Using a tender, Dodi and Diana left the *Jonikal* to swim in various places, snapped and tracked by Brenna. Later, from the shore, he obtained the famous photographs of Dodi and Diana embracing on the yacht, later entitled 'the Kiss'. Back in London, Jason Fraser sold the set of pictures for huge sums – a quarter of a million pounds was paid for the first rights by the *Sunday Mirror* which published them on 10 August. The *Sun* and the *Daily Mail* paid one hundred thousand pounds each for second rights. Diana seemed no less willing than Mohamed Fayed to publicize her new affair: Richard Kay, no doubt acting on information passed to him by Diana, confirmed that it was 'her first serious romance' since the divorce.[17] It was obvious that she wanted the world to know, her specific targets probably being Hasnat Khan and her ex-husband. On 7 August, when Diana dined with Dodi at 60 Park Lane on their return to London, a horde of photographers, doubtless acting on a tip-off, were there to record her arrival. Dodi at least was innocent of having given the information: when snapped boarding a boat to take them to the *Jonikal*, he looked genuinely surprised. Diana calmly looked the other way.

Diana left for Bosnia on 8 August for the landmines campaign with Bill Deedes, returning on the 11th when, still in the Fayed embrace, she and Dodi spent a romantic night at Oxted. Ten paparazzi were waiting outside the gates as they left guarded by Trevor Rees-Jones, an ex-soldier who had become Dodi's favourite bodyguard. Giving them the slip, they drove to 60 Park Lane for dinner. 60 Park Lane was the Fayed London headquarters, the complex in which Fayed occupied the lavish seventh floor with various other relations, including Dodi, dispersed around the other floors. It was like a hotel, with centralized service from one kitchen for all the apartments. It was also the headquarters of Fayed's security operations, a private army of some thirty armed ex-soldiers from the Military Police, the SAS and the Parachute Regiment. Unlike the highly trained Royalty and Diplomatic Protection Department, which had been taught specifically how to protect its principals and had a strict code of conduct, Fayed's bodyguards were under the direct control of whichever of the Fayeds, Mohamed or Dodi, they happened to be accompanying. It was well known among Fayed's employees that disobeying Fayed meant instant dismissal, an unspoken rule that was to have fatal results. When asked to do things of which they disapproved, the saying among the men was 'It's paying the mortgage'. 'You never challenged the Boss, even if you thought professional procedures were being compromised,' Trevor Rees-Jones said.[18]

That evening Diana and Dodi went to a private screening of *Air Force One*; as Trevor Rees-Jones drove out of the underground garage of the apartment, the car was besieged by cameramen. Dodi and Diana escaped being photographed by practically lying, giggling, on the floor. A few days later, on 15 August, when Diana left for a short holiday on a boat in Greece with Rosa Monckton, Fayed saw to it that they flew out and returned on his Gulfstream. For five days they managed to escape the notice of the paparazzi, with the sole exception of a tourist who snapped them. Next day his photograph was on the front page of the *Sun*. 'It's a hunt, Rosa, it's a hunt,' Diana told her friend.

The hunt was now on in earnest, partly orchestrated by the

distant Fayed but more closely, it would appear, by Diana herself. On 21 August, the day Diana returned on the Fayed jet to Stansted, Fayed had alerted not only Nigel Dempster but also the *Sun*. That same evening Diana flew to Nice to join Dodi for a second holiday on the *Jonikal*. At the jetty in the small port of St Laurent-du-Var, where they were to join the yacht, Jason Fraser and two French showbusiness photographers were waiting. Later they were joined by more. At Monte Carlo on 25 August Dodi and Diana decided to walk in the town, accompanied by Delorm and the two body-guards, Rees-Jones and 'Kez' Wingfield. They lost their way but remained unbothered by the media. It was on this expedition that Fayed would claim that Diana and Dodi picked out a special ring from the 'Tell Me Yes' range at the jewellers Repossi, which was later, according to him, to be presented to Diana as an engagement ring. Rees-Jones emphatically denied that they visited Repossi. (They had done so, however, on the earlier *Jonikal* trip on 5 August.) A fleet of paparazzi boats dogged the *Jonikal* from then on. After Monte Carlo Dodi was beginning to panic about the paparazzi, suspecting the crew of tipping them off. The two British bodyguards, Kez and Trevor, were telephoning requests for reinforcements, only to be turned down. Later, when the couple were trying to have a quiet romantic walk on the beach at Porto Venere, they were surprised by a single paparazzo; by now even Diana seemed upset and was seen in tears by the crew. On 27 August helicopters made three sorties to hover over the *Jonikal*, driving Diana below. Dodi began to fantasize about night-vision laser devices to disrupt the cameras or blind their operators. There was a sense that Diana was beginning to be bothered about his overreaction to things like mosquitoes, asking their stewardess, 'What are these Arab men like?'[19] Later, it was to be suggested by Diana's friends that, fiercely opposed as she was to drug use, she was beginning to be suspicious about Dodi's disappearances to the bathroom. On Friday 29 August they were at Cala di Volpe, on Sardinia, again when news filtered through that they would be leaving for Paris the following day.

Arriving at Le Bourget on a stifling hot August day, the party found the paparazzi waiting and this time in their most aggressive form – on motorbikes. Diana's face was set as she got into the Mercedes to drive to the city centre. They set off in two cars, Dodi and Diana in the Mercedes guarded by Rees-Jones and driven by the usual chauffeur, Philippe Dorneau. The back-up Range Rover with the luggage, valet, maid and masseuse, guarded by Wingfield, was driven by Henri Paul, assistant head of security at the Ritz, who had been personally greeted by Dodi. Outside the airport they were buzzed by paparazzi on motorbikes darting round them, oblivious to safety. An agitated Dodi told Dorneau to accelerate and lose them and at one stage Diana screamed at the driver to 'slow down' as she was worried there might be a collision with the bikes.[20] She tried to soothe Dodi. Outdistancing their pursuers, the couple stopped to visit the Villa Windsor, the home of Diana's ex-husband's great-uncle, the Duke of Windsor, and his wife for the last thirty and more years of their lives. Diana jumped out of the car without waiting for the door to be opened for her. According to the villa's security chief, Ben Murrell, 'Diana looked flustered and her face was red. She didn't look happy. Dodi was still sitting in the car by the time Diana walked into the house. It was obvious something had occurred during the journey . . . Diana looked shaken.'[21] The villa now stood empty of the furniture, which had been sent for auction. They spent precisely twenty-eight minutes there: Diana found it creepy, as she was to tell Richard Kay. Later Fayed was to claim that they spent two hours touring what he said was to be their future home together, accompanied at one stage by an interior decorator. Security cameras later proved this to be untrue. They then drove to the Ritz where Diana once again had use of the Imperial Suite. She had her hair done while Dodi visited the nearby Repossi jewellery shop, apparently to complete arrangements for the ring he had ordered for her and to inspect designs for more jewellery. The ring was then taken to the Ritz and given to Dodi who put it in his pocket.

Later, they left for Dodi's apartment on rue Arsène Houssaye to dress for dinner. There they were met by a noisy and aggressive troop of paparazzi shouting and pushing. 'This really upset the

31 Ibid.

32 Interview with the author 6/4/05.

33 William Tallon interview with the author 24/2/04.

34 Interview with the author 9/3/04.

35 Andrew Morton, *Diana: Her True Story – In Her Own Words*, pp. 36, 37.

36 Andrew Morton, *Diana: Her True Story – In Her Own Words*, p. 119.

37 Sarah Bradford, *Elizabeth: A Biography of Her Majesty The Queen*, p. 431.

38 Ibid., pp. 431–2.

39 Jonathan Dimbleby, *The Prince of Wales: A Biography*, p. 284.

40 Sarah Bradford, *Elizabeth: A Biography of Her Majesty The Queen*, p. 429.

41 Robert Spencer interview with the author, 26 June 2001.

42 Hugo Vickers, unpublished diary, 26 November 2004.

43 Jonathan Dimbleby, *The Prince of Wales: A Biography*, p. 287.

44 Robert Spencer interview with the author 26/6/01.

45 Andrew Morton, *Diana: Her True Story – In Her Own Words*, pp. 40, 41.

46 Rosalind Coward, *Diana: The Portrait*, p. 84.

47 Private information.

Chapter 6. The Beginning of the 'Fairy Tale' (pp. 91–106)

1 Andrew Morton, *Diana: Her True Story – In Her Own Words*, p. 41.

2 Ibid., p. 42.

3 Rosalind Coward, *Diana: The Portrait*, pp. 98–9.

4 Ibid., p. 99.

5 Ibid., p. 91.

6 Jonathan Dimbleby, *The Prince of Wales: A Biography*, p. 293.

7 Andrew Morton, *Diana: Her True Story – In Her Own Words*, p. 42.

8 Interview with the author 16/11/05.

9 Jonathan Dimbleby, *The Prince of Wales: A Biography*, p. 294.

10 Interview with the author 7/3/06.

11 Private information.

12 Interview with the author 9/5/01.

13 Interview with the author 9/5/01.

14 Jonathan Dimbleby, *The Prince of Wales: A Biography*, p. 294.

15 James Whitaker interview with the author June 2001.

16 Andrew Morton, *Diana: Her True Story – In Her Own Words*, p. 43.

17 Ibid., p. 43.

18 Interview with the author 9/5/01.

19 Interview with the author 9/5/01.

20 Interview with the author 16/11/05.

21 Private information.

22 Private information.

23 Andrew Morton, *Diana: Her True Story – In Her Own Words*, p. 43.

24 Ibid., p. 43.

25 Interview with the author 23/2/04.

26 Colin Tebbutt interview with the author 3/3/04.

27 Private information.

28 Interview with the author 16/11/05.

29 Interview with the author 16/11/05.

30 Interview with the author 16/11/05.

31 Interview with the author 16/11/05.

32 Interview with the author.

33 Interview with the author 25/10/05.

34 Jonathan Dimbleby, *The Prince of Wales: A Biography*, p. 298.

35 Andrew Morton, *Diana: Her True Story – In Her Own Words*, p. 45.

36 Private information.

37 Roy Greenslade interview with the author 20/9/05.

38 Andrew Morton, *Diana: Her True Story – In Her Own Words*, p. 45.

39 Private information.

40 Jonathan Dimbleby, *The Prince of Wales: A Biography*, p. 304.

Chapter 7. 'Di-mania' (pp. 107–25)

1 Interview with the author 25/10/05.
2 Patrick Jephson, *Shadows of a Princess. Diana, Princess of Wales 1987–1996*, p. 7.
3 Ibid.
4 David Hicks interview with author 2/6/93.
5 Stephen Barry, *Royal Service: My Twelve Years as Valet to Prince Charles*, p. 219.
6 Interview with the author 16/11/05.
7 Jonathan Dimbleby, *The Prince of Wales: A Biography*, p. 331.
8 Roy Greenslade interview with the author September 2005.
9 Sally Bedell Smith, *Diana: The Life of a Troubled Princess*, p. 140.
10 Ibid.
11 Private information.
12 Andrew Morton, *Diana, Her True Story – In Her Own Words*, p. 37.
13 Tim Clayton and Phil Craig, *Diana: Story of a Princess*, p. 15.
14 Jonathan Dimbleby, *The Prince of Wales: A Biography*, p. 332.
15 Ibid.
16 Ibid., p. 333.
17 Interview with the author 25/10/05.
18 Interview with the author 25/10/05.
19 Interview with the author 6/4/05.
20 Interview with the author 6/4/05.
21 Anthony Holden, *Charles, Prince of Wales*, pp. 204–5.
22 Private information.
23 Interview with the author 16/11/05.
24 Interview with the author 25/10/05.
25 Sally Bedell Smith, *Diana: The Life of a Troubled Princess*, p. 151.
26 Interview with the author 25/10/05.
27 Andrew Morton, *Diana: Her True Story – In Her Own Words*, p. 51.

Chapter 8. 'The Best Double Act in the World' (pp. 126–43)

1 Jonathan Dimbleby, *The Prince of Wales: A Biography*, letter from Charles to friends p. 395.

2 Interview with the author 25/10/05.

3 Letter from private collection.

4 Interview with the author 6/4/05.

5 Rosalind Coward, *Diana: The Portrait*, pp. 141–2.

6 Ibid., pp. 144–5.

7 Ibid.

8 Ibid., p. 142.

9 Ibid., p. 132.

10 Interview with the author 25/10/05.

11 Rosalind Coward, *Diana: The Portrait*, p. 156.

12 Patrick Jephson, *Shadows of a Princess*, p. 18.

13 Ibid.

14 Letter from private collection.

15 Interview with the author 15/5/04.

16 Sally Bedell Smith, *Diana: The Life of a Troubled Princess*, p. 134.

17 Interview with the author 25/10/05.

18 Mary Roberston, *The Diana I Knew*, p. 111.

19 Ibid., p. 108.

20 Jonathan Dimbleby, *The Prince of Wales: A Biography*, p. 381.

21 Ibid., p. 382.

22 Ibid., pp. 386–7.

23 Interview with the author September 2004.

24 Interview with the author September 2004.

25 Interview with the author 20/2/06.

26 *Time* magazine, 11 November 1985.

27 Interview with the author 25/10/05.

Chapter 9. 'Charles has gone back to his Lady' (pp. 144–59)

1 Ken Wharfe interview with the author 11/4/05.

2 Settelen tapes.

3 Ken Wharfe interview with the author 11/4/05.

4 Ken Wharfe interview with the author 11/4/05.

5 Settelen tapes.

6 Ibid.

7 Interview with the author 14/4/05.

8 Andrew Morton, *Diana: Her True Story – In Her Own Words*, p. 58.

9 Interview with the author 10/4/06.

10 Interview with the author 7/12/05.

11 Interview with the author 7/9/05.

12 Andrew Morton, *Diana: Her True Story – In Her Own Words*, p. 58.

13 Jonathan Dimbleby, *The Prince of Wales: A Biography*, p. 393.

14 Ibid., p. 394.

15 Ibid., p. 395.

16 Ibid.

17 Ken Wharfe interview with the author 11/4/05.

18 James Hewitt interview with the author 11/1/06.

19 James Hewitt interview with the author 11/1/06.

20 James Hewitt interview with the author 11/1/06.

21 James Hewitt interview with the author 11/1/06.

22 James Hewitt interview with the author 11/1/06.

23 James Hewitt, *Love and War*, p. 23.

24 Ibid., p. 20.

25 Ibid., p. 27.

26 Settelen tapes.

27 Interview with the author 11/1/06.

28 Interview with the author 25/10/05.

Chapter 10. A Dying Marriage (pp. 160–79)

1 Patrick Jephson, *Shadows of a Princess*, p. 63.
2 James Hewitt interview with the author 11/1/06.
3 Ken Wharfe, with Robert Jobson, *Diana: Closely Guarded Secret*, p. 77.
4 Interview with the author.
5 Andrew Morton, *Diana: Her True Story – In Her Own Words*, pp. 59, 59.
6 Interview with the author 16/11/05.
7 Jonathan Dimbleby, *The Prince of Wales: A Biography*, p. 397.
8 Interview with the author 9/11/05.
9 Mike Adler quoted in Rosalind Coward, *Diana: The Portrait*, p. 178.
10 Baroness Jay quoted in Rosalind Coward, *Diana: The Portrait*, p. 178.
11 Rosalind Coward, *Diana: The Portrait*, p. 179.
12 Interview with the author 23/2/04.
13 Rosalind Coward, *Diana: The Portrait*, pp. 183–4.
14 Ibid., p. 184.
15 Ibid.
16 Marguerite Littman interview with the author 8/12/04.
17 Victor Edelstein interview with author 22/5/01.
18 Private information.
19 Interview with the author 14/4/05.
20 *Sunday Times*.
21 Roy Strong, *The Roy Strong Diaries 1967–1997*, 10 December 1987, p. 431.
22 Dickie Arbiter interview with author 23/2/04.

Chapter 11. Diana Fights Back (pp. 180–96)

1 Squidgygate tapes 1989.
2 Sarah Bradford, *Elizabeth: A Biography of Her Majesty The Queen*, p. 444.
3 James Hewitt interview with the author 11/1/06.

4 James Hewitt, *Love and War*, p. 48.

5 Sally Bedell Smith, *Diana: The Life of a Troubled Princess*, p. 197.

6 Anthony Holden, *Charles, Prince of Wales*, p. 260.

7 Ken Wharfe, with Robert Jobson, *Diana: Closely Guarded Secret*, pp. 96–7.

8 Interview with the author 5/5/04.

9 Patrick Jephson, *Shadows of a Princess*, pp. 34–5.

10 Ibid., p. 37.

11 Ibid., pp. 38–9.

12 Ibid., p. 40.

13 Ibid.

14 Interview with the author 16/11/05.

15 Andrew Morton, *Diana: Her True Story – In Her Own Words*, p. 60.

16 Interview with the author 21/6/05.

17 Rosa Monckton, in Brian MacArthur (ed.), *Requiem: Diana, Princess of Wales 1961–1997*, pp. 64–5.

18 Patrick Jephson interview with author March 2004.

19 Sally Bedell Smith, *Diana: The Life of a Troubled Princess*, p. 189.

20 Andrew Morton, *Diana: Her True Story – In Her Own Words*, p. 29.

21 Patrick Jephson, *Shadows of a Princess*, p. 67.

Chapter 12. The War of the Waleses (pp. 197–215)

1 Close friend of Diana's in an interview with the author 16/11/05.

2 Sally Bedell Smith, *Diana: The Life of a Troubled Princess*, p. 203.

3 Interview with the author 30/10/04.

4 Patrick Jephson, *Shadows of a Princess*, p. 137.

5 Ibid., p. 147.

6 Ibid., p. 138.

7 Ibid., p. 141.

8 Sir William Heseltine interview with the author 15/7/96.

9 Patrick Jephson, *Shadows of a Princess*, pp. 131–2.

10 Sally Bedell Smith, *Diana: The Life of a Troubled Princess*, p. 205.

11 Richard Kay interview with the author 16/3/04.

12 James Hewitt, *Love and War*, p. 151.

13 Interview with the author 16/11/05.

14 James Hewitt, *Love and War*, p. 151.

15 Interview with the author 16/11/05.

16 Interview with the author 16/11/05.

17 Andrew Morton interview with the author 20/3/01.

18 Andrew Morton interview with the author 20/3/01.

19 Andrew Morton interview with the author 20/3/01.

20 Patrick Jephson interview with the author March 2004.

21 Patrick Jephson interview with the author March 2004.

22 Patrick Jephson interview with the author March 2004.

23 Patrick Jephson interview with the author March 2004.

24 Patrick Jephson interview with the author March 2004.

25 Andrew Morton interview with the author 20/3/01.

26 James Whitaker interview with the author June 2001.

27 Sally Bedell Smith, *Diana: The Life of a Troubled Princess*, p. 210.

28 Andrew Morton interview with the author 20/3/01.

29 Interview with the author 7/3/06.

30 Dickie Arbiter interview with the author 23/2/04.

31 Interview with the author 16/11/05.

Chapter 13. The Volcano Erupts (pp. 216–32)

1   Andrew Morton interview with the author 20/3/01.

2   Sarah Bradford, *Elizabeth: A Biography of Her Majesty the Queen*, p. 360.

3   Dickie Arbiter interview with the author 23/2/04.

4   Interview with the author 3/4/01.

5   Interview with the author February 2005.

6   Sally Bedell Smith, *Diana: The Life of a Troubled Princess*, p. 222.

7   Interview with the author 23/2/04.

8   Patrick Jephson, *Shadows of a Princess*, p. 235.

9   Ibid.

10 Interview with the author.

11 Jean Willis interview with the author.

12 Patrick Jephson interview with the author March 2004.

13 Jonathan Dimbleby, *The Prince of Wales: A Biography*, p. 484.
14 Interview with the author 29/12/93.
15 Sally Bedell Smith, *Diana: The Life of a Troubled Princess*, p. 228.
16 Sarah Bradford, *Elizabeth: A Biography of Her Majesty The Queen*, p. 467.
17 Patrick Jephson, *Shadows of a Princess*, p. 248.
18 Interview with the author 8/9/93.
19 Jonathan Dimbleby, *The Prince of Wales: A Biography*, p. 487.
20 Ibid., p. 488.
21 Patrick Jephson interview with the author March 2004.
22 Jonathan Dimbleby, *The Prince of Wales: A Biography*, p. 488.
23 Patrick Jephson, *Shadows of a Princess*, p. 267.
24 Patrick Jephson interview with the author March 2004.
25 Jonathan Dimbleby, *The Prince of Wales: A Biography*, p. 489.
26 Patrick Jephson, *Shadows of a Princess*, p. 272.
27 Jonathan Dimbleby, *The Prince of Wales: A Biography*, p. 491.

Chapter 14. The First Step Towards the Abyss
(pp. 233–53)

1   Patrick Jephson, *Shadows of a Princess*, p. 278.
2   Ken Wharfe, with Robert Jobson, *Closely Guarded Secret*, p. 265.
3   Interview with the author 5/5/04.
4   Interview with the author 16/11/05.
5   Interview with the author 5/5/04.
6   Interview with the author 16/11/05.
7   Interview with the author March 2005.
8   Interview with the author 30/10/04.
9   Interview with the author 30/10/04.
10 Sally Bedell Smith, *Diana: The Life of a Troubled Princess*, p. 258.
11 Interview with the author 4/11/04.
12 Interview with the author 4/11/04.
13 Ken Wharfe interview with the author 11/4/05.
14 Ken Wharfe, with Robert Jobson, *Closely Guarded Secret*, p. 186.
15 Ibid.

16 Ken Wharfe interview with the author 11/4/05.

17 Interview with the author.

18 Max Hastings, *Editor: An Inside Story of Newspapers*, pp. 336–7.

19 Patrick Jephson, *Shadows of a Princess*, p. 412.

20 Douglas Hurd, *Memoirs*, p. 474.

21 Ibid., p. 556.

22 Interview with the author February 2005.

23 Patrick Jephson, *Shadows of a Princess*, p. 297.

24 Ibid., p. 297.

25 Ibid., pp. 297–8.

26 Ken Wharfe, with Robert Jobson, *Closely Guarded Secret*, p. 231.

27 Patrick Jephson, *Shadows of a Princess*, p. 307.

28 Andrew Morton, *Diana: Her True Story – In Her Own Words*, p. 57.

29 Paul Burrell, *A Royal Duty*, p. 183.

30 Ken Wharfe interview with the author 11/4/05.

31 Ken Wharfe, with Robert Jobson, *Closely Guarded Secret*, p. 218.

32 Ibid., p. 221.

33 Ibid., p. 241.

34 Ibid., p. 229.

35 Ibid., p. 248.

Chapter 15. The Inconsequential Years (pp. 254–68)

1 Patrick Jephson, *Shadows of a Princess*, p. 293.

2 Interview with the author 27/6/05.

3 Interview with the author 16/11/05.

4 Sally Bedell Smith, *Diana: The Life of a Troubled Princess*, p. 258.

5 Ibid.

6 Interview with the author 16/11/05.

7 Sally Bedell Smith, *Diana: The Life of a Troubled Princess*, p. 260.

8 Ibid., p. 259.

9 Andrew Morton interview with the author 20/3/01.

10 Sister Bridie Dowd interview with the author 20/1/06.

11 Sister Bridie Dowd interview with the author 20/1/06.

12 Sister Bridie Dowd interview with the author 20/1/06.

13 Interview with the author.

14 Interview with the author.

15 Patrick Jephson, *Shadows of a Princess*, p. 293.

16 Interview with the author February 2004.

17 Interview with the author 5/5/04.

18 Interview with the author 23/2/95.

19 Sally Bedell Smith, *Diana: The Life of a Troubled Princess*, p. 265.

20 Jonathan Dimbleby, *The Prince of Wales: A Biography*, p. 608.

Chapter 16. Towards a New World (pp. 269–80)

1 Brian MacArthur (ed.), *Requiem: Diana, Princess of Wales 1961–1997*, p. 102.

2 Interview with the author 16/11/05.

3 Patrick Jephson, *Shadows of a Princess*, p. 343.

4 Brian MacArthur (ed.), *Requiem: Diana, Princess of Wales 1961–1997*, p. 102.

5 Ibid., p. 101.

6 Ibid., p. 102.

7 Ibid., pp. 99–100.

8 Patrick Jephson, *Shadows of a Princess*, p. 345.

9 Ibid., p. 346.

10 Interview with the author 28/9/94.

11 Interview with the author 15/11/94.

12 Interview with the author 20/7/05.

13 Michael Shea interview with the author 1/2/95.

14 Patrick Jephson, *Shadows of a Princess*, p. 345.

15 Interview with the author 2/2/04.

16 Interview with the author 2/2/04.

17 Interview with the author 2/2/04.

18 Interview with the author 2/2/04.

19 Piers Morgan, *The Insider*, p. 106.

20 Ibid., p. 115.

21 Ibid., p. 118.

22 Ibid., p. 157.

23 Brian MacArthur (ed.), *Requiem: Diana, Princess of Wales 1961–1997*, p. 123.

24 Ibid., p. 124.

25 Paul Burrell, *A Royal Duty*, p. 203.

26 Ibid., p. 203.

27 Brian MacArthur (ed.), *Requiem: Diana, Princess of Wales 1961–1997*, p. 89.

28 Ibid., p. 96.

29 Interview with the author February 2005.

30 Interview with the author February 2005.

31 Brian MacArthur (ed.), *Requiem: Diana, Princess of Wales 1961–1997*, p. 89.

Chapter 17. Fall from Grace (pp. 281–300)

1 *Mail on Sunday*, 20 August 1995.

2 Patrick Jephson, *Shadows of a Princess*, p. 351.

3 Interview with the author November 1994.

4 Patrick Jephson, *Shadows of a Princess*, p. 356.

5 Brian MacArthur (ed.), *Requiem: Diana, Princess of Wales 1961–1997*, p. 97.

6 Patrick Jephson, *Shadows of a Princess*, p. 354.

7 Ibid., p. 356.

8 Interview with the author 4/11/04.

9 Judy Wade, *The Truth: The Friends of Diana, Princess of Wales, Tell Their Stories*, p. 87.

10 Sally Bedell Smith, *Diana: The Life of a Troubled Princess*, p. 283.

11 Interview with the author 23/2/04.

12 Interview with the author March 2005.

13 Richard Kay interview with the author 16/3/04.

14 Interview with the author 4/11/04.

15 Interview with the author 4/11/04.

16 Paul Burrell, *A Royal Duty*, p. 322.

17 Colin Tebbutt interview with the author 3/4/04.

18 Ken Wharfe interview with the author 11/4/05.

19 Andrew Morton, *Diana: In Pursuit of Love*, p. 179.

20 Ibid., p. 178.

21 Sally Bedell Smith, *Diana: The Life of a Troubled Princess*, p. 282.

22 Interview with the author February 2005.

23 Interview with the author February 2005.

24 Brian MacArthur (ed.), *Requiem: Diana, Princess of Wales 1961–1997*, p. 96.

25 Sally Bedell Smith, *Diana: The Life of a Troubled Princess*, p. 284.

26 Sarah Bradford, *Elizabeth: A Biography of Her Majesty The Queen*, p. 481.

27 Interview with the author 5/5/04.

28 Patrick Jephson, *Shadows of a Princess*, p. 367.

29 Ibid., p. 369.

30 Paul Burrell, *A Royal Duty*, p. 219.

31 Interview with the author 6/1/05.

32 Paul Burrell, *A Royal Duty*, pp. 221–2.

Chapter 18. Out on a Limb (pp. 301–20)

1 Patrick Jephson, *Shadows of a Princess*, p. 552.

2 Ibid., p. 560.

3 Paul Burrell, *A Royal Duty*, p. 222.

4 Ibid., pp. 225–6.

5 Ibid., p. 226.

6 Ibid.

7 Ibid., pp. 226–7.

8 Interview with the author 5/5/04.

9 Interview with the author 27/6/05.

10 Interview with the author 6/1/06.

11 Interview with the author June 2005.

12 Brian MacArthur (ed.), *Requiem: Diana, Princess of Wales 1961–1997*, p. 80.

13 Ibid., p. 80.

14 Ibid., p. 81.

15 Ibid., pp. 81–2.

16 Ibid., p. 83.

17 Kate Snell, *Diana: Her Last Love*, p. 86.

18 Ibid., p. 67.

19 Interview with the author 5/5/04.

20 Interview with the author 5/5/04.

21 Interview with the author 5/5/04.

22 Colin Tebbutt interview with the author 3/3/04.

23 Pamela Harlech interview with the author October 2004.

24 Cheryl Barrymore interview in the *Daily Mail* (21 October 2002).

25 Ibid.

26 Allan Starkie, *Fergie: Her Secret Life*, p. 76.

27 Ibid., p. 117.

28 Ibid., p. 206.

29 Sarah, The Duchess of York, *My Story*, p. 72.

Chapter 19. Stirring Beneath the Surface (pp. 321–37)

1 Richard Kay interview with the author 16/3/04.

2 Cited in Paul Burrell, *A Royal Duty*, p. 242.

3 Interview with the author 25/10/05.

4 Interview with the author February 2005.

5 Kate Snell, *Diana: Her Last Love*, p. 135.

6 Interview with the author February 2004.

7 Interview with the author February 2004.

8 Interview with the author February 2004.

9 Interview with the author January 2004.

10 Interview with the author January 2004.

11 Interview with the author February 2004.

12 Interview with the author February 2004.

13 Interview with the author 23/2/05.

14 Private information.

15 Sarah Bradford, *Elizabeth: A Biography of Her Majesty The Queen*, pp. 244–5.

16 Interview with the author February 2004.

17 Interview with the author September 2004.

18 Interview with the author September 2004.

19 Interview with the author September 2004.

20 Interview with the author 14/4/05.

21 Interview with the author 11/4/05.

22 Interview with the author 11/4/05.

23 Interview with the author 11/4/05.

24 Interview with the author 11/4/05.

25 Interview with Richard Kay 16/3/04.

26 *Report to His Royal Highness The Prince of Wales by Sir Michael Peat and Edmund Lawson QC*, 13 March 2003, p. 10.

27 Ibid., p. 11.

28 Ibid., p. 12.

29 Ibid., p. 13.

30 Ibid., p. 25.

31 Ibid., p. 36.

32 Ibid., p. 39.

33 Ibid., p. 43.

34 Ibid., p. 49.

35 Interview with author 6/2/04.

36 Interview with author 7/2/04.

Chapter 20. Diana the Hunted (pp. 338–55)

1 William Deedes.

2 William Rees-Mogg, in Rosalind Coward, *Diana: The Portrait*, p. 260.

3 Richard Kay interview with the author 16/3/04.

4 Interview with the author February 2006.

5 Meredith Etherington-Smith interview with the author 25/1/03.

6 Meredith Etherington-Smith interview with the author 25/1/03.

7 Meredith Etherington-Smith interview with the author 25/1/03.

8 Meredith Etherington-Smith interview with the author 25/1/03.

9 Meredith Etherington-Smith interview with the author 25/1/03.

10 Meredith Etherington-Smith interview with the author 25/1/03.

11 Meredith Etherington-Smith interview with the author 25/1/03.

12 William Deedes interview with the author 19/1/04.

13 Brian MacArthur (ed.), *Requiem: Diana, Princess of Wales 1961–1997*, p. 135.

14 William Deedes interview with the author 19/1/04.

15 Brian MacArthur (ed.), *Requiem: Diana, Princess of Wales 1961–1997*, p. 136.

16 Ibid.

17 Paul Burrell, *A Royal Duty*, p. 281.

18 Ibid.

19 William Deedes interview with the author 19/1/04.

20 Interview with the author March 2004.

21 Interview with the author March 2004.

22 William Deedes interview with the author 19/1/04.

23 Rosalind Coward, *Diana: The Portrait*, p. 294.

24 Ibid., p. 266.

25 Meredith Etherington-Smith interview with the author 25/1/03.

26 Meredith Etherington-Smith interview with the author 25/1/03.

27 Meredith Etherington-Smith interview with the author 25/1/03.

28 Meredith Etherington-Smith interview with the author 25/1/03.

29 Meredith Etherington-Smith interview with the author 25/1/03.

30 Meredith Etherington-Smith interview with the author 25/1/03.

31 Meredith Etherington-Smith interview with the author 25/1/03.

32 Meredith Etherington-Smith interview with the author 25/1/03.

33 Meredith Etherington-Smith interview with the author 25/1/03.

34 Meredith Etherington-Smith interview with the author 25/1/03.

35 Meredith Etherington-Smith interview with the author 25/1/03.

36 Brian MacArthur (ed.), *Requiem: Diana, Princess of Wales 1961–1997*, p. 113.

37 Paul Burrell, *A Royal Duty*, p. 300.

38 Ibid.

Chapter 21. Fatal Summer (pp. 356–72)

1 Tom Bower, *Fayed: The Unauthorized Biography*, pp. 6–7.
2 Ibid., p. 25.
3 Interview with the author February 2005.
4 Tom Bower, *Fayed: The Unauthorized Biography*, p. 159.
5 Pamela Harlech interview with the author October 2004.
6 Pamela Harlech interview with the author October 2004.
7 Richard Kay interview with the author 16/3/04.
8 Tom Bower, *Fayed: The Unauthorized Biography*, p. 413.
9 Interview with the author 18/2/04.
10 Richard Kay interview with the author 16/3/04.
11 Tom Bower, *Fayed: The Unauthorized Biography*, pp. 416–17.
12 Interview with the author 16/11/05.
13 Interview with the author 16/11/05.
14 Interview with the author 16/11/05.
15 Richard Kay interview with the author 16/3/04.
16 Interview with the author 16/11/05.
17 Interview with the author.
18 Trevor Rees-Jones, *The Bodyguard's Story: Diana, the Crash and the Sole Survivor*, p. 15.
19 Ibid., p. 72.
20 Martyn Gregory, *Diana: The Last Days*, p. 50.
21 Ibid., p. 49.
22 Ibid., p. 56.
23 Ibid., p. 57.
24 Trevor Rees-Jones, *The Bodyguard's Story: Diana, the Crash and the Sole Survivor*, p. 79.
25 Brian MacArthur (ed.), *Requiem: Diana, Princess of Wales 1961–1997*, p. 63.
26 Ibid., p. 55.
27 Colin Tebbut interview with the author 3/3/04.
28 Trevor Rees-Jones, *The Bodyguard's Story: Diana, the Crash and the Sole Survivor*, p. 86.
29 Colin Tebbutt interview with the author 3/3/04.

Chapter 22. Death in Paris (pp. 373–88)

1 Daniel Eyraud, vascular surgery team, cited in Martyn Gregory, *Diana: The Last Days*, p. 74.
2 Martyn Gregory, *Diana: The Last Days*, pp. 74–5.
3 Colin Tebbutt interview with the author 3/3/04.
4 Colin Tebbutt interview with the author 3/3/04.
5 Colin Tebbutt interview with the author 3/3/04.
6 Andrew Morton, *Diana: In Pursuit of Love*, p. 250.
7 Ibid., p. 251.
8 Interview with the author February 2004.
9 Rosalind Coward, *Diana: The Portrait*, p. 302.
10 Colin Tebbutt interview with the author 3/3/04.
11 Colin Tebbutt interview with the author 3/3/04.
12 Rosalind Coward, *Diana: The Portrait*, p. 304.
13 Ibid.
14 Paul Burrell, *A Royal Duty*, p. 297.
15 Interview with the author 20/7/05.
16 Interview with the author 20/7/05.
17 Interview with the author 23/2/04.
18 Dickie Arbiter interview with the author 23/2/04.
19 Dickie Arbiter interview with the author 23/2/04.
20 Private information.
21 Dickie Arbiter interview with the author 23/2/04.
22 Meredith Etherington-Smith interview with the author 25/1/03.
23 Brian MacArthur (ed.), *Requiem: Diana, Princess of Wales 1961–1997*, p. 6.

Select Bibliography

Barry, Stephen P., *Royal Service: My Twelve Years as Valet to Prince Charles*, Avon Books, New York, 1984

Bedell Smith, Sally, *Diana: The Life of a Troubled Princess*, Aurum Press, 1999

Berry, Wendy, *The Housekeeper's Diary: Charles and Diana Before the Breakup*, Barricade Books, Inc., New York, 1995

Bower, Tom, *Fayed: The Unauthorized Biography*, Pan Books, 2001

Bradford, Sarah, *Elizabeth: A Biography of Her Majesty The Queen*, rev. edn, Penguin Books, 2002

Burchill, Julie, *Diana*, Weidenfeld & Nicolson, 1998

Burrell, Paul, *A Royal Duty*, Michael Joseph, 2003

Campbell, Lady Colin, *Diana in Private: The Princess Nobody Knows*, Smith Gryphon, 1992

Clarke, Mary, *Little Girl Lost: The Troubled Childhood of Princess Diana by the Woman who Raised Her*, Birch Lane Press, New York, 1996

Clayton, Tim, and Phil Craig, *Diana: Story of a Princess*, Hodder & Stoughton, 2001

Courtney, Nicholas, *Diana: Princess of Wales*, Park Lane Press, 1982

Coward, Rosalind, *Diana: The Portrait*, HarperCollins, n.d.

Deedes, William, *Brief Lives*, Macmillan, 2004

Delorm, René, with Barry Fox and Nadine Taylor, *Diana & Dodi: A Love Story*, Tallfellow Press, Los Angeles, 1998

Dimbleby, Jonathan, *The Prince of Wales: A Biography*, Little, Brown, 1994

Ferguson, Ronald, *The Galloping Major: My Life and Singular Times*, Macmillan, 1994

Goldsmith, Lady Annabel, *Annabel: An Unconventional Life*, Phoenix, 2004

Graham, Caroline, *Camilla – The King's Mistress: A Love Story*, Blake Publishing, 1994

Graham, Tim, with text by Tom Corby, *Diana, Princess of Wales: A Tribute*, Weidenfeld & Nicolson, n.d.

Greenslade, Roy, *Press Gang: The True Story of How Papers Make Profits from Propaganda*, Macmillan, 2003

Gregory, Martyn, *Diana: The Last Days*, Virgin Publishing, 1999, revised and updated by Virgin Books, 2004

Hastings, Max, *Editor: An Inside Story of Newspapers*, Pan Books, 2003

Hewitt, James, *Love and War*, Blake Publishing, 1999

——, *Moving On*, Blake Publishing, 2005

Holden, Anthony, *Charles, Prince of Wales*, Weidenfeld & Nicolson, 1979

——, *Charles: A Biography*, Fontana Paperbacks, 1989

——, *Charles: A Biography*, Corgi Books, 1999

Hurd, Douglas, *Memoirs*, Abacus Books, 2004

Jephson, Patrick, *Shadows of a Princess. Diana, Princess of Wales 1987–1996*, HarperCollins, 2000

——, photographs by Kent Gavin, *Portraits of a Princess: Travels with Diana*, Sidgwick & Jackson, 2004

Junor, Penny, *Diana, Princess of Wales*, Sidgwick & Jackson, 1982

——, *Charles, Victim or Villain?*, HarperCollins, 1998

Kortesis, Vasso, *The Duchess of York*, Blake Publishing, 1996

Levin, Angela, *Raine and Johnnie: The Spencers and the Scandal of Althorp*, Weidenfeld & Nicolson, 1993

MacArthur, Brian, ed., *Requiem: Diana, Princess of Wales 1961–1997 – Memories and Tributes*, Arcade Publishing, 1997

Morgan, Piers, *The Insider*, Ebury Press, 2005

Morton, Andrew, *Inside Kensington Palace*, Michael O'Mara Books, 1987

——, *Diana: Her True Story – In Her Own Words*, revised edn, Michael O'Mara Books, 1997

——, *Diana: Her New Life*, Michael O'Mara Books, 1994

——, *Diana: In Pursuit of Love*, Michael O'Mara Books, 2004

Pasternak, Anna, *Princess in Love*, Bloomsbury, 1994

Pontaut, Jean-Marie, and Jerome Dupuis, *Enquête sur la mort de Diana*, Editions Stock, Paris, 1998

Rees-Jones, Trevor, with Moira Johnston, *The Bodyguard's Story: Diana, the Crash and the Sole Survivor*, Little, Brown, 2000

Report to His Royal Highness The Prince of Wales by Sir Michael Peat and Edmund Lawson QC, 13 March 2003

Riddington, Max, and Gavan Naden, *Frances: The Remarkable Story of Diana's Mother*, Michael O'Mara Books, 2003

Robertson, Mary, *The Diana I Knew*, Judy Piatkus, 1998

Rogers, Rita, *From One World to Another . . .*, Pan Books, 1998

Sancton, Thomas, and Scott MacLeod, *Death of a Princess: An Investigation*, Weidenfeld & Nicolson, 1998

Sarah, The Duchess of York, with Jeff Coplon, *My Story*, Simon & Schuster, 1996

Seward, Ingrid, *The Queen and Di*, HarperCollins, 2000

Shanley-Toffolo, Oonagh, *The Voice of Silence: A Life of Love, Healing and Inspiration*, Rider, 2002

Simmons, Simone, with Susan Hill, *Diana: The Secret Years*, Michael O'Mara Books, 1998

Snell, Kate, *Diana: Her Last Love*, Granada Media, 2000

Souhami, Diana, *Mrs Keppel and Her Daughter*, HarperCollins, 1996

Spencer, Charles, *Althorp: The Story of an English House*, Viking, 1998

——, *The Spencer Family*, Viking, 1999

Starkie, Allan, *Fergie: Her Secret Life*, Michael O'Mara Books, 1996

Strong, Roy, *The Roy Strong Diaries 1967–1997*, Weidenfeld & Nicolson, 1997

Wade, Judy, *The Truth: The Friends of Diana, Princess of Wales, Tell Their Stories*, Blake Publishing, 2001

Wharfe, Ken, with Robert Jobson, *Diana: Closely Guarded Secret*, revised and expanded paperback edn, Michael O'Mara Books, 2003

Whitaker, James, *Diana v. Charles*, Signet, 1993

Wilson, Christopher, *The Windsor Knot: Charles, Camilla and the Legacy of Diana*, Citadel Press, New York, 2002

Ziegler, Philip, *Mountbatten*, HarperCollins, 1985

Permissions

The author and publisher are grateful for permission to reproduce the following copyright material:

From *Diana: The Portrait* edited by Rosalind Coward. Reprinted by permission of HarperCollins*Publishers* Ltd. Copyright Rosalind Coward 2004

From *The Prince of Wales: A Biography* by Jonathan Dimbleby. Reprinted by permission of David Higham Associates. Copyright Jonathan Dimbleby, Little, Brown 1996

From *Diana: The Last Days* by Martyn Gregory. Reprinted by permission of Virgin Books. Copyright Martyn Gregory 1999, 2000, 2004, Virgin Books Ltd.

From *Shadows of a Princess: Diana, Princess of Wales 1987–1996* by Patrick Jephson. Reprinted by permission of HarperCollins*Publishers* Ltd. Copyright Patrick Jephson 2001

From *Diana: Her True Story – In Her Own Words* by Andrew Morton. Reprinted by permission of Michael O'Mara Books Ltd. Copyright Andrew Morton 2003

From *Diana: Closely Guarded Secret* by Ken Wharfe. Reprinted by permission of Michael O'Mara Books Ltd. Copyright Ken Wharfe 2002

From *The Insider* by Piers Morgan, published by Ebury Press. Reprinted by permission of The Random House Group Ltd. Copyright Piers Morgan 2005

From *Raine and Johnnie: The Spencers and the Scandal of Althorp* by Angela Levin. Reprinted by permission of Weidenfeld & Nicolson, an imprint of The Orion Publishing Group. Copyright Angela Levin 1993

From *Fayed: The Unauthorized Biography* by Tom Bower. Reprinted by permission of Pan Macmillan. Copyright Tom Bower 2003

From *Fergie: Her Secret Life* by Allan Starkie. Reprinted by permission of Michael O'Mara Books. Copyright Allan Starkie 1996

From *Love and War* by James Hewitt. Reprinted by permission of Blake Publishing. Copyright James Hewitt 1999

From *The Bodyguard's Story: Diana, the Crash and the Sole Survivor* by Trevor Rees-Jones. Reprinted by permission of Little, Brown. Copyright Trevor Rees-Jones 2000

From *Requiem: Diana, Princess of Wales 1961–1997* edited by Brian Mac-Arthur, published by Arcade Publishing, New York, NY. Text copyright 1997 by Brian MacArthur

From *The Duchess of York* by Vasso Kortesis. Reprinted by permission of Blake Publishing. Copyright Vasso Kortesis 1996

While every effort has been made to obtain permission from the owners of copyright material reproduced herein, the publisher would like to apologize for any omissions and will be pleased to incorporate missing acknowledgements in any future editions.

Acknowledgements

I owe a great debt of gratitude to all those people who have been kind enough to help me with this book, those named below and those who have preferred not to be named. I have also been fortunate to have the taped memories of members of the royal circle recorded over a decade ago when the events described in this book and people's reactions to them were still fresh. If I have omitted anyone who should have been included, I ask their forgiveness.

A&H Associates; Dickie Arbiter LVO; Sally Bedell Smith; Michael Bentley; Mark Bolland; Tom Bower; Lord Carlile of Berriew QC; Phil Craig; Sir Geoffrey Dear QPM, DL; The Rt Hon. Lord Deedes; Sister Bridie Dowd DC, OBE; Victor Edelstein; Meredith Etherington-Smith; Tess Gilder; Robert Golden; Roy Greenslade; Geordie Greig; David Griffin RVM; Linda Hall; Pamela, Lady Harlech; Nicholas Haslam; James Hewitt; Stuart Higgins; Anthony Holden; Patrick Jephson; Richard Kay; Timothy Leese; Brian Lapping; Marguerite Littman; Christopher Loyd CVO; Robert Low; Colin and Annabel Mackay; Andrew Morton; M.J. Rockall for his kindness in making available to me his collection of Diana letters; the Reverend Michael Seed SA; Ian Shapiro of Argyll Etkin Ltd, London for giving me access to Diana documents and letters; James Sherwin; Robert Spencer; Dr Will Swift; William Tallon RVM★ Gold; Colin Tebbutt MVO; Hugo Vickers for kindly making available to me his unpublished diary and extensive collection of royal newspaper cuttings covering the Diana years; Judy Wade; Lord Wakeham PC, JP, DL, FCA; Christopher Warwick; Nigel West; Kenneth A. Wharfe MVO; James Whitaker.

I am grateful to Martin Morse Wooster for his help with American sources, Lucy Pullan for her research in newspaper archives, to Camilla Eadie and Lizzie Grant for their skilful transcriptions and general help, to Lynda Marshall for her help in picture research, and to Douglas Matthews for compiling the index.

My agent, Gillon Aitken, has been a great support, assisted by Ayesha Karim and Sally Riley. At my publishers, Viking in London, I should like to express my gratitude to Helen Fraser, Tom Weldon and Keith Taylor. Above all, Carly Cook has accompanied me almost every step of the way, going far beyond the call of duty in collecting and designing the pictures illustrating Diana's life, editing the book and seeing its completion down to the most minute and often tedious detail. Richard Collins has once again proved the most intelligent and skilful of editors. In the early stages of the book no one could have done more to encourage me than Antonia Till. Above all my husband, William Bangor, has provided me with moral support throughout and practical expertise on proof checking.

Index